"As global persecution c  leadly international conflicts mu to be informed about the dange s sisters and brothers around t vides insights, information, and inspiration to urgently act and pray on their behalf."

—Frank Wolf, former U.S. Congressman, 1981–2014

"I've spent much of my political career working toward the advancement of religious freedom for all people, everywhere. Sadly, religious freedom is under attack around the world. *Heroic Faith* details the harsh realities far too many Christians face merely for practicing their faith. I pray that learning about their plight through this book will open your heart and challenge you to act. To truly make a difference regarding the monumental challenge of religious persecution, it will require all of us."

—Samuel Brownback, former Ambassador-at-Large for
International Religious Freedom, and
former U.S. Senator and governor of Kansas

"This book could not come at a more critical time. Across the globe, oppressive regimes deny their people the fundamental right to religious freedom. The Chinese Communist Party alone restricts the faith of some 100 million Christians. In *Heroic Faith*, you will read some of their stories. As a former leader of a house church in China, I've seen the risks many Christians take just to practice their faith. We owe it to them to make the world aware of their plight, and as Christians, we should be stirred to action to walk with them. This book is a starting place for you to do just that."

—Bob Fu, author of *God's Double Agent*
and founder and president of ChinaAid

"This important new book about the international persecution of Christians couldn't be better timed. Reliable reports say some 360 million Christians live in places where they experience high levels of persecution and discrimination. Yet, at the same time, accounts of their courage, sacrifice, and suffering are still not widely known, even among Christians. I think you'll be both inspired and prayerful as you encounter some of these faithful believers and their stories in the pages of *Heroic Faith*."

—Nina Shea, director, Hudson Institute
Center for Religious Freedom

"As the persecution of Christians is increasing rapidly throughout the world, this timely book calls our attention to what is occurring in key areas. It incorporates a general survey of major regions and detailed descriptions of what is happening on the ground, coupled with inspiring tales of faith and sacrifice. All this is also set in an illuminating historical and security context provided by General Boykin."

—Paul Marshall, Wilson Distinguished Professor of
Religious Freedom at Baylor University

"Christians are the most persecuted group in the world today. *Heroic Faith* details the plights of Christians who are simply trying to practice their faith in some of the most hostile places on Earth. I have seen firsthand the price so many pay to follow Jesus—I have heard their stories, and experienced persecution myself. When I was wrongfully imprisoned in Turkey, I deeply wanted to know I had not been forgotten. I expect many of the victims of persecution whose stories are featured in this book feel the same. My hope is that by reading this book, God would stir your heart to pray for them and to not forget, because God does not forget."

—Andrew Brunson, author of *God's Hostage*

HEROIC FAITH

HOPE AMID GLOBAL PERSECUTION

LELA GILBERT AND ARIELLE DEL TURCO

WITH LTG (RET.) JERRY BOYKIN

FIDELIS
PUBLISHING

FIDELIS PUBLISHING

ISBN: 978-1-737176367
ISBN (eBook): 978-1-737176374

Heroic Faith
Hope Amid Global Persecution

Edited by Amanda Varian
Cover Design by Hannah Eichelberger
Interior Design by Xcel Graphic

For information about special discounts for bulk purchases, please contact BulkBooks.com, call 1-888-959-5153 or email cs@bulkbooks.com

Fidelis Publishing, LLC Sterling, VA • Nashville, TN fidelispublishing.com. Publishing in cooperation with Family Research Council.

Manufactured in the United States of America
10 9 8 7 6 5 4 3 2 1

CONTENTS

FOREWORD

RAMPANT RELIGIOUS PERSECUTION IS ONE OF THE great tragedies of our time. It strikes at the very core of the human heart, dictating what a person may believe or how they should live.

As the former chairman of the bipartisan U.S. Commission for International Religious Freedom (USCIRF), I traveled to Sudan in 2020 and saw with my own eyes the difference religious freedom could make for people who formerly suffered for their faith under a hostile, Islamic regime. At the time of my visit, Sudan had just installed a civilian-led transitional government after the brutal regime of Omar al Bashir fell after thirty years.

My trip to Sudan taught me something crucial: people flourish with religious freedom. When the transitional government began to secure the fundamental human rights denied to them under Bashir's regime, it was like a breath of fresh air for many Sudanese people. Before, converting from Islam to any other religion was punishable by death. But under the new transitional government, Christian converts from a Muslim background could speak about their faith openly.

The positive impact of the increase of religious freedom—although progress was being made and it was not yet perfect—was evident in Sudan. The drastic change in a country once a notorious suppressor of religious freedom for so long gave hope to advocates who feared the country was a lost cause. The success proved that change was possible; even in the most challenging cases. Now, Sudan's future is again uncertain after a military coup (another reminder of the fragility of religious freedom globally), but the Sudanese people have been given a taste of freedom—including religious freedom—and that will not easily be forgotten or surrendered.

Religious freedom is core to who we are as humans. We naturally seek to answer life's biggest questions—about who we are, where life itself comes from, what our purpose is, and where we are going. These answers are found in our Christian faith. This makes the freedom to choose and live out our faith essential to living a fully human life. It's no wonder oppressed Sudanese converts rejoice when they are offered the chance to live with religious freedom for themselves.

Americans know better than most the deep importance of religious freedom. It is called our "first freedom" not merely because it is enshrined in the First Amendment to the U.S. Constitution, but because it is central to America's founding. Some of the earliest Europeans to emigrate to the New World were people who were persecuted for not worshiping according to the dictates of their home country's state-approved churches. They came to America seeking the freedom to practice their faith in every aspect of their lives, and that has been our understanding of religious freedom for most of our almost two and a half centuries as a country.

Although far from perfect, America has been a beacon for religious freedom ever since.

In the West, we too often take for granted the basic freedoms we have inherited. We do so to our detriment. When business owners face lawsuits for operating their business according to their religious convictions or when government officials target churches disproportionately, this is a dangerous erosion of our freedoms. Yes, the desperate circumstances faced by those around the world remind us why it's important to vigilantly protect this freedom. America will not be able to promote religious freedom globally if we do not maintain it within our borders.

When the American government, or other governments for that matter, publicly and privately push for greater religious freedom worldwide, it can make a positive difference. This is important because religious freedom isn't simply an American right, it's a fundamental human right for all humanity. The release of prisoners of conscience, including American missionary Andrew Brunson and Sudanese Christian Mariam Ibraheem, testify to the impact government pressure can have. The United States government must continue to work on this issue.

Christians in particular are regularly targeted because of their faith. Sadly, we rarely hear about Christian persecution. Such information does not make mainstream headlines, but that does not minimize the importance of persecuted Christians to God. Nor does it excuse our failure to pray for the persecuted church or advocate on their behalf.

The first step to make a difference is to know what's happening. That's why the book you are now holding, *Heroic Faith*, is so important. My colleagues at Family Research Council—Lela Gilbert and Arielle Del Turco—are tireless advocates for international religious freedom. They've spent years researching the causes and impacts of Christian persecution. This book offers a survey of Christian persecution around the world and highlights the real-life stories of its survivors. My friend and Family Research Council's Executive Vice President, LTG (RET.) Jerry Boykin, offers insight on how global Christian persecution affects national security and what the U.S. government should do.

By reading this book, I hope you are motivated to pray for the persecuted, learn from their stories of truly heroic faith, and then be led to give action to your prayers by engaging on the issue of international religious freedom.

As USCIRF commissioner, I adopted Leah Sharibu as a religious prisoner of conscience to advocate for. She's a Nigerian teenager, kidnapped by Boko Haram in 2018 at fourteen years old. She was abducted from her all-girls school along with dozens of other classmates. Yet, while the other girls were released, Leah is the only one who remains a captive. Her classmates say it's because she refused to renounce her Christian faith when Boko Haram terrorists demanded she do so. This book tells more of her story. Leah represents so many Christians who face unfathomable torture, abuse, pressure, intimidation, and oppression simply because they put their faith in Jesus Christ. Yet, they respond with grace and remain strong in their faith.

One day, I hope to meet Leah Sharibu and thank her for her unshakable faith. Until that day, I will carry on fighting for religious freedom for Leah and for all people, everywhere. I hope you will do the same.

—Tony Perkins, president of Family Research Council
and former chair of the U.S. Commission
on International Religious Freedom

INTRODUCTION

I N TODAY'S WORLD, STORIES OF INTERNATIONAL
discrimination, violence, and even bloodshed increasingly
appear all too often in our news reports. And more than
a few Christians are beginning to reflect on one particular
"big idea:" religious liberty. Some of us are giving serious
thought to what those words really mean and how such an
ideal can be achieved. Even in the United States, concerns
about restrictions on freedom of religion are intensifying.
Those worries are significant and worthy of consideration.
But a look beyond our borders is even more telling, opening
our eyes to worrisome events that transpire in other lands
every day.

As we examine the picture more closely, our concerns
quickly broaden beyond those who share our faith in Jesus
Christ; they necessarily extend to others who face great difficulties in their own chosen form of religious observance. A
global view of how religious freedom or its absence presents
itself quickly demonstrates how expressions of faith and

worship often involve living dangerously. It also provides a much-needed perspective, helping us understand the times in which we live.

The book you're holding in your hands contains a selection of stories from across the globe, bringing to light real-life examples of courage, faith, and determination. Its pages will carry your imagination to faraway lands with different cultures, climates, and cuisines. And it may well inspire you, encourage you, or even compel you to take action, to reach out, to really want to "do something."

On the other hand, this isn't a book filled with good news and happy endings. It is true in some cases you'll discover miracles have happened, troubled scenarios have been repaired, and unlikely souls have come to faith. However, reports from far too many Christian organizations, human rights groups, and international observers underscore what has been informally pointed out for years—the persecution of Christians abroad is mounting exponentially.

According to a 2020 report from Pew Forum, "In 2018, Christians reportedly were harassed in 145 countries, up from 143 countries in 2017."[1] According to this report, the number of countries was only 95 in 2008, which means that harassment has jumped 52 percent in one decade. The same Pew report lists Muslims as the second most abused religious group. And we will examine two clear cases in which Muslim ethnic groups are enduring horrendous mistreatment—most notably in China and Burma (Myanmar).

Meanwhile, David Curry, president and CEO of Open Doors, wrote this about his organization's 2022 World Watch List: "More than 360 million of our Christian brothers and sisters live in places where they experience high levels of persecution and discrimination. That's 1 in 7 Christians, worldwide."[2]

CHRISTIANS AROUND THE WORLD

So who are these Christians? And where? And how do they live their lives? In his book *Their Blood Cries Out*, Paul Marshall offers this eloquent portrait:

> Christians are African women who rise at dawn to greet the rising sun in a wailing chant of thanks to God. They are Indian untouchables cleaning up excrement from the streets. They are slaves in Sudanese markets. They are Chinese peasants flip-flopping in rice fields or pedaling bicycles through Shanghai. They are Mexican tribal people, driven from their ancestral homes. They are Filipina maids, misused throughout the world. They are Russian Orthodox priests, hit by cars which mysteriously careen onto the sidewalk. They are Arab women who have been raped and had acid poured on them to remove distinguishing Christian marks. And overwhelmingly, they are people who, given a moment's time, space, and freedom, live life with joy, enthusiasm, and gratitude.[3]

This portrait of such an array of lifestyles, traditional distinctions, and racial origins makes one wonder why seemingly ordinary, harmless, and vulnerable men, women, and children are the targets of cruelty and violence. In the pages that follow, we will look at the variations of culture, of governmental authority and of religious rigidity that contribute to attacks on Christians. At the same time, they not only harm and even kill Christians, but also others who belong to vulnerable faith groups, such as the Yazidis in Iraq and the Baha'is in Iran. We'll also consider the primary propagators of Christian persecution in specific international regions and states.

You'll discover, when we look toward the East, three of the most brutal regimes in the world—China, North Korea, and Afghanistan—are located there. For twenty years Open Doors World Watch List placed North Korea as the #1 persecutor of Christians. Only in 2022, after the sudden and disastrous U.S. withdrawal, did Open Doors replace North Korea with Afghanistan as the world's worst abuser, due to the predatory violence of the radical Islamist Taliban. North Korea is now listed as #2.[4]

China, meanwhile, has become notorious in recent years for its abuses of Uyghur Muslims, Tibetan Buddhists, Falun Gong practitioners, and, of course, Christians as well—Catholic and Protestant alike. An anti-religious crackdown continues to surge in China even as we write.

Both China and North Korea are ruled by hardline communist regimes, influenced by Mao Tse-tung's radical form of Marxist ideology. This belief system rejects all religions, which are disallowed as threats to the authority of the states and its leaders. As we'll see, there is no room for a Higher Power in the eyes of communist leaders and governments. The cruel enforcement of religious bans has been exposed in those two countries, as well as in many others.

Meanwhile, if we survey the Middle East and Africa, we find another source of violent persecution—like that in Afghanistan—radical Islamist ideology. This is evident in Iran, Iraq, Saudi Arabia, Turkey, and increasingly across both East and West Africa. This dangerous and potentially deadly belief system has led to the formation of groups like ISIS, al-Shabaab, al-Qaeda, Boko Haram, Iran's Islamic Revolutionary Guard Corps (IRGC), and sponsored militias. These, in varying degrees of ferocity, demand conversion to Islam, and may imprison or execute those who refuse to convert.

Other motives for religious persecution can lie within the myopic vision of nationalist parties, tyrannical dictators, or other intransigent regimes such as the military juntas in Burma/Myanmar, in Eritrea, and in some Latin American countries. It may also result from increasingly aggressive religious ideology, such as the radical Hinduism escalating in India's BJP ruling party. Ethnic groups can also become violent, particularly when religious disputes play into their identity. Antisemitism is an ancient form of this danger, which combines both religious and ethnic intolerance, fueled by ancient libels, leading to discrimination, persecution, and violence. The Holocaust provides the most horrifying example of the attempted genocide of an entire race of people.

In later pages, we'll also look carefully at violations of religious freedom that don't necessarily fall along geographical lines. Examples include apostasy and blasphemy laws, "hate speech" violations, and the forbidding of conversion from one religious faith to another.

Apostasy laws punish people who "apostasize" and convert away from Islam. Across much of the Muslim world, apostasy laws—backed by social pressure—are used to deter apostasy and sometimes punish even allegations of the crime. These laws prevent Muslims from freely choosing their faith—whether Christianity or anything else.

Blasphemy laws generally prohibit insults to religion and are the most widespread of these three types of laws. In many places, while still on the books, such laws are no longer enforced or even used. But in other places, again in many Muslim-majority countries, they are often abused when allegations of blasphemy are made against religious minorities—often with no evidence—to settle unrelated disputes and vendettas.

Anti-conversion laws, quite simply, prohibit people from converting to another religion. Primarily in place in parts of the Hindu and Buddhist world, anti-conversion laws are used by governments to maintain a majority of the population within their preferred religion. While threats to religious freedom arise from other sources, these three types of laws and the cultural support behind them are major threats to the freedom to choose one's faith—and thus to religious freedom worldwide.

Punishment for those convicted of violating such laws can include marriage annulment, property confiscation, prison sentences, or death sentences. Additionally, a mere allegation of a violation often results in intense social hostility from one's community and family members, who retaliate with anything from slight harassment all the way up to violence resulting in death. Drafted out of the ashes of the Holocaust, the Universal Declaration of Human Rights (UDHR) proclaims in Article 18 that "[e]veryone has the right to freedom of thought, conscience and religion; this right includes freedom to change his religion or belief, and freedom, either alone or in community with others and in public or private, to manifest his religion or belief in teaching, practice, worship and observance."[5] The laws and the social acceptance behind them are a direct threat to religious freedom as articulated in the UDHR.

Such encroachments on international religious freedom are often correctly ascribed to radical Islam, because there are clearly articulated Islamic *hadith*—religious laws—against Muslims abandoning their faith. Blasphemy, which involves speaking ill of Islam, the Prophet Mohammad, or the Koran, is also forbidden, and is too often enforced with legalized death penalties. Accusations, arrests, and assassinations are the tragic result of blasphemy legislation in countries like Pakistan, where death penalties for blasphemy are enshrined in national law. However, random brutalities based on the same "rules" also take place in non-Islamic countries like Uganda, for example, even though it has a population that is 80 percent Christian.

Interestingly, variations of these same kinds of demands also exist in ardently secular regimes such as China, North Korea, and other radical political dictatorships. In these places, the danger lies in speaking against the state's ideology or its leadership, because such regimes demand full devotion and loyalty. Thus, in that context, words of disrespect and defiance of the state become a form of secularized blasphemy. Meanwhile, divergence from legalities and resisting a state's absolute power quickly morphs into a humanistic form of apostasy. Some examples of those restrictions will be described in the following chapters.

Myriad problems exist for minority religious groups beyond the free world. And there's really no question about just how difficult and challenging it has become in some places to be a follower of Jesus Christ. For that matter, depending on the place and time, it can be challenging to belong to any minority religion or even to choose atheistic belief in countless locations. A commitment to freedom of conscience carries a remarkably high price tag in most of the world, and too often it is far higher than many of us might have imagined.

In recent years, the Pew Research Center has found increasing governmental and social hostility toward religious believers worldwide. The global level of government restrictions on religion reached an all-time high in 2018, the most recent year studied. Pew found that 56 countries have "high" or "very high" restrictions on religion. While the specific threats to religious freedom vary in type and intensity, one common source is the legal and cultural support for apostasy, blasphemy, and/or anti-conversion laws, which often threaten the freedom to choose and/or change one's faith.

LEGISLATION TO SUPPORT INTERNATIONAL RELIGIOUS FREEDOM

Thankfully, during previous decades in the United States, there have been believers and activists with remarkable foresight. Cries for help were heard from Africa, Asia, and the Middle East, eventually reaching the ears of politicians, diplomats, and advocates in the U.S. government.

During the late 1990s, as persecution against Christians swelled, a discussion about it—and what to do about it— grew more intense and animated in America. Coalitions were formed, workshops were scheduled, and articles were published. Such discussions finally reached the halls of Congress, and in 1998 the International Religious Freedom Act was signed by President Bill Clinton. Its rather dense and lengthy definition explains that it expressed,

> . . . United States foreign policy with respect to, and to strengthen United States advocacy on behalf of, individuals persecuted in foreign countries on account of religion; to authorize United States actions in response to violations of religious freedom in foreign countries; to establish an Ambassador at Large for International Religious Freedom with the Department of State, a Commission on International Religious Freedom, and a Special Adviser on International Religious Freedom with the National Security Council.[6]

Then the Frank R. Wolf International Religious Freedom Act of 2015 (H.R. 1150, S. 2878) was signed by President Barack Obama. That law was meant to strengthen American efforts to combat persecution of religious minorities throughout the world. Named for Frank Wolf—a great congressional champion of religious freedom—the Act called for the integration of international religious freedom into American foreign policy, for mandatory religious freedom training for foreign service officers, and for coordination between the Ambassador-at-Large for religious freedom and the National Security Council.

The development, crafting, and signing of these congressional acts clearly requires the U.S. government to take religious liberty into account in diplomatic disputes, in international policy negotiations, and when shaping trade agreements. Perhaps most importantly, these acts reflect the spirit and resolve of a majority of American voters, who are learning to speak out and demand that their legislative representatives speak out for religious freedom around the globe.

As we experience increasing threats of discrimination and persecution in the U.S., it is important for us to learn from our brothers and sisters who suffer deeply and dangerously. How do they cope? How do they face injury and death? They may not look like us or live the way we do, but they are our Christian family. What can they teach us?

Pastor Andrew Brunson, an American Christian missionary who suffered two years of solitary confinement in a Turkish prison for false charges, has an important perspective on the issue of religious freedom. He says we should prepare for persecution ourselves, because it may well strike the Western world sooner rather than later. And how should we prepare ourselves? Let's take the time to learn from those who continue to suffer across the world and prepare our hearts and minds to follow their example.

**LTG (RET.) JERRY BOYKIN:
HOW AMERICAN VALUES CAN IMPACT
INTERNATIONAL RELIGIOUS FREEDOM**

As we begin to think carefully about religious freedom, it's important for us to remember how the United States of America first began and how deeply religious belief was integrated into our nation's founding.

Our country was built upon a rock-solid foundation of religious principles with a deep concern for religious freedom. American values were anchored in Judeo-Christian ethics, and our Constitution and founding documents provide non-Christians with the freedom and opportunity to practice their faith—or lack of it—as well. Even if we don't share someone else's faith personally, we still have a fundamental responsibility to respect it as long as it does not threaten the Constitution or other's rights.

Obviously, we cannot demand democracy from other people, just as we can't shove our own faith upon others. But we can demonstrate our American "First Freedoms," and historically that's what we've done. The First Amendment was the initial articulation of unalienable rights by the Founding Fathers after they signed the Constitution. They came right back and created the Bill of Rights—which makes the issue of America's religious freedom, along with other "first freedoms," very clear.

Since the beginning, the understanding that we live according to America's first principles has impacted our foreign policy. What would we have done in World War II Europe, were it not for the common foundation of Christian faith? As a nation, we rejected Nazism morally and we opposed it militarily. We were in the Pacific because the

Japanese attacked us. But that wasn't true of the Nazis. We condemned the vile Nazi ideology as a matter of principle.

As a Christian myself, I believe our foreign policy needs to be based largely on rooting out those who are just plain evil. And that means calling out those who persecute and victimize others because of their faith. For example, I'm all for Islam being able to practice every one of its five pillars—up to the point those beliefs lead to jihad, to the denial of human rights, and to the use of force to compel others to convert to Islam.

Clearly, there are occasions when a loss of religious freedom can endanger national security. I approach this from two perspectives—domestic and foreign. Of course, voices on the Left try to convince us we were not founded on Judeo-Christian principles. But the truth is, we were. As John Adams said to the Massachusetts Militia in 1798,

> We have no Government armed with Power capable of contending with human Passions unbridled by morality and Religion. Avarice, Ambition, Revenge or Gallantry would break the strongest Cords of our Constitution as a Whale goes through a Net. *Our Constitution was made only for a moral and religious People. It is wholly inadequate to the government of any other.* [Emphasis added][7]

Adams clearly declared that our American Constitution is only suited to moral and religious people. We were founded on Judeo-Christian principles with the expectation we would live by them and that our values as individuals would be influenced by a Judeo-Christian foundation in our Constitution. At the same time, our Constitution also gave us the First Amendment, which protects our unalienable Freedom of Religion. This was not solely freedom to worship, but specifically freedom to choose and practice our faith. It is constitutionally declared we as a people would always be able to observe our chosen religious practices, as long as they do not violate the laws of the land or infringe on the rights of others.

But what does this have to do with religious freedom in other countries? When we see clear violations of human rights abroad, including the persecution of religious groups—too often affecting Christians—how should we respond? And perhaps more specifically, should we recognize religious freedom as a national security issue?

ACTIVATING THE ELEMENTS OF NATIONAL POWER

Sometimes the challenges we face as a nation are great, and the abuses we observe are widespread. On occasion we become aware lives are unjustly threatened and are perhaps even being lost in countries with whom we have diplomatic relations. This can affect both the country in question and the United States. In those cases, America has an array of useful tools with which to influence adversaries. Every American Embassy in the world is able to put to use specific elements of national power: diplomatic information, military, economic, financial, intelligence, and law enforcement options—sometimes shortened to the acronym DIMEFIL.

How can these elements be used to defend vulnerable people and/or endangered Americans? One example took place in the Balkans in the 1990s, when the United States activated every element of national power. We tried to end the war, to separate the warring factions, and then to help them rebuild their society so we could help permanently stop the ongoing genocide. We used every element of national power to do so.

America can apply those same principles when we're hoping to address abuses of religious freedom abroad. We can decide which ones would best be applied to a particular situation in a specific region. And only rarely would this be limited just to one element. In fact, I can't think of an example in which only military action, for example, or only diplomatic negotiation took place on its own. Of course, what makes our diplomacy strong and credible is the fact we can back it up with our military. We can also back it up with our economic strength.

We might say to one national leader, "We can provide economic incentives for you. We can help you to do better financially than you're doing right now for your people, and you'll be more prosperous in the long run." We might also suggest, "We can develop an intelligence relationship with you."

Suppose we are dealing with a country that suffers from a consistent incursion of troublemakers coming across its borders. Maybe we tell them, "We'll share intelligence with you and tell you what we see, when we see it, and who is specifically trying to infiltrate and why. We will provide you all of the information that you need." Another example of information might be something like this: "We can provide some helpful information to help you learn how to grow coffee instead of cocaine."

When dealing with religious freedom violations, our elements of national power are the tools we should encourage our government to use whether they are overlooking, harboring, or provoking violations. In every country with which we have international relations, we have an American embassy. And one of the key things that those embassies are supposed to be doing is reporting back through the U.S. Ambassador and the Chief of Station: What's going on in those countries? What is the leader up to? What are the people saying? All this can and should be done smoothly because the embassy's Chief of Station has a clandestine network of agents who are providing him with a constant flow of information, meant to keep the ambassador informed. We learn what's going on in countries around the world primarily through our embassies.

THINKING REALISTICALLY ABOUT THE MILITARY

Sometimes when Americans learn about abuses taking place in other countries, popular opinion may push toward the U.S. taking "military action." But in fact, that is rarely the right answer to our religious freedom questions. In fact, sometimes U.S. military support ends up doing more harm than good, particularly when we offer to train local forces to fight on behalf of their own people. In the Special Forces in which I served, our mission was to organize, train, and equip indigenous forces. Our forces do that well, although it can prove difficult when those native soldiers have values that are incompatible with ours.

And what about religious freedom in our own military? It is our goal to train up young people who are the products of this 245-year-old nation, which—as we've seen—is founded on Judeo-Christian principles, values, and ethics. We want America's troops to have come from an environment that retains their ability—thanks to our Constitution—to practice their own religion. With that kind of a military population, we have a pretty good chance of fielding a very good self-defense force—a strong and moral military that understands its own ethics and morality.

We train all kinds of people in our military, and all of them are not people of similar faith. Some may even call themselves atheists but—as that old saying goes—there are no atheists in a foxhole. I can tell you from my own experience our troops are looking for a Higher Power when their lives are on the line and their future is in danger. They're looking for some kind of divine intervention. But whatever faith our individual troops practice, religious freedom begins at home. We need a military populated with young men and women who respect and care about the faith of others—especially those believers who practice their faith in foreign lands and continue to suffer for it.

CHAPTER 1

ASIA: PERSECUTION FROM ALL SIDES

OZENS OF LOCAL SECURITY GUARDS AND OFFICERS raided Xingguang Church, a Protestant church not registered with the Chinese government, in May 2020.[1] The small group of Christians was singing hymns in a private home in China's Fujian province when they were interrupted by authorities from the local Ethnic and Religious Bureau. These officers pushed their way into the house without warning and without proper legal documents.

Authorities insisted the gathering was illegal. When church members started recording the raiding incident on their phones, the officers yelled at them to stop. When the officers saw neighbors also filming the incident, they removed the family for recording the raid.

Pastor Yang Xibo of Xingguang Church told Radio Free Asia, "The state security police came banging at the door, then they kicked it down and dragged those in the way outside the doorway, dragging them to the ground."[2] This was not Xingguang Church's first chaotic raid. Authorities previously raided the church and accused the pastor of "violating several articles of the religious regulations."[3]

The experience of Pastor Yang Xibo and Xingguang Church is all too common in China. To submit a church to the authority of the state-sanctioned church associations is to submit to the influence of the Chinese Communist Party (CCP). Churches that refuse to do so, like Xingguang Church, often face harassment from the government. Although the Chinese government has quietly tolerated house churches in the last few decades, recent years have seen an uptick in the harassment and even the forced closure of house churches. Yet, millions of Chinese believers persist in gathering every week. All because they want to worship God as they see fit, even with the risks involved.

SNAPSHOTS OF HUMAN RIGHTS IN ASIA: A DOWNWARD SPIRAL

While China has rightfully been the focus of many human rights controversies in recent years, Christians and others suffer on account of their faith across Asia. While Asia is home to some of the fastest growing high-tech societies, it also has both tight government restrictions on religious practice and terrifying and sometimes violent social hostility to religious minorities, which are often Christian.

A snapshot of the experiences of some Christians provides a glimpse into the dire challenges faced by many:

- **In North Korea,** a Soviet-style dictatorship rules the people with an iron fist. Christianity is practiced with the utmost secrecy, and getting caught with a Bible is enough to warrant a death sentence.

- **In Vietnam,** the legacy of the communist regime continues to place pressure on Christians and is a cause of intimidation for believers.
- **In Pakistan,** Islamist mob violence and social discrimination blends to form a dangerous concoction for Christians. Marginalized from the broader society, Christians are often left with little recourse when injustices are committed against them, enabling oppression to thrive.
- **In India,** the dangerous Hindu nationalist movement asserts Christians and other non-Hindus have no place in Indian society. This exclusive narrative allows hatred to thrive and enables attackers to harm Christians with impunity.
- **In Nepal,** Christianity is multiplying despite monumental pressure.
- **In Sri Lanka,** the Buddhist majority makes life difficult for the Christian minority.
- **And in China,** the ruling Chinese Communist Party is among the world's most notorious violators of religious freedom, and with good reason. The challenges believers face there are diverse and troubling. As China rises as a global power, it is all the more disturbing its government maintains tight control and repressive measures against minorities.

SUFFOCATING REPRESSION IN CHINA

Housed in an inconspicuous low-rise office building in Chengdu, China, over 500 members of Early Rain Covenant Church comprised one of the most influential house churches in China. Bold and unashamed of their faith, these

Christians do not bother to keep a low profile, although their status as an unregistered church makes them vulnerable to being shut down at the whim of the government. Early Rain runs a seminary and a Christian school, in addition to ministries that serve the most marginalized in Chinese society, including orphans, the families of prisoners of conscience, and the unborn.[4]

Given the trailblazing streak of this church, it is no surprise they chose Wang Yi to be their pastor. When Wang Yi converted to Christianity in 2005, he was already a prominent lawyer, public intellectual, and professor known for his human rights work. In 2006, he was invited to the White House to meet with George W. Bush along with two other notable Chinese Christians. Early Rain Covenant Church installed this former firebrand lawyer as their pastor in 2011.[5]

In his new role as a pastor, he did not cower from the possibility of backlash from the government. In 2015, Pastor Wang honored the 60th anniversary of the sacrifice of Wang Ming Dao, one of China's most influential house church pastors in the 1950s. He was arrested with his wife and coworkers after publishing an article that explained why they refused to join the Three–Self Patriotic Movement (TSPM) in order to be recognized by the government. This arrest signaled the beginning of persecution against house churches which has ebbed and flowed since that time.

In Wang Ming Dao's honor, Pastor Wang Yi and Early Rain published their own version of Luther's 95 Theses, affirming the Chinese house church's position on faith before government and society at large. Thesis 81 is among many that surely raised the ire of government officials:

> We believe that in today's China, only by completely parting with the "Three-Self" system, completely ending the cooperation in Caesar's conspiracy, solely relying on the Bible and the Lord Jesus' Great Commission, proclaiming our faith, ordaining officers, re-establishing church properties, recounting the remnants, can we restart building one-by-one a true and independent "local church."[6]

Pastor Wang's internationally known public profile likely spared him from an immediate harsh punishment in response. But the Chinese government's patience soon waned.

Pastor Wang knew there was a strong possibility he would one day be arrested. He prepared for that eventuality by writing a document he titled "My Declaration of Faithful Disobedience." His congregation was instructed to release the declaration if he were ever detained by the government for more than forty-eight hours. The day he prepared for came on Sunday, December 9, 2018, when he, his wife, and more than 100 members of Early Rain Covenant Church were arrested. By December 12, the declarations had begun to inspire Christians around the globe. It offers a beautiful description of what he calls "faithful disobedience," contrasting this from political activism or civil disobedience. He wrote:

> I firmly believe that the Bible has not given any branch of any government the authority to run the church or to interfere with the faith of Christians. Therefore, the Bible demands that I, through peaceable means, in meek resistance and active forbearance, filled with joy, resist all administrative

policies and legal measures that oppress the church and interfere with the faith of Christians.

I firmly believe this is a spiritual act of disobedience. In modern authoritarian regimes that persecute the church and oppose the gospel, spiritual disobedience is an inevitable part of the gospel movement.[7]

He was secretly tried at the Chengdu Intermediate People's Court on December 26, 2019. On December 30, Pastor Wang Yi was sentenced to nine years in prison on false charges of "illegal business activity" and "inciting to subvert state power" and fined 50,000 RMB.[8] It was a harsh punishment that surprised even the most cynical China hawks.

Pastor Wang was far from a national security threat, or even an opponent of the Chinese government. Upon his arrest, the congregation of his church released a statement emphasizing this. They testified that Pastor Wang "has taught that even when the church is being persecuted, Christians should be willing to submit to the government's physical restrictions of them as well as to the depravation of their property."

The national security charge of "inciting to subvert state power" is familiar to many Chinese dissidents. The ruling Chinese Communist Party (CCP) often feels threatened by anyone who publicly disagrees with the state or even pledges allegiance to authorities outside of Party control, and that includes God. This makes dissidents—and sometimes people of faith who refuse to comply to state regulation—perceived opponents of the state itself.

As of this writing, Pastor Wang remains in prison, serving out his sentence. Meanwhile, the government continues to harass Early Rain church leaders and members. In April 2020, several Early Rain leaders and congregants were arrested by the Public Security Bureau while they participated in a church service held via Zoom in their homes.[9]

Following the rise of General Secretary Xi Jinping, religious adherents of all faiths have been under increased pressure, though five religions are legally recognized: Protestantism, Catholicism, Islam, Buddhism, and Daoism. However, even state-sanctioned religious institutions are subject to state supervision and government surveillance. Xi has also started to enforce old laws which were previously neglected, including a ban on foreign-based religious organizations for their proselytizing in China.[10]

The PRC's constitution promises in Article 36 that citizens "enjoy freedom of religious belief."[11] Yet, the constitution includes an important caveat by indicating this applies only to "normal religious activities," a term which is not defined.[12] The constitutional declaration that Chinese citizens enjoy freedom of religious belief has never provided any real protections for those of faith.

Open Doors estimates that there are approximately 96.7 million Christians in China.[13] China allows legal status for Protestant churches that are part of the Three-Self Patriotic Movement (TSPM) and the government-run China Christian Council (CCC). However, state-sanctioned churches that submit to these authorities still experience a high degree of government interference.

In 2018, President Xi issued new regulations for religious affairs and gave the officially atheist CCP power to enforce them.[14] The United Front Work Department (UFWD) was also restructured in 2018 to more effectively oversee China's religious affairs and "sinicize" (modify by Chinese influence) organized religion.[15] A "Five-Year Plan for the Sinicization of Christianity" began in 2018 to promote "Chinese

Christianity."[16] Churches and believers who refuse to compromise their faith by accepting the sinicization of Christianity will likely face punishment.

The Bible itself has been a recent target of the Chinese government and its "Great Firewall" which facilitates the censorship of anything the Party feels does not suit its purpose. The Bible is on the list of targets. Bible apps have been removed from the App Store in China. It now requires the use of a virtual private network (VPN) to download Bible apps in China.[17]

Popular Christian accounts on the Chinese app WeChat have also been removed. Users who tried to access the social media pages see messages that the pages had violated "internet user public account information services management provisions." Some Bible apps have been entirely removed from the platforms of Chinese tech companies Huawei and Xiaomi.[18]

Physical Bibles are also unavailable for purchase on Chinese websites. In March 2018, China's largest online stores, including Taobao, Jingdong, Amazon.cn, and others, suddenly stopped showing results for searches for the Bible. In December 2020, four Chinese Christian businessmen from Shenzhen were tried in court for selling audio versions of the Bible online.[19] The businessmen were arrested as part of a campaign to "eradicate pornography and illegal publications."

Earlier that same month, Christian businessman Lai Jinqiang was tried in Shenzhen on charges of "unlawful business operation" for his business which sold audio Bible players. His company, the "Cedar Tree Company," reported the highest sales of audio Bible players in China, distributing around 40,000 units per month.

Instead of allowing people to choose what they will read and how they will access their religious texts, China requires all Bible sales be funneled through official channels only.

Bibles can be purchased at state-approved church bookstores regulated by the government.

Even worse than suppressing the Bible is the Chinese government's attempt to change the Bible. As a part of its five-year plan to sinicize religion and make it more acceptable for the goals of the government, one strategy is "reinterpreting the Bible and writing annotations for it" from a socialist viewpoint.

Though the full text has yet to be revealed, the Chinese government's previous manipulation of the Bible has been bizarre. In one textbook at the government-run University of Electronic Science and Technology, John 8 was shamefully distorted.

In the biblical version, an adulterous woman is brought to Jesus, and her accusers ask if she should be stoned to death because of her sins. Jesus disperses the angry crowd with His response, "Let him who is without sin among you be the first to throw a stone at her" (v. 7). The CCP's version states the crowd leaves, yet Jesus tells the woman, "I too am a sinner. But if the law could only be executed by men without blemish, the law would be dead," before stoning her Himself.

Former communist countries have a long history of hindering access to the Bible. Missionaries like Brother Andrew famously served persecuted believers living under communist repression in the Soviet Union.[20] Now, the CCP continues the legacy of communist crackdowns on the Bible. As its attacks on the Bible continue to mount, the Chinese government should know they will never succeed. No earthly forces can crush the power of the gospel and the hope it has brought to millions of Chinese believers.

China's crackdown on Christianity has had visible consequences. In the Zhejiang province alone, the Chinese government removed crosses from 1,200 to 1,700 Christian churches in 2015–2016.[21] At times, officials have replaced the crosses with Chinese flags. In the provinces of Jiangxi and Henan, portraits of Jesus have been forbidden, even in private homes. Chinese authorities have also forcibly removed door plaques on Christian homes that convey religious themes with sayings such as "God loves the world" and "The Lord gives peace."[22]

In 2019, witnesses reported the Ten Commandments were removed from nearly every Three-Self church and replaced with quotes from President Xi.[23] Churches have been shut down for their failure to comply with this instruction. The government has also started to install surveillance cameras in churches to monitor the content of sermons.[24] China's restrictions on churches are not conducive to fostering a sincere faith. And the sheer volume of restrictions makes it difficult to live within the law. Minors and college students are barred from entering all churches.[25]

Beijing is fine with allowing Christianity as long as it can be used as a platform to advance the Communist Party. Churches and individual Christians who refuse to let their faith be used as a platform to promote government-sponsored communist propaganda can face real danger. What have come to be known as "house churches" (whether they meet in a house or not) lack government approval. The house church movement started under Mao when Christians were forced to worship secretly in homes or face persecution.[26] House churches were especially important during the Cultural Revolution.[27] Today, some house churches have hundreds of members. It is estimated that two-thirds of Chinese Christians attend a house church.[28] In 2020, ChinaAid found that residents reporting suspected illegal house church activity can earn rewards of up to 5,000 RMB (or $700 USD).[29]

Religious restrictions apply not just to Chinese Christians, but also to foreign missionaries and foreign persons living in China. According to a 2019 report by ChinaAid, a "work plan" created by the Chinese government seeks to "resolutely destroy" the activities of foreign missions groups, cracking down on supposed "international religious infiltration."[30] The suppression of foreign religious groups includes the shutting down of facilities, propaganda and misinformation campaigns, and surveillance of individual members' lives and online activity.[31]

Yet, it is not just Protestant churches that feel the burden of government restrictions and control. On September 22, 2018, the Chinese government and the Vatican reached a "provisional agreement" on the appointment of bishops, which was renewed in 2020. This issue had strained Vatican-China relations for decades. Before 2018, the Catholic Church in China which remained loyal to the Vatican was dubbed the "Underground Catholic Church."[32] Two state-run institutions, the Chinese Catholic Patriotic Association (CPCA) and the Council of Chinese bishops, oversee the bishops who are recognized by both the Vatican and the Chinese government.[33] Following the Vatican-China Deal of 2018, the Vatican considered the CPCA and the underground Catholic Church as the unified Chinese Catholic Church.[34] The text of the deal was never disclosed, yet it reportedly allows the Chinese government to nominate bishops, while the Pope has the power to veto nominees.[35]

Under Chinese law, priests and bishops are required to register with the state and to sign a document agreeing to the principles of independence, autonomy, and self-administration of the Church in China.[36] Some priests and bishops have declined to join the CPCA for reasons of conscience, and the Vatican has requested that the CCP respect such conscientious objectors.[37] While the Vatican and the Chinese government are cooperating more now than in the past several decades, critics question why the atheistic Chinese regime should have a role in choosing bishops. The two-year deal was renewed for another two years in October 2020.[38]

Christians are among many religious groups to face repression in China. Tibetan Buddhists have long endured harsh treatment. Their devotion to the Dalai Lama is perceived as disloyalty to the People's Republic of China, verging on treason. In response, since 2009, 156 Tibetans have self-immolated in protest of China's abuses. Falun Gong practitioners are also subject to arrest and imprisonment, and credible reports indicate many Falun Gong political prisoners have been executed for organ harvesting.[39]

Even a community of less than 1,000 Jews in Kaifeng has been victimized by Party authorities, who in 2018 stormed through a study center's gates, tore loose and trashed a metal Star of David, and ripped Hebrew scriptural quotations off the walls. The authorities also put a stop to any foreign funding for the group.

Yet, no religious group has endured as intense of a crackdown in recent years as Uyghur Muslims. Mihrigul Tursun is a survivor of a massive "re-education" internment camp in Xinjiang. It is incredibly rare to hear from a survivor of one of the camps. Detainees are rarely released. And when they are, they are closely monitored and intimidated by the Chinese government.

The camps are designed to erase the faith and culture of Uyghur Muslims, an ethnic and religious minority, and force them to adopt the norms, language, and non-religious tendencies preferred by the CCP. Detainees are subjected to daily Communist Party indoctrination sessions, inhumane living conditions, and torture. It is estimated that China currently detains at least one to three million Uyghurs in these facilities.[40]

A Uyghur Muslim originally from Xinjiang, Mihrigul was living in Egypt with her husband following her education. When she had triplets in 2015, she took her babies back to China so that her parents could help her care for them. When she arrived at the airport in Xinjiang with her two-month-old triplets, Chinese authorities seized her children from her while she was questioned and beaten. Authorities then took her directly to prison where she was held without any idea if or when she might be released.

Following her release from prison two months later, she rushed to pick up her children from the hospital where the authorities had kept them. Upon her arrival, she was informed that operations had been performed on all three of her children. A day later, it resulted in the death of one of her sons. Despite her pleas, she was denied the request to see her son.

Mihrigul was again taken into custody—this time to a "reeducation" camp. There, Chinese authorities repeatedly tortured her. They put a metal device on her head which transmitted electric shocks sending a searing pain which could be felt even in her veins and bones. The pain was so great she begged the guards to kill her—convinced that death would be better than enduring more torture.[41]

She was placed in Cell 210, a small room that held sixty-eight women. One woman in the cell hadn't been allowed to leave the room in thirteen months—not even to shower. Occasionally, women were taken from the cell and never heard of again.

Mihrigul witnessed nine women die in the cell due to the brutal conditions of the camp over the course of her detention. When the police came to remove a body of the deceased, all the women were instructed to lie down on the floor. The police did not enter the room to pick up the body. Rather, they used a metal contraption to pick the body up by the neck and drag it out of the cell, as if trash was being picked up off the ground.

At one point, Mihrigul was even sentenced to death and the police asked her how she wanted to die. Thankfully, Mihrigul was released in April 2018 after having been detained for ten months in total. She was allowed to return to Egypt to seek medical treatment for her two remaining children who had Egyptian citizenship. Even after seeking refuge in the United States, the nightmare did not end for Mihrigul. She struggled to sleep at night. The images of the nine women who died kept coming to her mind. In her dreams, Chinese authorities wanted to kill her.

China continues to shamelessly deny the true nature of these camps. Chinese leaders try to sell the narrative that these camps are merely "free vocational training" centers. There is ample evidence to prove what is really going on in Xinjiang. Satellite images, Chinese government budget reports, and witness testimonies such as Mihrigul's reveal the truth of China's brutal oppression of religious minorities.

Major reports concerning a widespread program of forced sterilization and abortion in Xinjiang prompted former Secretary of State Mike Pompeo's determination that the Chinese government is committing an ongoing genocide in Xinjiang.[42] The genocide determination is significant, and it will inevitably affect U.S.-China relations moving forward.

The stories of forced sterilization and abortion against Uyghur women is heartbreaking. When Gulzia Mogdin was visiting from Kazakhstan, authorities in Xinjiang discovered WhatsApp on her phone, a punishable offense that prompted extra scrutiny. Police took her to the hospital, where medical workers discovered she was pregnant with her third child. The authorities forced Mogdin to have an abortion, threatening to detain her and her brother if she resisted. She later told the Associated Press, "I cannot sleep. It's terribly unfair."[43]

Ultimately, the CCP demands residents to find their identity in being Party members, not religious believers. And so, the Chinese government finds itself at odds with all faiths unless believers are willing to make the tenets of Chinese communist ideology central to their faith. The freedom to practice a religion that includes state-imposed doctrine is no religious freedom at all. Yet, even as Beijing works to control religious belief, Christianity has managed to flourish in China. Although proselytizing is illegal, Christianity has still rapidly expanded in China since 1980. Researchers estimate China is on course to have more Christians than any other country in the world by 2030.[44]

COMPLETE DENIAL OF FREEDOM IN NORTH KOREA

Ji Hyeona is one of the few Christians who have managed to escape North Korea. Successful defections from the world's most isolated country are rare, and firsthand accounts from Christians in this country that has outlawed religion for decades are even more rare.

Hyeona first encountered a Bible in North Korea after her mother traveled across the border into China to find food during the devastating North Korea famine in the 1990s.[45] In addition to bringing food for her family, she also brought back a small Korean-language Bible. Hyeona read the treasured prize every day.

One day, she was summoned to the local Ministry of State Security, the dreaded secret police known as the *bowibu*. Hyeona had no idea why she had been taken. The *bowibu* agents beat her until she was bloodied. It was her first experience being tortured.

The agents interrogated her, demanding to know if she had come into contact with any South Korean intelligence agents. "I don't know what you're talking about," she said. Finally, a *bowibu* agent placed Hyeona's Bible on the desk in front of her. "This is what this is all about," he said.

Hyeona felt her heart stop. She knew what all North Koreans know. In North Korea, if the government discovers you believe in any god or gods besides Kim Il-sung and the Kim family dictators, you will be sent to a political prison camp or executed.

She had to think quickly. She told the security agents she found it outside while she was on a walk. She said she had even been about to turn it in to the authorities, but she did not have the time. This was a lie, but Hyeona felt it was the only way to get out of the situation alive. Agents left her with the threat if she were ever caught with a Bible again, she would not escape punishment.

Eventually, Hyeona escaped from North Korea four separate times. The first three times, she was discovered by Chinese authorities and repatriated back into the custody of North Korean authorities. Upon her arrival in North Korea, she was always sent to Prison Camp #11, a labor reform prison camp. There, she and other detainees were made to work like slaves. Working conditions at the camps were dire. Detainees often died from overwork, malnourishment, and easily treatable illnesses such as diarrhea.

During her third repatriation back to North Korea, Hyeona was pregnant. The North Korean regime considers half-Chinese babies to be "mixed-race," and therefore undesirable and not worthy of life. When North Korean security agents discovered Hyeona was pregnant, they took her into a private room and lifted her onto a desk. There were no hospital beds or basic equipment, and she was given no anesthesia.

A doctor forced her legs apart and began shredding her baby apart in her womb. Many women endure the tragic torture of a forced abortion in North Korea. She said, "Every night, I heard the screams of women going through forced abortions in the prison camp." On her fourth escape from North Korea, she finally made it to South Korea.

Too many North Korean Christians have stories a lot like Hyeona's. North Korea is an atheist nation in which religious believers, especially Christians, have endured decades of targeted persecution. Yet, Open Doors estimates that a little over one percent of the population (approximately 300,000 people) is Christian. Although religion is not allowed in North Korea today, Christianity once flourished in the land now controlled by North Korea. The early part of the twentieth century witnessed a period of immense growth of Christianity in the country, earning Pyongyang the title "Jerusalem of the East." Many of today's North Korean Christians learned of the faith because it was passed down by their families from this time. Notably, Kim Il-sung's parents were reported to be practicing Christians.

This changed abruptly when a communist regime took power in 1948. Kim Il-sung took measures to suppress Christianity almost immediately. Restrictions on churches and religious practice grew tighter with time. Throughout the late 1940s and 50s, Christians were systematically imprisoned, driven into exile, and executed.

With the enforced absence of public religious expression, Kim Il-sung successfully consolidated power and built a personality cult around himself. To reinforce his status as a god-like dictator and to affirm the Communist Party's agenda, the government promoted the ideology of *Juche*, often translated as "self-reliance."[46] The sentiment behind *Juche* is a rejection of dependence on others and the conviction that a proper show of revolutionary spirit will enable North Korea to survive on its own as a socialist state.

Christians are prohibited from openly practicing their religion, and those caught doing so are subject to severe punishments.[47] In a country estimated to be the home of nearly a half million Christians, there are only five churches. Possession of a Bible can be life-threatening. One North Korean defector testified that "many North Korean refugees have Bibles with them when they are repatriated. If they are caught carrying a Bible, they are punished. In North Korea, you can get away with murder if you have good connections. However, if you get caught carrying a Bible, there is no way to save your life."[48]

Those who follow Christianity do so at enormous risk, forcing them to often live out their faith in an isolated manner. Christians must keep their faith a secret, sometimes even from their own families. Because of the severe lack of places of worship, Christians in North Korea are often isolated from a faith community. They cannot meet with large groups of fellow believers for worship, for fear of someone informing the regime.

Believers know the cost of getting caught is high. The punishment is often immediate imprisonment in a political prison camp or even execution.[49] The UN's 2014 commission of inquiry report found those who are discovered to have been in contact with Christian churches "may be forcibly 'disappeared' into political prison camps, imprisoned in ordinary prisons or even summarily executed."[50] North Korea punishes crimes to the third generation of the offender, so if the government discovers a Christian, the Christian's family is often sent to a prison camp as well.

While current North Korean dictator Kim Jong-un denies the existence of any prison or labor camps, satellite images capture glimpses of large land tracts guarded with towers and barbed wire. A 2019 U.S. State Department report on North Korean prisons describes two different types of labor camps:[51] the *kwanliso*, or political prison camps, and the *kyohwaso*, or re-education labor camps. Christians, thought to be a foreign threat to the authority of the regime, are sent to the *kwanliso*. The conditions of the *kwanliso* are known to be extremely dire, with prisoners forced to perform hard labor much of the day. They receive meager, starvation-level food rations. These political prison camps are sometimes called "absolute control zones" and prisoners remain there for the rest of their lives. It is estimated that 50,000 Christians are held in these camps. Reports indicate detainees endure torture, including beatings with electric rods or metal poles, forced submersion in water, and use for medical experimentation.

The trial of Otto Warmbier in 2016, an American student who was accused of subversion by North Korean authorities after he allegedly took down a propaganda poster on a tour, demonstrates the regime's paranoia about Christianity.[52] Though Warmbier was Jewish, the court proceedings repeatedly mentioned the offense of Christianity, and connected his crime to the influence of a friend from an American Methodist church. The court sentenced Warmbier to fifteen years of hard labor, but he was sent by medical transport to his hometown of Cincinnati, Ohio after only seventeen months, where he died days after returning to the United States.

After they escape, many defectors say they had never heard of religion or Christianity while in North Korea. The closest thing they can compare to a religion in North Korea is the enforced worship of the Kim dictatorship. Religion is not spoken of out loud in the hermit kingdom. After decades of propaganda and state-controlled education, many North Koreans lack basic knowledge about world religions.

In his book *Under the Same Sky*, North Korean defector Joseph Kim recounts when he fled to China, a woman instructed him to seek help at churches and to locate them by looking for crosses on buildings. To her surprise, she had to show him what the famous Christian symbol looked like.

The regime has proven it is obsessed with preventing North Koreans from seeing any religious imagery. When a large Christmas tree structure was lit in December 2014 in a South Korean town two miles from the border with the North, the regime threatened to shoot it down and accused South Korea of "psychological warfare." The North Korean regime's abusive attempts to suppress religion is a tragic spiritual reality for the millions of people who will never be given the freedom to choose and live out their faith.

Shrouded in secrecy, North Korea remains one of the world's most mysterious countries. The secretive nature of North Korea makes it difficult for American leaders and activists to address these human rights issues. Even though options are limited, the gravity of the situation calls on Western countries to take every action possible to relieve the suffering of the North Korean people, who have no chance of speaking up for themselves.

After decades of intense and strategic efforts to suppress religion, religion remains in North Korea. This is a testament to the importance of religion—and religious freedom—to humanity. Although the North Korean government tries to replace religion with state-promoted *Juche*, this empty substitute for religion centered on the ruling Kim family will not satisfy the human soul. Despite the dangers, Christians and others will still choose to practice their faith with courage in North Korea.

STRUGGLES IN VIETNAM

In Vietnam, like China and other countries, the effects of communist rule linger and affect how the state interacts with religion—always for the worse. Pastor A Dao knows the struggle of being a faithful leader in such a society well. He is the leader of the Montagnard Evangelical Church of Christ in Gia Xieng village, Kontum Province of Vietnam. The Montagnard tribes represent various indigenous groups in the Central Highlands of Vietnam. Christians belonging to these ethnic minority groups are doubly targeted by the government.

Pastor A Dao spoke at a conference in East Timor about religious freedom in 2016. He emphasized the challenges his church was facing from the government regulations and harassment. Unfortunately, this act of public advocacy for religious freedom provoked the ire of Vietnamese authorities.

He was arrested shortly after his return from the conference in August 2016. In April 2017, he was sentenced to five years' imprisonment for supposedly "helping individuals to escape abroad illegally."[53] Pastor A Dao refused to confess to the false charges Vietnamese authorities were trying to force him to admit. For his integrity, Pastor A Dao was tortured.

Members of the Montagnard Evangelical Church of Christ were interrogated. Vietnamese authorities instructed them to cut off contact with "foreign reactionaries." This was not the first time these brave members of the congregation had endured government abuse. Pastor A Ga, the church's previous pastor, was also imprisoned for his bold Christian leadership. The church is prominent among churches not registered with the government, inducing the government to take strong actions to repress their leadership.

After serving four years of his five-year prison sentence, Pastor A Dao was finally released in September of 2020. The ordeal cost him several years of his life and had a chilling effect for other pastors in Vietnam. U.S. Representative Glenn Grothman (R-Wis.) had advocated for Dao through the Tom Lantos Human Rights Commission's Defending Freedoms Project and advocated for him publicly, as did U.S. Commission on International Religious Freedom (USCIRF) Commissioner James Carr. Upon Pastor A Dao's release, Rep. Grothman said it "shows the importance of American elected officials speaking out against oppression and promoting the importance of religious freedom throughout the world."[54]

In Vietnam, all churches must be registered with the government. Yet pastors belonging to ethnic minority groups, including Hmong and Montagnard, have great difficulty registering their churches. Vietnamese bureaucrats often reject applications for churches to register based on bogus occupancy limitations.[55]

Furthermore, many churches choose not to register with the government. They would rather teach what they know from Scripture to be true than to register with the government and give it a large say in what the church teaches. Registered churches are closely monitored by the government. House churches may be raided and shut down for illegal activity, particularly affecting those in the Central Highlands.

The ruling Communist Party in Vietnam considers some Christians to be a dangerous segment of society with the capacity to mobilize large numbers of people. Many Christians in Vietnam—around 10,000—belong to the country's ethnic minority groups, including the Hmong and Montagnard. These groups are essentially rendered stateless as authorities refuse to issue them registration documents and identity cards.[56] Ethnic Christians often have their homes destroyed, forcing them to flee and seek refuge in Cambodia. Yet, in several cases, Christians who flee abroad cause the Vietnamese government to put pressure on the Cambodian government, prompting Cambodia to deport the fleeing Christians back to Vietnam.[57]

Vietnam continues to enforce burdensome regulations on religion. In January 2018, the National Assembly passed the *Law on Belief and Religion*. This thirty-page law came with an implementing decree with fifty-three separate permission forms.[58] Historic churches in Vietnam, including the Catholic Church, are not subject to the level of harassment experienced by house churches. Yet, the government often forcibly takes or even destroys properties belonging to the Catholic Church. In one instance, thugs working for the government attacked members of a Benedictine monastery, eventually forcing the monastery to give up its land.[59]

The growth of the church among the Hmong has Vietnamese authorities particularly worried. Authorities, especially in rural areas, have even published literature criticizing them.

Pastor Trung Ton was an outspoken advocate for religious freedom and social justice causes. He was arrested in July 2017 and charged with attempting to "overthrow the people's government." He received a twelve-year prison sentence in April 2018. This hard punishment was not the end of his family's suffering. His wife, Thi Lanh, has been harassed by authorities and arrested, though she was quickly released.[60] Tragically, Pastor Ton's son has been tortured by authorities. At one point, they blindfolded him and beat his head with an electric baton. He required medical treatment to recover.

Despite the trauma, the family remains committed to their faith and to advocating for religious freedom for others.

The Vietnamese church is brave and full of faith. *Christianity Today* told the powerful story of Dang Van Sung and his wife, Diep Thi Do, living under tight communist control:

> In 1953, they went to work with the Stieng minority tribe in Binh Phuoc province. Just before Communist forces captured the area in April 1975, he was taken prisoner and never heard from again.
>
> For six years, Mrs. Diep went into hiding, unable and afraid to contact any local Christians. Eventually she surfaced, and one day while in the market she met a group of Christians. Recognizing her, they pled with her to become their pastor.
>
> She did more than that. Battling the government, she pressed the Communist state to open closed churches. In time, they agreed. In Phuc Long, she built a church seating 2,000, the largest church building in the country at the time.[61]

The courageous faith of Christians in Vietnam demonstrates the hope provided by the gospel will survive and even grow despite the repression of communist and post-communist regimes that seek to impede people's ability to worship God in their own way.

MOB VIOLENCE AND LEGAL OPPRESSION AGAINST CHRISTIANS IN PAKISTAN

When Maira Shahbaz was ordered by a Pakistani court to resume living with the man who had kidnapped her, she broke down in tears in the courtroom. The court's decision came several months after three armed men had intercepted Maira while she was walking home and forced her into a car, shooting wildly into the air as they drove away.[62] One of the men, Mohamad Nakash, forged a fake marriage certificate and claimed she had converted to Islam.

Maira's parents desperately sought custody to recover their daughter. Although her parents had the legal birth certificate proving Maira was only fourteen years old, Nakash's forged marriage documents falsely claimed she was nineteen years old. Even the imam whose signature was allegedly on the marriage certificate denied the certificate's legitimacy.

In July 2020, the Faisalabad District and Sessions Court removed Maira from her abductor's custody and placed her in a women's shelter until a ruling could be made. Unfortunately, the Lahore High Court chose to send Maira back to the abusive arms of her captor the following month. The court ruled the young Christian girl had voluntarily converted to Islam and her marriage to the twenty-eight-year-old Nakash was legal, even though he already had another wife. Polygamy is legal in some circumstances in Pakistan, but rarely practiced.

In cases of forced marriage, "the women are reportedly questioned in front of the men they were forced to marry, creating pressure to deny coercion." Maira's parents' lawyer Sumera Shafiq stated this happened to Maira too. He said, "The girl was subjected to threats from her rapist, so she had to state in favor of him in court."[63]

After the High Court ruling, Maira successfully escaped from Nakash and went into hiding with her family in September 2020.[64] But Maira has not yet found safety. She still receives death threats from her abductor and his supporters who label her an apostate. As of this writing, Maira and her family are seeking asylum in the United Kingdom.[65]

While there are no official estimates, likely hundreds of Christian and Hindu girls in Pakistan are forced to convert to Islam and marry Muslim men. Victims are usually taken by men looking for brides and, once legally converted, are quickly married off to their abductors. This abusive practice depends upon several nefarious factors: Islamic clerics who are willing to solemnize the underage marriages, magistrates who make the marriages legal, and corrupt authorities who refuse to investigate despite the obvious criminal nature of these marriages.[66] Pakistan's failure to protect religious freedom and respect its people's human dignity fosters a culture in which such heinous practices can thrive.

Islam is the state religion of Pakistan, but its constitution states, "Subject to law, public order, and morality, every citizen shall have the right to profess, practice, and propagate his religion."[67] The right to religious freedom should never have a qualifier. The State Department's International Religious Freedom Report in 2020 cited intelligence that the Pakistani government "was inconsistent in safeguarding against societal discrimination and neglect, and that official discrimination against Christians, Hindus, Sikhs, and Ahmadi Muslims persisted to varying degrees . . ."[68] Members of religious minority communities claim that authorities at the federal and provincial levels apply Pakistani secular law inconsistently.[69]

Blasphemy laws have long oppressed Christians and others in Pakistan. Such laws forced one married couple in Pakistan to languish apart in separate prisons, unable to see each other or their four children. Shafqat Emmanuel remains paralyzed from the waist down following an accident in 2004. His wife, Shagufta Kausar provided for her family by working as a cleaner. Shafqat and Shagufta lived simple lives on a church compound before their world came crashing down and a years-long nightmare ensued due to Pakistan's draconian blasphemy laws.

The saga began in June 2013, when a Muslim cleric claimed he received a blasphemous text message from Shagufta's phone. The cleric said he showed the text to his lawyer, and both subsequently claimed they received more inflammatory texts from the phone registered to Shagufta. The alleged texts were written in English.

There are a few problems with this dubious story. Shagufta and Shafqat come from a poor background and are illiterate. They could not have crafted such a text in their native Urdu, and certainly not in English. The couple suspects the cleric's accusation is retaliation for an argument between their children and their neighbors.

Blasphemy laws prohibit insults to religion and are utilized against Muslims and non-Muslims alike. Section 295-B of the Pakistani penal code states whoever "defiles, damages or desecrates a copy of the Holy Qur'an" can be punished with imprisonment for life.[70] Section 295-C states insults against the Prophet Muhammad are punishable by life imprisonment or death.[71]

Nonetheless, authorities arrested the couple and charged them both with "insulting the Qur'an" and "insulting the Prophet." In April 2014, Shafqat and Shagufta were sentenced to death, and it was not until June 2021 they were finally acquitted following substantial international pressure including a resolution from the European Parliament highlighting their case.

Blasphemy laws violate the freedom to live out one's faith through expressing one's beliefs. The mere fact that blasphemy laws remain on the books legitimizes and emboldens violence against non-Muslims who are perceived to have insulted Islam. Even when someone accused of blasphemy is acquitted, mobs have often form, threatening to punish perceived blasphemers themselves.[72] This trend contributes to an environment in which government officials are afraid to enforce justice.

People around the world are likely to associate Pakistan's brutal blasphemy laws with Asia Bibi, a Pakistani Christian who spent eight years on death row for the supposed "crime" of blasphemy. Her conviction was finally set aside by the Pakistani Supreme Court in 2018.[73]

Bibi had been accused of blaspheming the Prophet Mohammed during an argument with several women after she shared a drink with them, thereby making the water ceremonially "unclean." She was subsequently convicted and spent the following eight years awaiting her execution.

Following Bibi's release, thousands of Islamists demonstrated in the streets. They demanded she be put to death. Mobs formed to threaten her life, even though the courts had freed her. After her acquittal, the threats to Bibi's life and the lives of her family members were so great they required protective custody. She was finally granted asylum in Canada.

Blasphemy laws are not the only means by which Christians in Pakistan experience discrimination. Employment is a continuing struggle for Pakistan's religious minorities. In Pakistan's largest cities, sewage cleaners plunge clogged sewers by hand, often surrounded by cockroaches and without the protection of gloves or masks. The work is essential to maintain Pakistan's dilapidated sewage system. But it is also highly dangerous, and sometimes costs workers their lives.

For sewage cleaner positions, the most hazardous and filthy of jobs, local governments prefer to hire Christians. Last July, one Pakistani newspaper advertisement was so obvious as to say only Christians need apply for jobs as sewer cleaners. "I have seen death from very near," Pakistani street sweeper Michael Sadiq told the *New York Times*.[74] He described how his friend died after getting swept away by "putrid black water" in the sewers.

Most Christians in Muslim-majority Pakistan are descendants of lower-caste Hindus, who converted to Christianity by the thousands. The discriminatory legacy of the former Indian caste system haunts them to this day. Often derogatorily called "*chuhras*" by fellow Pakistanis, these lower-caste Christians are considered "untouchables" or "unclean."

As some of the poorest people in Pakistan, Christians have limited options for work. They have high illiteracy rates and are often resigned to menial jobs as farmhands, sanitation workers, or street sweepers. But these jobs carry stigmas of their own, reinforcing cultural discrimination against them. According to International Christian Concern, at least 80 percent of Pakistan's street sweepers, janitors, and sewer workers are Christians.[75] Street sweeping, like sewage cleaning, is a dangerous job thought to be too demeaning for Muslims. One Catholic street sweeper in Gujranwala was killed when he was hit by a police car in the road.[76]

Christians are a small and marginalized minority in Pakistan, making them vulnerable to discrimination in the judicial system, the economy, and society at large. This provides opportunities for extremists to target Christians. The international community should be focused on calling Pakistan to a higher standard of human rights for Christians and others who suffer from oppression there.

Changing Your Faith Is Dangerous in India

For many Westerners, India is an exotic travel destination, offering colorful cultural sites and warm-hearted, hospitable people. However, thanks to the current Hindu nationalist leadership of the Bharatiya Janata Party (BJP), India is increasingly marred by religious conflict and Christian persecution. The Purty family's double tragedy serves as a sad example of this. And for some Indian Christians, their story is not unusual.

Chamu Hassa Purty was a Christian pastor from Sandih village in Jharkhand State. Late one night in October 2015, he was asked to pray for a sick child. He rushed to the family's home, prayed for the boy, and helped the parents admit him to a local hospital. Shortly after Pastor Purty returned to his own home, eight armed men forced their way into his house. He and his wife urgently warned their daughters, Sharon and Neelam, to immediately leave the house through a back entrance.

In an interview with *Morning Star News*, Sharon recalled, "As we were about to move, two of them held us and brought us back to the front room. They fired at my father many times . . ." Pastor Purty died of gunshot wounds that night.[77]

After the murder, the Purty family left their village and rarely returned. But due to the COVID-19 pandemic in 2020, it became necessary they return to their former home. Soon after, attackers once again appeared at the Purty house. Sharon and her younger brother answered the door and found themselves confronted by two gunmen.

"Is this the house of the pastor who was killed?" one of the intruders demanded. Sharon stared at him as he ranted,

"That pastor was killed but you didn't learn your lesson. You're still assembling in large numbers for Christian prayers. And where's the woman who's working as a spy?"

"There are no spies here . . ." she responded. At that moment Neelam, hearing angry voices, entered the room. The gunman shouted, "She's the one! She's the spy!" He aimed his gun and pulled the trigger.

"Our father was shot to death in that same room," Sharon Purty later recalled. "We cried for help as the two gunmen jumped on a motorbike and fled." Her sister, Neelam Purty, sustained serious injuries and was bleeding heavily. She was rushed to a hospital, where it was determined that a bullet was embedded in her thigh and her thighbone was shattered. Only after major surgery was she able to begin her painful recovery.

The police were notified and evidence was recorded, yet the gunmen were never apprehended. Attacks like those against the Purty family are on the rise in India due to a dangerous ideology gaining steam in the world's largest democracy—Hindu nationalism. It asserts that India is a nation for Hindus, marginalizing Christians and other minorities.

This movement often inspires mob attacks against Christians. Such attacks, when committed by Hindus, are rarely rebuked by the present Indian government, and the legal system often fails to bring perpetrators of mob violence to justice. One Indian pastor was dragged out of his church mid-service by a mob of Hindu nationalists and beaten for hours.[78] Yet when the police arrived, they charged the pastor with violating a blasphemy law rather than charge the radicals for their violent assault.

Even Indian laws pose a threat to minorities, though according to the constitution, India is a secular country. Yet, anti-conversion laws remain on the books in several Indian states. These laws are intended to prevent forced conversions, while in reality, they restrict the right to change one's faith and discourage conversion away from Hinduism. Some Hindu nationalist leaders are deeply paranoid about Hindus converting to Christianity or other religions. One former member of parliament and member of the BJP party called Christian missionaries "a threat to the unity of the country."[79]

Anti-Christian sentiment has also affected travelers to India. American pastor Bryan Nerren was only allowed to return home after being detained in India for over seven months. "I am back with family and friends at home," the Tennessee pastor finally told *Morning Star News*.[80] "It is a wonderful time."

Authorities first interrupted Pastor Nerren's two-week trip to India and Nepal in October 2019, arresting him as he got off his flight in Bagdogra. Officials questioned him about failing to pay duty on $40,000—funds meant to go toward two ministry conferences—he brought with him when he arrived in New Delhi.

Yet, Pastor Nerren had done nothing wrong. He maintained he was never told to pay a duty. He was also not carrying enough money to be charged for evading tax duty. The real issue was his Christian mission. According to his lawyers, Indian officials "specifically asked if he was a Christian and if the funds would be used to support Christian causes." After spending six days in jail, Pastor Nerren was required to pay a $4,000 fine. He was released but was banned from leaving the country.

The targeted interrogation about Pastor Nerren's faith reflects a growing problem in India. Since the 2014 election of Prime Minister Narendra Modi, who rose to power with the BJP, things have been going from bad to worse for religious minorities.

Inflammatory rhetoric from national leaders, a growing exclusionary movement that ostracizes religious minorities, and draconian blasphemy and anti-conversion laws form a perfect storm for the persecution of Christians in India. India's dire religious freedom problems deserves far more international attention than they receive. India is the world's most populous democracy, making it all the more disappointing its government is failing to protect the fundamental human right to freedom of religion.

CHURCH GROWTH AMID CRACKDOWNS IN NEPAL

In Hindu-majority Nepal, Christianity is the fastest-growing religion. In 1961, Nepal only had 458 Christians according to the census. Fast-forward to 2011, and Nepal counted almost 376,000 Christians. Though it is spreading quickly, Christians remain a small minority at 1 to 2 percent of the population.

Christian communities in Nepal are young and dynamic, composed primarily of converts to Christianity. The growth of Christianity has made Nepali authorities nervous, as Hindu nationalists maintain paranoid fears that Christians are preying on Hindus to convert them and erode the Hindu majority in Nepal.

The extended legal battles that Pastor Hari Tamang was forced to endure illustrates well the danger of anti-Christian sentiment in Nepal. His legal battles with the state began when a woman who ran an orphanage that was being shut down came to Pastor Tamang for help, and he was quick to offer his assistance.

She had brought the children with her and Pastor Tamang helped provide food and shelter for the group, who had no place else to go. After ten days of supporting the children, the police arrived and took Pastor Tamang into custody. He was shocked to find out he had been charged with trafficking and attempted religious conversion.[81]

His bail was set at 50,000 Nepali rupees (around $423 USD). Pastor Tamang paid his bail, and the prosecutors soon dropped the trafficking-related charges. However, they did not drop the charge of attempted conversion of the children. The case went on for more than four years, and at the time of this writing, Pastor Tamang still makes regular court appearances over this case. He claims that the government targeted him for his faith. He is hardly the only Christian to make such a complaint.

In 2021, Hindu nationalists distributed fake documents on social media that framed Christian groups for having a master plan to cause ethnic divisions between Hindus in order to convert them.[82] The forgeries were meant to prove that two major Christian groups—Nepal Christian Society (NCS) and National Churches Fellowship of Nepal (NCFN)—were conspiring to draw Hindus into converting to Christianity by dividing lower-caste and upper-caste Hindus.

Given the irrational widespread fear of conversions, Hindu nationalists try to prevent religious conversions through the enactment of anti-conversion laws. Anti-conversion laws, quite simply, prohibit people from converting to another religion. Primarily in place in parts of the Hindu and Buddhist world, anti-conversion laws are used by governments to keep a majority of the population following the state's preferred religion.

These laws are supposedly meant to serve the purpose of preventing people from being tricked and "induced" into changing from any faith to any other faith, but often end up discouraging the sharing of one's faith—often due to action taken against quite ordinary proselytizing on the grounds it is "tricking" people into "fraudulent" conversions. These laws end up having a chilling effect on simply sharing one's faith, even if it is done in a noncoercive manner.

Nepali law criminalizes proselytism.[83] Foreign nationals can be deported for converting people to Christianity. In August 2019, authorities accused four Christians—Tul Bahadur Pariyar, Rupa Sonam, Chandrakali Rawat, and Bhim Kumari—of "preaching Christianity." Upon their arrest, authorities seized a bag containing Christian tracts and resources. The four Christians were charged under the anti-conversion law which can carry up to a five-year prison sentence.[84] The simple act of sharing one's faith should not mean a possible prison sentence. Yet, for Christians in Nepal, this is a real fear.

Sometimes, the government is outwardly belligerent toward Christians. The forced demolition of a church to make way for school grounds drew one congregation to tears.[85] Rupantaran Khristiya Church served Christian families in the Naya Basti slum area before the pastor and church elders were given just five minutes to remove their equipment and any items they wished to keep before the church was torn down. The destruction of religious sites is a problematic trend around the world. The carelessness shown by local authorities fosters social hostility toward minorities.

Much like in India, Hindu nationalism is on the rise in Nepal. Political parties, such as the Rastriya Prajantra Party (RPP), are working to make Nepal an officially Hindu state—tying the majority religion to the country's national identity. In 2016, the government caved to Hindu nationalist pressure and tried to remove the official status of Christmas as a national holiday.[86] It reversed its decision on Christmas eve of the same year. But this attack on Christmas demonstrates the lengths Hindu nationalists in Nepal will go to alienate Christian culture from the mainstream.

Social discrimination remains a problem for Nepali Christians. Open Doors reported the story of one Christian woman given the alias Bhumika, who said that "In my village they do not allow me to fetch water from the village well, and we're not allowed to even touch the handle of the water pump." All because of her Christian faith. She said, "Often I went secretly at night to fetch water."[87]

Bhumika's neighbors would go to her house to disrupt her small prayer meetings with other believers. Bhumika's husband was a convert to Christianity, and the couple faced discrimination from his own family. Her in-laws even blamed the couple's Christian faith whenever someone in the family became ill.

Despite the pressure, the church in Nepal continues to demonstrate impressive growth. Tej Rokka, a Nepali pastor, was sent to an orphanage by his father after his mother's death. The orphanage was run by an Indian missionary, and Rokka came to accept Christ there. Today, Rokka believes that 90 percent of the orphans he was raised with have founded their own ministries, just like he did.[88] This is a powerful testimony to the power of faith, even in a hostile environment.

SCATTERED VIOLENCE IN SRI LANKA

Usually a celebratory day for Christians around the world who remember the resurrection of their Savior, Easter Sunday in Sri Lanka in 2019 was a terrifying and mournful occasion. A coordinated bombing of multiple churches and hotels across multiple cities claimed the lives of more than 250 people and injured hundreds more.[89] Some of the bombs detonated within ongoing Easter services themselves.

According to the *Washington Post*, survivor Delicia Fernando was prepared for a normal Easter celebration.[90] First, she would go to mass at St. Anthony's Shrine, one of Sri Lanka's most famous churches, and then go to her parents' house for a large family lunch. She attended the 8:00 a.m. Mass as planned, but when Mass was well under way, the congregation stood up to pray and was immediately met with the loud ripping sound of an explosion.

The sounds of screams and the confusion caused by falling debris soon followed. Delicia and her two adult children fled the church. Later, when they got the chance to look for her husband, they found him dead under pieces of the damaged building.

Many survivors of the attacks had similar stories. The victims were diverse, coming from different stations in life. One thing united them—they were attacked on Easter Sunday by terrorists who wished to strike fear into the Christian community. A radical Muslim terrorist group claimed responsibility for the attack.

Christians, most of whom are Catholic, make up 7 percent of the population of Sri Lanka. Yet, Christianity is marginalized by the Buddhist majority and treated like a foreign religion and a product of colonialism.[91]

Christianity's social stigma also extends into education. The Christian faith is often not taught as a subject in state-run public schools, and students get little exposure to learning about the religions or beliefs of others.[92] This caught the attention of UN Special Rapporteur on Freedom of Religion Ahmed Shaheed in 2019, prompting him to call for reform in the education system in Sri Lanka because it required students to choose only one religion to learn about for the duration of their education. The failure to properly foster religious understanding through education hardly helps ease the longstanding religious and ethnic tensions in Sri Lanka.

Much of the pressure faced by Christians in Sri Lanka is social. The families of converts to Christianity often try to persuade them away from their newfound faith. Communities socially exclude those who convert away from the majority faith. The social exclusion felt by many new Christians in Sri Lanka is painful. Withstanding the social pressure takes commitment and perseverance.

LTG (RET.) JERRY BOYKIN:
REFLECTIONS ON AMERICAN INTERESTS
AND CONCERNS IN ASIA

America has myriad interests in the continent of Asia, and not the least of these is our commitment to protect and support our friends there—friends who are very important to our national security. One good example is the Philippines, which has proven to be a strategic U.S. ally. We've kept American military air and naval bases there for decades. Thailand is another very reliable ally—one that still remembers World War II and recalls that America was very influential in protecting them during those years.

We also have trade agreements with several Asian countries. And at the same time, the shipping lanes in the Pacific Rim are critical to America's international trade. In fact, they are so critical that our country must have alliances—as well as freedom of navigation—in order to keep those shipping lanes open and international trade alive. It would be a significant blow to our economy if they were challenged.

Today, South Korea and Japan are our two most prominent allies in the region. Here is how those relationships began. In the summer of 1950, the U.S. sent Task Force Smith into South Korea. It was a force made up primarily of troops under General Douglas MacArthur's command and it was pulled together very quickly. These fighters were not properly equipped or even well trained. But when the South Koreans had been pushed by North Korea just as far as they could be pushed without going into the ocean, Task Force Smith entered the fray.

The North Koreans were still pushing hard, but the new American task force was able to turn the tide of war, which was marked by MacArthur's landing at Inchon. He and his troops got in behind the North Koreans and threatened to cut off their supply lines and their lines of communications. And that's when the breakout of the Pusan Perimeter was enabled, and we fought them all the way back across the border. The Korean War speaks for itself. And it was not just the U.S. and the South Koreans. It was really a United Nations effort.

The U.S. has kept military forces there since the armistice was signed by the warring factions. The American troops in South Korea have developed a solid relationship with the South Koreans. In fact, I think it is one of the strongest relationships America has among her allies, with the possible exception of Israel and Great Britain.

U.S. troops have been in Korea since 1950. We've shuffled troops around and we've reduced their numbers from time to time. But still we have a U.S. presence there, prepared to be part of any effort to push back the North Koreans across the border and to defeat them, should they be foolish enough to try to cross that border into South Korea again.

The South Koreans, although originally Buddhist, have long been open to the gospel and are very much a Christian nation. So, we've had more than just an economic and military alliance. We also had a theological alliance with these people.

Meanwhile, North Korea is a radically atheistic country. If you stop and look at the difference between North and South Korea, only the names are similar. In terms of the way they think, of their values, of what they see for the future, they are profoundly different. North Korea has been the #1 worst persecutor of Christians for more than twenty years—as long as such records have been kept.

North Korea is an existential threat to South Korea, because if North Korea gets a nuclear weapon, it would only take a couple of bombs to wipe out most of the South Korean population. They'd wipe out a lot of American soldiers as well, and in response we would ultimately make a parking lot out of North Korea. The whole idea that Kim Jong-un—a guy who is clearly not completely stable—would have any kind of nuclear weapon really is a frightening thought.

So, today, what can the U.S. do to deter North Korea while also supporting our allies? One priority is military exercises with the South Koreans. Those exercises not only build interoperability, but they also send a strong message to Kim Jong-un. And these are not just land exercises but naval exercises as well. This is designed to make sure when conflict arises, we can operate together and each country understands the tactics of the other.

And what else can we do? We are heavily sanctioning North Korea. And if it weren't for the fact the Chinese continue to bust those sanctions, we would be hurting the North far more. I think the Russians and the Chinese—regardless of what they say—are clandestinely supporting North Korea and taking some of the bite out of our sanctions.

But what more can we do? Well, as mentioned before, there's another element of power called intelligence. And we can share what we know with South Korea and Japan, both of which have skin in the game. We can provide robust intelligence for them including the primary thing intelligence is designed for: I&W—Indications and Warnings.

Indications and Warnings are the primary mission of the intelligence community. We can not only take note of these facts ourselves, but we can provide I&W to Japan as well as South Korea. We can also furnish them with routine intelligence—we continually give them good, useful information. That ranges from intelligence on the North Korean nuclear program down to intelligence on specific individuals like Kim himself: What's he doing? What's he planning? What's his next move?

Like Iran, North Korea is an excellent place for covert action to take place. How might that look? Think about this: every time the Iranians go out to fire a missile and that missile blows up on a launch pad, there are a couple of possibilities. One is bad luck. The other is that we can easily assume it's probably Israeli covert action. Every time a nuclear scientist gets in his car and it blows up, it is probably Israeli covert action. They may not call it that, and they may even deny it, but it's the same principle.

So just use your imagination when you think about North Koreans. What could be done to stop progress in their nuclear program? What could be done to remove some of their scientists or top nuclear people? What could be done with regards to their delivery capabilities such as missiles?

Imagination is the key word here, and covert action is certainly a possibility.

CONCERNS ABOUT CHINA'S AGGRESSIVE AMBITIONS

One of the key obstacles in dealing with North Korea is China, which provides both open and clandestine assistance to North Korea's rogue regime. This complication has intensified in recent years. And meanwhile, the present adversarial situation between the U.S. and China is very much complicated by China's ambition to seize Taiwan—its population and commercial assets—as if it were China's own.

In 1979, some thirty years after the Communist Party conquered the Chinese government, President Jimmy Carter shut down the U.S. Embassy in Taiwan and recognized only mainland, communist China as a nation state. Until then, America had a robust presence in Taiwan. We had a military advisory group there training the Taiwanese. We considered them strong allies, and then Jimmy Carter slammed the U.S. Embassy shut.

That was a huge strategic mistake because it meant we were ceding the security of Taiwan to the Chinese with nothing in return. Today, the Chinese want Taiwan just as they wanted Hong Kong. And it's not surprising. If you had visited Hong Kong in its heyday, you'd have seen its economy was incredible. Tourism was one of their biggest moneymakers. At the same time, they bought and sold goods and products from all over the world. Hong Kong was long a model of financial success; Taiwan's accomplishments are similar.

And now the Chinese want Taiwan. They have wanted it ever since it was separated from mainland China. Of course, this is nothing new to America's leaders. For many decades, really since World War II, the U.S. has been determined not to let Taiwan fall back into Chinese hands. Therefore, we've had contingency plans, and we've modified them over time as circumstances changed, technology improved, and intelligence reports dictated further modification.

But what are we most likely to do if and when the Chinese launch an invasion of Taiwan? How are we going to respond?

The question of whether we will defend Taiwan can only be answered by one person: the President of the United States. Some presidents are more likely than others to execute our contingency plan, which would mean pitting U.S. forces against Chinese forces—by air, land, and sea. My guess is not every president would be willing to do that. So yes, China is an existential threat to Taiwan, which really is a separate and independent nation. Meanwhile, the United States does not have an embassy there, and we are unable to activate our elements of national power: diplomatic, information, military, economic, financial, intelligence, and law enforcement options. Thank you, Mr. Carter.

China fully intends to seize Taiwan, and they are preparing for the conflict. They're building islands from which they can launch airplanes and ships, and islands where they can run intelligence stations, including monitoring communications and activity in the shipping lanes. They have similar outposts on *terra firma* and in some other Pacific regions. And they're building ports on small coral reefs. The Chinese are systematically setting themselves up so that they'll ultimately be able to launch an operation to capture Taiwan swiftly.

AMERICAN CHRISTIANS' RESPONSIBILITIES TO CHINA'S BELIEVERS

Whether or not the U.S. is prepared to confront China's political and military aggression, we Christians certainly need to stand strong with our Christian brothers and sisters there. There are millions of Christians in China's underground church. There are also many believers in the government-approved churches—the Protestant Three-Self Church and the Chinese Patriotic Catholic Church. But sadly, many of those registered churches are compromised because the government plants spies in their services to report back on various attendees and issues.

I think China's leaders fully realize it was Christianity, and the desire for religious freedom, that greatly influenced the American Founders' decision to separate from the King of England and the British Crown. I also think those same Chinese authorities fear this whole idea of Christianity places an imperative upon new believers in Christ not to continue to live under communist tyranny. It places Christianity above communism, because the God of the Bible is the Highest Authority on earth.

The Chinese genuinely fear Christians and what Christians might be able to do. They fear seeing them coming together and rallying and becoming a problem for the government, forcing them either to slaughter Christians or to back away. And there's a real sense of danger in the mind of the regime that these Christians might take over. To the government, Christian beliefs may sound a little foolish—just a bunch of quotes from an old book. But it sounded foolish in 1776 too. It also sounded insane to believe that a bunch of ragtag militiamen could form a government and defeat the

British army, which at the time was world's biggest, most powerful military. The Chinese are very concerned about that. That's why the persecution of Christians increases whenever the regime moves to increase its authority.

At the same time, there are also some other very bad actors persecuting Christians in the Asia region. There is intense and at times deadly persecution in Pakistan, and now we see thousands are threatened in Afghanistan. And in India, where supposedly peaceable Hindus now run the government, there is increasing abuse of Christians as well as Muslims. Another sad example is Burma, now known as Myanmar. Deadly government attacks on one Muslim tribe—the Rohingyas—continues there. And the Christians in Myanmar, more than three million of them, are scattered among several tribes. They are also suffering greatly.

WHAT IS THE ROLE OF AMERICAN CHRISTIANS?

It's important, as we think of Asia's persecuted Christians, to look at our non-governmental responsibilities to them— not only in several troublesome nations but in China itself. We can try to influence our government officials on one hand. But within our own Christian communities, we need to keep sending people into these countries to train new church leaders. This is essential, because in most restricted countries, only a dozen believers or less are legally able to gather for worship for security reasons. And when people come to know Christ, they need not only pastors but also reliable Bible teachers—well-trained instructors who can take new Christians to the next level of their spiritual walk. We should assist in training the leaders of the underground churches, while also keeping diplomatic pressure on the Chinese and other repressive regimes.

It is essential we protest the mistreatment of China's Uyghur Muslims. Far more than a million of them have been arrested and badly abused in prison camps by the Chinese communist regime who claim they are "terrorists." Because they are being so brutalized, their cause has become a humanitarian issue as much as a religious or theological one. So yes, by all means, let's support the Uyghurs and the persecuted Christians as well. Because, just as might be the case with Iran and its despotic leaders, China's Christians may be the very thing that brings down the Chinese government as we know it today.

Gordon Chang has written a book called *The Coming Crisis in China*. And he foresees just that—a huge crisis for the present government. When that comes to pass, wouldn't you like to know there are millions of Chinese people who trust God, millions of people who know Jesus as their personal Savior, millions of people who are united with us in our common faith? And wouldn't you like to know when things start to come apart in China, there is a vast body of Christians already there with leadership capabilities? They already have the motivation, and they already have the necessary courage to step into the fray. Even now, as in Iran, many of them are risking their lives for their faith. It brings a certain level of comfort to know about these godly people who are already active in the faith. And with a little support from believers in the United States, they can make a huge difference.

CHAPTER 2

AFRICA: THERE'S A WAR GOING ON

O N FEBRUARY 19, 2018, A BEAUTIFUL TEENAGER named Leah Sharibu was among more than 100 girls kidnapped by Boko Haram terrorists in Dapchi, Nigeria. Their abduction took place at 5:30 in the afternoon, when the girls were unexpectedly seized at Dapchi Girls' Science and Technical College.[1]

During the incident, four or five girls died in the back of a truck as they were violently transported to Boko Haram's encampment. Thankfully, following a month of horrific captivity, and after enduring death threats and unspeakable abuses, nearly all the surviving girls were freed by their captors on March 21.

One girl, however, was left behind—Leah Sharibu.

Before long, it become clear that she had not returned home for one simple reason: the other girls were all Muslim, but Leah was Christian and had refused to renounce her faith.

In August 2018, *The Cable*, a Nigerian news source, obtained a recording of Leah, begging President Muhammadu

Buhari to rescue her and reunite her with her family: "I am Leah Sharibu, the girl that was abducted in GGSS Dapchi. I am calling on the government and people of goodwill to intervene to get me out of my current situation."[2]

Leah's appeal resulted in absolutely no response from anyone; no intervention took place.

Later, when she heard that her classmates were being set free, Leah asked one of them to carry a note to her mother, Rebecca Sharibu.[3] "My mother, you should not be disturbed," she wrote. "I know it is not easy missing me, but I want to assure you that I am fine where I am. . . . I am confident that one day I shall see your face again. If not here, then there at the bosom of our Lord Jesus Christ."

Her mother later said, "She did an amazing thing by refusing to renounce Christ, and I'm very proud of what she has done. I'm not sure if I was even in her position at 14 years old that I would have even done what she has done."[4]

In the summer of 2019, *Heroic Faith's* coauthor Lela Gilbert met Rebecca Sharibu in Washington, D.C. She had come to seek help from the United States, and her heartache was evident on her weary and sorrowful face. When Gilbert asked her what she had most recently heard about her daughter, she said (through a translator), "We don't even know where Leah is. We have not seen her. We have not heard from her. I have no idea."[5]

Around six months later, on January 26, 2020, *The Cable* again reported about Leah, this time claiming that she had been "impregnated by one of the commanders of the sect, and she was delivered of a baby four days ago."[6] It was impossible to confirm the story, although it implied that Leah was probably still alive. It has since been rumored she has had another child fathered by her captors.

However, today there is no further news about Leah Sharibu. But Nigeria's abuses of religious freedom continue to accelerate. In fact, the carnage has been described by some as a slow-motion genocide.[7]

According to a U.S. Commission on International Religious Freedom (USCIRF) report released in February 2021, estimates suggest the conflict with groups like Boko Haram and the Islamic State in West Africa Province (ISWAP) has resulted in the deaths of more than 37,500 people since 2011. There is a reasonable basis to believe these groups have committed war crimes and crimes against humanity.

USCIRF Chair Tony Perkins adopted Leah as a prisoner of conscience, personally advocating for this brave hostage who refuses to renounce her faith.[8] Yet sadly, not much has changed. Meanwhile, Open Doors listed Nigeria among the top ten persecutors of Christians on its 2021 World Watch List.[9] And massacres of Nigerian Christians have only increased.

Meanwhile, as we mark year after year following her abduction, Leah Sharibu remains a captive. Mercifully, across the world, faithful prayers continue for her freedom. But reports about her have dwindled into silence, despite repeated pleas from international human rights groups and Christian organizations appealing for her release.

As the world's attention is diverted to other crises, other violence, and ever-increasing Christian persecution elsewhere, the significance of Leah's brave devotion to her faith continues to resonate. A few months ago in an eloquent opinion piece, Nigeria's *Guardian* summed up the significance of Leah's capture, her faithful witness at just fourteen years of age, and her continued detention by the Boko Haram insurgents:

The story of her capture and her continued detention by the Boko Haram insurgents as a result of her
defiance of compromise and refusal to renounce her
faith is the stuff of legend. . . . Leah Sharibu alone
was not released because she refused to renounce
her faith and convert to Islam as demanded by her
captors. Still missing and in captivity till the present
. . . she has since become the symbol of Nigeria's
refusal to succumb to agents of darkness, hell-bent
on dividing the country and appropriating a section of the nation's territory to themselves. By her
principled stand, the battle for the soul of Nigeria
became one between a young girl with a heart and
a garrison of devils without souls.[10]

SNAPSHOTS OF A TROUBLED CONTINENT

Leah Sharibu is one memorable face among untold thousands
of Nigerians who have been abducted, wounded, orphaned,
or murdered because of their Christian faith. We will return
to Nigeria's uniquely tragic plight more than once in the
pages that follow. Its story has come to be, at least for now,
the most shocking and tragic in all of Africa.

But first, it's important to begin our account of Africa's
turmoil with a broader-stroke—an overview of what is taking
place among Africa's far-flung and Christian communities.
To get an idea of the population numbers, Pew Research
Center reported in 2010:

Just a little more than a century ago, most Africans (76%) practiced traditional African religions.
According to historical estimates from the World

Religion Database, in 1900, just 14% of the people living in Sub-Saharan Africa practiced Christianity; even fewer were Muslim (9%). Today, however, Africa is overwhelmingly populated by followers of these two religions. The number of Christians has grown 70-fold, and now a majority of Sub-Saharan Africans are Christian (57%). The Muslim population has grown 20-fold, and now nearly three-in-ten (29%) Sub-Saharan Africans are Muslim.[11]

Meanwhile, the continent is beset by crippling poverty, widespread political corruption, the COVID pandemic, and ever-increasing Islamist terrorism. As a result, millions of Africans suffer under the continuous threat of violence. And no African population experiences these misfortunes as acutely as the continent's 685 million Christians.

In January 2021, Britain's *Guardian* related that worldwide "more than 340 million Christians—one in eight—face high levels of persecution and discrimination because of their faith, according to the 2021 World Watch List compiled by the Christian advocacy group Open Doors. This was a 60 percent increase over the previous year in the number of Christians killed for their faith."[12] *The Guardian*'s account went on to say more than 90 percent of the global total of 4,761 deaths were those of African Christians.

As we've seen, those numbers have only increased in 2022. Here is a quick snapshot of some distressing examples. We'll look at some of them more closely in the pages that follow.

- **In Mozambique**, stunning recent reports in November 2020 revealed Islamic State (ISIS) had attacked innumerable civilians, abducting women and children and torching homes. Al

Jazeera described fifty innocent people—many of them Catholics—being "herded" to their death on a soccer field. There, they were systematically decapitated and dismembered. Due to a hapless and futile government response, ISIS has continued its ferocious assaults, most recently on January 2, 2021.[13]

- **In Democratic Republic of Congo (DRC)**, ISIS stated on July 4, 2021 it attacked a Christian village in the Ituri region. ISIS claimed its fighters engaged Congolese Army soldiers, killing one and seizing his weapon before killing several Christian civilians and burning down their homes.[14]

- **In Sudan,** there has been increasing hope for the country after the demise of the murderous dictator President Umar Hassan Ahmad al-Bashir. His bloodstained thirty-year rule ended in April 2019, and a Sovereignty Council—a joint civilian-military-executive body—has held tenuous power since November 2019.[15] Today, there is continuing upheaval amidst fragile optimism for slow, steady improvement in that devastated country. As for religious freedom, Open Doors explains, "Although Sudan has taken significant steps . . . Christians from a Muslim background still face extreme persecution from their families and communities. These believers no longer face the death penalty for leaving Islam, but may be attacked, ostracized or otherwise discriminated against if their faith is discovered."[16]

- **In South Sudan,** the hope of a promising new nation welcomed the North/South

Comprehensive Peace Agreement (CPA), signed in January 2005. This event was met with euphoria and dreams of peace and prosperity. But tragically, a decade later, chaos rules. Four hundred thousand people have died since the fledgling country's declared independence, and unbridled violence, hunger, political abuse, and corruption prevail. The country is 60 percent Christian and most of the conflict is political and ethnic—virtually all South Sudanese suffer hunger and deprivation equally. It seems that little expectation for quick resolution exists.[17]

- **In Somalia**, the notorious site of "Black Hawk Down," Christians must vigilantly hide their faith. Sources informed FRC that one family was recently jailed for having converted to Christianity from Islam as well as being accused of evangelizing—a capital crime under strictly enforced Sharia law. Yet, surprisingly, Christianity is growing in Somalia, with small underground "churches" made up of handfuls of new believers continuing to grow, while secretly hidden from the dark threat of oppression and persecution.

- **In Ethiopia**, Abune Mathias, head of Ethiopia's Orthodox Church, said in early 2021 that atrocities amounting to genocide are being committed in Tigray—a war-torn ethnic region in northern Ethiopia. These were the cleric's first comments on the conflict in the region that broke out in November 2020 and has killed untold thousands. And neighboring Eritrea, which is the other party to the conflict, has its own brutal reputation. In fact, Eritrea was listed as the sixth worst persecutor of Christians in the world in 2020. By all accounts, it is difficult to find any of the involved combatants without fault in this horrifying conflict.[18]

- **In Libya**, ISIS beheaded twenty Egyptian Coptic Christians and one Ghanian believer on a beach in 2015. Today, Open Doors reports the country is the fourth worst persecutor of Christians in the world. Few stories are told in media reports about specific abuses in the war-torn nation. However, Open Doors 2021 World Watch List explained, "In Libya, there's no freedom of speech, no freedom of religion and very limited possibility of public church life. Christians from a Muslim background face violent pressure from their family and community to renounce their faith. These brave souls—as well as foreign Christians—are also vulnerable to abduction or murder by Islamic militants and crime groups. Sharing your faith publicly is illegal; those who do try, risk violent opposition and arrest."[19]

- **In Burkina Faso**, savage carnage has erupted, with more than a million Christians displaced. "The terrorism activities have hit us so quickly!" one pastor explained. "These groups moved in and took control . . . Many areas of Burkina's northern and eastern regions have now become 'no-go' areas."[20]

- **In Algeria**, the 22nd worst persecutor in 2022, alongside Morocco (the 27th) and Tunisia (35th), Christian converts are the primary targets of persecution in North Africa, not just due to family and extended family accusations and abuses, but also imposed by local ethnic leaders and elders. Their new faith is opposed—sometimes violently—by both family and community. Additionally, it is difficult, if not impossible, for converts from Islam to live out their faith forthrightly. If they speak openly about their belief in Jesus Christ, they can also lose their inheritance, their children, and occasionally, their lives.[21]

- **In Nigeria**, the location of the most continuous and ever-increasing Christian persecution in Africa, brutal violence is rapidly ripping apart the fabric of the nation. Mass murders are committed almost entirely at the hands of three Islamist terrorist groups: Boko Haram, Islamic State in West Africa Province (ISWAP), and Fulani jihadis. Hardly a week passes without accounts of mass kidnappings of Nigerian schoolchildren. Christian clergy are abducted and too-often murdered. Aid workers are gunned down, villages are torched, and churchgoers are massacred. Today, to complicate matters further, a separatist movement in the country's southwest is resisting the government.

THE BIG PICTURE: ENDANGERED CHRISTIANS ACROSS THE AFRICA CONTINENT

Across Africa's heartland stretches the so-called "Group of Five" (G5) nations—Chad, Mali, Mauritania, Burkina Faso, and Niger. In this region Christians and non-radicalized

Muslims face continuous threats and attacks. These onslaughts are of deepening concern to international military analysts and religious freedom advocates alike, thanks to the tireless brutality of ISWAP, Boko Haram, and al-Qaeda.

In North Africa, Christians face local dangers, while the encroachment of terrorist groups, such as Iran's proxy Hezbollah, continue to worry both military and civilian observers.

Likewise, reports from East Africa warn that ISIS, al-Qaeda, al-Shabaab, and other Islamist groups are strengthening their numbers and increasing their hold over territory.

Many if not most well-informed observers believe that we are seeing the beginning of an ever-worsening Africa-wide scenario. The *Wall Street Journal* explains that ISIS is transforming itself into a different kind of enemy by "embracing an array of militant groups as if they were local franchises. . . . After its dreams of imposing draconian Islamist law in a self-declared Syrian and Iraqi state were crushed, ISIS successfully relocated and injected itself into localized conflicts in Nigeria, Libya, and across the Sahel."[22]

Olivier Guitta, Managing Director of GlobalStrat, ominously predicts the dawning of a new Caliphate. He writes:

> Islamic State's historical strong franchises have included the spinoff of Boko Haram in Nigeria that is part of Islamic State in West Africa Province (ISWAP). More recently the Islamic State in the Greater Sahara has made huge progress almost supplanting al-Qaeda as the top dog in the region. . . . The future looks unfortunately bright for IS[IS] in a continent with lots of fragile, corrupt quasi-failed states that could allow the birth of a Caliphate in mini territories in Mozambique, the Sahel and possibly Nigeria.[23]

The obvious and best-known threat to most African countries is Sunni Muslim jihadis—groups like ISIS, al-Shabaab, and al-Qaeda. But they are not alone in their African ambitions. There is another force at work in Africa, more quietly seeking to fulfill its own vision of Islamist conquest: The Islamic Republic of Iran.[24] Recently, Iranian President Raisi declared, "In the new Iranian government, all our capabilities will be devoted to deepening cooperation with African countries."[25]

The Iranian campaign to "export the Revolution"—even into Africa—has long been carried out through Islamic Revolutionary Guard Corps (IRGC) and its many proxies—most famously through Lebanon's Hezbollah. In 2018, Middle East Institute reported that "Iran told Hezbollah that it needed to recruit and train Nigerians to establish a stronghold there so that it could serve as an operational base for the rest of Africa, mainly to thwart Israeli and western ambitions in the region."[26] Iran was said to be providing Hezbollah-style military training to hundreds of Nigerians in camps throughout Northern Nigeria.

In Somalia, *Foreign Policy* related in July 2020 that Iran "has a proxy network . . . and uses facilitators to provide support to violent extremist organizations to counter the influence of the United States and Persian Gulf states, including using Somalia to funnel weapons to Houthi rebels in Yemen and to transit weapons to other countries such as Kenya, Tanzania, South Sudan, Mozambique, and the Central African Republic."[27]

In Ethiopia, as the *New York Times* reported in February 2021, the country's intelligence agency uncovered a cell of fifteen people who were "casing the embassy of the United Arab Emirates. [It also uncovered] a cache of weapons and explosives. . . . It claimed to have foiled a major attack with the potential to sow havoc in the Ethiopian capital, Addis Ababa."[28] American and Israeli officials say the operation was the handiwork of Iran.

Likewise, the countries of Morocco and Algeria are taking note of Iran's ever-encroaching activities. Adjacent to Morocco lies Western Sahara and its separatist movement, the Polisario Front. The United States recently recognized Western Sahara as part of Morocco thanks to its signing of the Abraham Accords. It is widely claimed that Polisario's soldiers are being directly trained for combat by Lebanese Hezbollah, an Iranian proxy, well known for its criminal and terrorist activities.

When reflecting on Iran's activities, it is noteworthy that Iran continues to be among the top ten persecutors of Christians in the world.

ISIS, al-Qaeda, and various other Sunni terror groups are aggressively seeking to fulfill their vision for Islamist conquest and an ever-widening Caliphate. Meanwhile, one of Iran's primary motivators is a Shiite belief in the reappearance of the Twelfth Imam, and the need to prepare for his return. This belief was openly declared by former Iranian president Mahmoud Ahmadinejad.[29]

Whether emanating from Sunni or Shiite plans and plots, the threats to those Africans who have come to believe in Jesus Christ are real and increasing. A closer look at several countries will quickly illustrate the escalating dangers faced by innumerable Christians and others.

MURDEROUS RAMPAGES IN MOZAMBIQUE

A woman sat in a state of shock, an arm around each of her two little children. The little family was disheveled and exhausted.

When asked what had happened to her, she first explained Mozambique's government soldiers never arrived to protect them from the Islamist jihadis who invaded their village, killing dozens of people. She and her children ran for their lives days before. And where they were going next was unclear.[30]

She tried to explain how painful it was to recall the massacre, but it was evident she was deeply traumatized.

Finally, she went on to say, "They arrived with trucks at dawn and started shooting and shot my husband and children. They killed so many people and they raped women."

Her story was but one of many. In 2020, Al Jazeera posted a breathtaking headline: "ISIS-linked attackers behead 50 people in northern Mozambique." The subhead was equally horrifying: "Witnesses say the assailants herded victims onto a football pitch in the village of Muatide where the killings were carried out."[31]

In the midst of a pandemic, and in the throes of an angrily contested U.S. presidential election, it wasn't surprising to encounter disconcerting news headlines. But the gruesome description of innocent people "herded" to their death on a soccer field, where they were systematically decapitated and dismembered, seems more suitable to a horror film than a present-day news report.

Despite the declaration of an African branch of ISIS taking credit for the killings and its religious tone, there has been discussion about the cause of the violence. For example, *New York Times* and Al Jazeera suggest that poverty and inequality led to the attacks. This is similar to the argument that climate change is the primary source of the genocidal Fulani attacks on Christian villages in Nigeria.

Writing about the beheadings, *New York Times* journalist Declan Walsh quoted Sam Ratner, a contributing editor at *Zitamar News*. "While the militants claim to be targeting Christians, in practice they make little distinction between their victims. ISIS propaganda says they burned a Christian village or killed Christian soldiers," Ratner said. "But on the ground, we're not seeing a lot of differentiation between Christians and Muslims. They do not appear to be targeting churches in particular, for instance."[32]

It is true that northeastern Mozambique where the attacks took place is an oil-rich region, and there is wealth to be gained through massacres and the confiscation of property. There have been attacks on oil company convoys and other petroleum-related entities. Perhaps some of the violence is indeed the work of opportunistic criminal enterprises.

Still, the fact remains ISIS has taken credit for the attacks. And ISIS has openly and repeatedly declared its hostility toward Christians, while massacring tens of thousands of believers in multiple international locations, and with terrifying frequency across Africa.

Christians comprise some 57 percent of the population of Mozambique, while the country's Muslim population is around 32 percent. The region in which the most recent attacks took place, Cabo Delgado, is primarily Muslim.[33] However, reports from UK researchers suggest that at least one of the two towns attacked during the recent massacre—Muidumbe—is largely Catholic.[34]

While reporting on the November 10 beheadings, Catholic News Agency pointed out that in Mozambique during Holy Week 2020, "insurgents perpetrated attacks on seven towns and villages in Cabo Delgado province, burning down a church on Good Friday, and killing 52 young people who refused to join the terrorist group."[35]

In July, CBN News interviewed Bishop Luiz Fernando Lisboa of Mozambique's Pemba Diocese. He described the world's response to the atrocities that are taking place in his country and across the world as "indifference." He explained:

> The extremists burned several Christian chapels. . . . They attacked the church and burnt the benches and a statue of Our Lady, made of ebony. They also destroyed an image of the Sacred Heart of Jesus, to whom the parish is dedicated. Fortunately, they were unable to burn the building itself, only the benches. The world still has no idea what is happening because of indifference, and because it seems that we have already become accustomed to wars. There is war in Iraq, there is war in Syria, and there is also now a war in Mozambique.[36]

Without a doubt, the world looks tragically indifferent to Bishop Lisboa and his community. He has seen more than his share of death and destruction. But is indifference the real reason the world "has no idea" what is happening?

The fact is that violence against Christians in far-flung locations is rarely reported by Western mainstream news sources—unless the shock-value propels the story into the headlines, however briefly. And even when such tragedies are reported, as we've seen above, the religious aspect of the violence is either underplayed or explained away altogether. More realistic accounts about international religious persecution often appear from small online publications or organizations such as *Morningstar News*, International Christian Concern, and *Article 18* (in Iran), or in larger outlets like Catholic News Service and Christian Broadcasting Network (CBN).

Although some of these less prestigious periodicals may have limited readership, they do their best to make the truth about religious persecution known to their Western readers."

They give voice to local clergy, laypeople, eyewitnesses, and victims.

The fact is that indifference is not an option for faithful believers in today's shattered world. However, those of us who want to know the plight of our fellow Christians may have to search for the facts and choose to inform ourselves about the dangerous circumstances that lie behind them. Then perhaps we can find opportunities to share those stories with our friends and our faith communities, and when possible, to seek action from appropriate authorities—secular and religious.

SOMALIA'S CHRISTIAN PRISONERS AND COURAGEOUS WITNESSES

The East African country of Somalia is best known to most Americans for three unsettling reasons. First of all, as we've seen, many learned about Somalia thanks to the tragic "Black Hawk Down" battle—the event, the book, and the film. The country is also infamous for attacks by Somali pirates on international shipping routes. And, today, the ruthless jihadi group al-Shabaab—apparently with links to al-Qaeda—continues to torment its Somali homeland as well as the surrounding African nations.

Is Somalia a place for intrepid American tourists to visit? In 2020, the State Department scored it as a "Category 4" risk with a concise comment: "Do not travel to Somalia due to COVID-19, crime, terrorism, civil unrest, health issues, kidnapping, and piracy."

And what about being a tempting site for Christian missionaries eager to reach out to Muslims? Certainly not. According to Open Doors World Watch List, Somalia is the third worst persecutor of Christians in the world.[37]

Sharia law prevails in most of the country, and where it is not officially enforced, the fierce implementation of apostasy and blasphemy laws (whether official or unofficial) is handled by locals, and particularly by those who support the anti-Christian goals of al-Shabaab—whether officially affiliated with the terror group or not.

As the 2020 U.S. State Department report explains, al-Shabaab continues to impose its own interpretation of Islamic practices and Sharia on other Muslims and non-Muslims, including executions as a penalty for alleged apostasy in areas under its control, according to media and UN sources. It also notes that 2019 was one of the deadliest on record for fatalities from al-Shabaab attacks, with numbers already more than 1,200.[38]

With all that in the background, in autumn 2020, friends in Africa alerted Family Research Council about a Christian family that had recently been arrested in Hargeisa. The Somaliland Police accused the couple of abandoning Islam, and even more dangerously, of evangelizing the people of Somaliland. According to a report about the incident from Somali Bible Society (that must remain unnamed), "The spokesperson's speech was peppered with threats against local Christians."

The report went on to say the arrested man had been tortured; his wife had delivered a baby by C-section a short time before the arrest and required urgent medical attention, and the baby needed maternal care and breastfeeding.

We weren't particularly surprised to learn that Christians were attacked in Somalia. More amazing was after so many war-torn years and violent incidents, any Christians remained there at all. And not only do they remain, but according to reports, there are hundreds of new believers who continue to worship in secret underground churches—small gatherings comprised entirely of less than a dozen brave and faithful local converts from Islam.

In early 2021, a trial took place in Hargeisa that could cost the lives of six Somali Christians—all of them courageous converts from Islam who have been accused of "crimes" that might carry a death sentence. According to court documents, the accusations against these believers included, "disrupting the religious activities of the republic of Somaliland (Islamic religion), uniting and inciting against the law . . . because you have all been involved in spreading the Christian Protestant religion in Somaliland, and disrupting the faith of the Muslim community in the Republic of Somaliland by proselytizing and encouraging them to leave Islam and convert to Christianity . . ." (source must remain unnamed).

The court's evidence for these life-and-death accusations included:

- Two books about Christianity and written in Somali that were taken from the house of the accused;
- A letter written in Somali about the Christian religion;
- Bibles written in English and Bibles written in Amharic;
- Numerous other books and extensive data from the defendants' computers.

For Somali Christians under such circumstances, the threat is not insignificant. These brave and bold Christians face a potentially painful future, yet they continue not only worshiping privately, but reaching out to others and teaching them about the story of Jesus—who He is and how He willingly gave His life for them. Now, 2,000 years later and at grave risk, they continue to follow in His footsteps.

UPHEAVAL IN ETHIOPIA, BRUTAL PERSECUTION IN ERITREA

One of the most complex conflicts in Africa has raged for months between Ethiopia and Eritrea over Tigray, a hotly contested region that lies between the two countries. The two countries who are often pitted against each other for various reasons have both been battling a revolutionary movement in Tigray, which in just a matter of months has cost more than 50,000 lives on all sides. In May 2021, Abune Mathias, Patriarch of the Ethiopian Orthodox Church, declared that a genocide was taking place in that vicious war. And reports of rape and violent sexual abuse of women are widespread.

Ethiopia is more than half Christian and is, in fact, the site of one of the earliest Christian communities in the world. Meanwhile, neighboring Eritrea—which was once part of Ethiopia—is listed by Open Doors as the sixth worst persecutor of Christians in the world.[39] Their 2021 report explains that "Christians from non-traditional denominations face the harshest persecution in Eritrea, both from the government and from the Eritrean Orthodox Church (EOC—the only Christian denomination recognized by the government). Government forces monitor phone calls and conduct countless raids that target Christians and can lead to arrest and imprisonment without trial. Many Christians are held in the country's intricate tunnel system of inhumane prisons. Their loved ones may not know where they are or even if they're still alive."[40]

Eritrean detainees are often locked up into metal shipping containers situated in desert sites and without insulation or other protection from either bitter cold or scorching weather. They are deprived of water, food, and sanitation. They are frequently beaten and tortured.

Such was the experience of Helen Berhane, once a popular Eritrean gospel singer and speaker. Her arrest and imprisonment are illustrative of Eritrea's brutality toward evangelical and Pentecostal Christians. She was first arrested shortly after releasing a cassette tape of gospel songs in May 2004. She spent much of her two and a half years of captivity in one such container. She was also regularly tortured, and when she was released after two and a half years she was permanently disabled. So brutal was her torture and so severe her injuries that she left the prison in a wheelchair and continues to suffer with substantial health concerns.

"The only reason they let you go is when they torture you to death," Helen told the *Washington Post* in 2015.[41] "They don't want you to die in prison, it's not their responsibility, so they send you home to die." Berhane went on to say the situation in Eritrea is getting worse and huge numbers of people continue to flee the country. While many are escaping from religious persecution, others are fleeing compulsory military conscription and poverty.

Both political, ethnic, and religious upheaval have troubled Ethiopia in recent years, while Eritrea continued with its brutality unabated for generations. The recent Tigray brutality continues at the time of this writing. It is proving to be one of the most brutal and inhumane conflicts in Africa. And, as is the case in so many other African crises, Christians are caught in the midst of the violence and are unable to spare themselves and the lives of their children.

In a more hopeful message, however, Voice of the Martyrs' Pastor Eric Foley reports the church in the Tigray region has been a beacon during all this chaos. "People are gathering in the churches, and they're grieving at the churches. They're bringing dead bodies to the churches to bury them in mass graves. The Gospel is still making a way for people to have hope. The Christians who are hearing the Word of God are acting on it. They're opening their homes and sharing bread. They're doing all of the things that Jesus taught us to do."[42]

West Africa: Islamist Encroachment, Bloodshed and Fleeing Refugees

"One evening in late June, gunmen stormed a village in northern Burkina Faso," the *Washington Post* reported, "and ordered people who had been chatting outside to lie down. Then the armed strangers checked everyone's necks, searching for jewelry. They found four men wearing crucifixes— Christians. They executed them . . ."[43]

Burkina Faso is one of several vulnerable African nations frequently targeted for terrorism and Christian persecution. Along with Nigeria—where reportedly more than 1,200 Christians were killed by jihadists in the first six months of 2020—the "Group of Five" (G5) in Sub-Saharan West Africa deserves attention: Burkina Faso, Chad, Mali, Mauritania, and Niger. These obscure countries are facing alarming circumstances that rarely make their way into our American news-cycle—especially in an election year.[44]

Premier Christian News reported, "Churches across the north of Burkina Faso are being left deserted as Christians flee escalating violence from armed Jihadist groups. More than one million people are now displaced in the West African nation in what the UN Refugee Agency has said is now 'the world's fastest-growing humanitarian and protection crisis.' Although the violence does not affect Christians exclusively, there is no doubt that they are specifically targeted."[45] In related news, according to the UNHCR, in Burkina Faso, "Five per cent of the country's entire population—an astonishing one in 20 people—is now displaced in the world's fastest-growing humanitarian and protection crisis."[46]

Religious freedom advocates are deeply troubled by the ever-escalating violence inflicted by ISWAP, Boko Haram, and al Qaeda. These terrorist groups are expanding in alarming numbers. Some African countries have agreed to host foreign fighters to train and defend local military and law enforcement units. But due to the present draw-down of American troops in the region, there is little likelihood of the U.S. being involved.

For those of us watching from afar, the situation in West Africa is both tragic and infuriating. It is doubtful whether American or other foreign forces will be engaged in assisting beleaguered Christians there any time soon. Yet, like the faithful believers who persistently call out for help, we need to stand alongside them in their appeals for divine intervention. Because, truthfully, any good news about West African Christians' struggle against terrorist groups would be an enormously welcome answer to prayer. At this point we might even call it a miracle.

THE GENOCIDE AGAINST CHRISTIANS IN NIGERIA

In July 2021, International Christian Concern said Nigeria is "the world's biggest killing ground of Christians today, but few are aware of it. In the last eighteen years, an estimated 50,000 to 70,000 Christians have been murdered by radical Islamic militant groups, while another 2 million people have been displaced. Of these groups, Fulani terrorists have become the greatest threat to Nigerian Christians and have killed the majority of the 3,462 Christians who were murdered in 2021."[47]

Caroline Cox, a life peer in the U.K.'s House of Lords and a resolute human rights advocate focusing on persecuted Christians, has traveled to Nigeria innumerable times since the early 2000s. The poorly reported violence there has grown significantly more deadly in the decade since. The Baroness recounts not only the number of deaths but the stories of survivors—many of whom have been maimed and remain homeless and grieving over the loss of their closest loved ones. Here are some quotes from her humanitarian organization HART's November 2019 report:[48]

- "They shot Sarah's husband and children and so she begged them to kill her too, but they refused, saying that they wanted her to cry and bear the pain."—Deaconess Susan Essam, Jos
- "My sister was raped, and her wrists cut off before she was shot through the heart. They took my brother, his wife and all their six children, tied and slaughtered them like animals." —Margaret, Ngar village
- "They were hacking and killing people, making sure that those that were shot were finished off . . . They wore red to conceal blood splashes on their clothes as they butchered their victims." —Lydia, Ningon village

- "I saw my brother-in-law's body on the ground, hacked to pieces by a machete. Our home was destroyed. The hospital was burnt. They tried to burn the roof of the church by piling up the chairs, like a bonfire."—Antonia, Karamai
- "Every day we carry new corpses to the cemetery. They kill farmers. They destroy our homes and churches. They kidnap and rape women."—Pastor, Maiduguri in Borno
- "We could see bullets whizzing. Everything was destroyed. In our whole village, only two of the homes were not burnt. Almost 50 people were killed."—Ta'aziya, Karamai
- "They attacked me with a machete twice, once to the neck and once to my hand. I lost consciousness. When I woke up, I saw my daughter on ground—she was dead—with my chopped finger in her mouth."—Veronica, Dogon Noma
- "Only me and my husband remain. Our home is destroyed. Nothing survived. We have to beg for food."—Asabe, Karamai

Certainly much of the huge African continent is in a state of chaos and calamity. It is well documented that Christian communities, churches, clergy, and leadership suffer exceptional levels of death and destruction whenever and wherever jihadis attack. But no country better exemplifies this tragic reality than Nigeria.

As we've seen, as the most populous and commercially significant African nation, Nigeria is the site of what is often described as a slow-motion genocide. Tens of thousands of Christians have been massacred there in recent years primarily at the hands of three notorious Islamist terrorist groups, and local observers assert that some of these groups cooperate with each other, and others may even have discreet support from the current Nigerian government.

Hardly a day passes without accounts of mass kidnappings of Nigerian schoolchildren, Christian clergy and aid workers gunned down, villages torched, and churchgoers massacred. Not so long ago, while hundreds of terrified girls were being kidnapped from their school and held for ransom, extremists released a video of a Christian pastor, Bulus Yikura, pleading for his life. Calling on President Muhammadu Buhari and other politicians, Yikura exclaimed: "If you want me alive, I beg you in your capacity as president, the governor and our local government chairman to save me from this suffering." Buhari did nothing, but thankfully, Yikura's ransom was paid and he was released by his captors—the ISIS-affiliated Boko Haram terror group. But tens of thousands of Nigerians have not been so fortunate. More than can be counted have died at the hands of their assailants.[49]

In a recent conversation, one of America's most highly respected experts on international religious freedom, former U.S. congressman Frank Wolf, expressed his deep concern about Africa. Nigeria's deteriorating security and rapidly escalating violence serves as a warning to the rest of the continent, and indeed, to the whole world, Mr. Wolf explained.

> Boko Haram is committing genocide against Christians. In fact, Boko Haram has killed more civilians in Nigeria than ISIS slaughtered in Iraq and Syria combined. Meanwhile, Fulani militants are committing crimes against humanity and genocidal massacres against Christians. . . . Nigeria may

very well implode. And with continuing economic, political, and security deterioration, refugees will soon flee that troubled continent by the millions.[50]

Slowly—far too slowly—the United States and other global leaders are beginning to wake up to the horrifying levels of violence suffocating Nigeria and other countries in Africa. We can only hope that effective, responsive actions will finally be taken. But much more needs to be done.

BLACK LIVES MATTER EVERYWHERE, INCLUDING IN NIGERIA

For good reason, there was a national outcry in the United States about the brutal death of George Floyd, a black man who died under the knee of a white police officer in Minneapolis. Videos of Floyd's struggle for life shocked and horrified viewers. Anyone with a sense of human decency was appalled by the story, as well as by other law enforcement injustices.

Not long thereafter—with a backdrop of the COVID pandemic's global menace—round-the-clock global media reports focus on the shattered streets of New York, Minneapolis, and beyond while the impassioned slogan "Black Lives Matter" filled U.S. airwaves.

Of course, the slogan is true. Yet before, during, and after the George Floyd-related race riots in America, atrocious violence against black women, children, and men was surging in Nigeria. It had been doing so for years in such increasing numbers it remains difficult to keep up with the horrible statistics. And this raises the question:

Why don't those black lives seem to matter to the rest of the world?

Consider the numbers: According to Genocide Watch, "credible statistics show that from June 2015 to February 2020, between 11,500 and 12,000 Christians were murdered by Boko Haram, Jihadist Fulani Herdsmen, and 'Bandits/Highway Kidnappers.'"[51]

Most Americans are familiar with Boko Haram, whose killers and kidnappers were initially spotlighted by Michelle Obama's #bringbackourgirls campaign in 2016. Her hashtag campaign was inspired by Boko Haram's mass kidnapping of 276 girls from a school in Chibok, Nigeria in April 2014. As of the time of this writing, some 112 of the Chibok girls have never been found.

For some years, Boko Haram committed the most killings of Christians in Nigeria. Yet, since June 2015, Genocide Watch reports, "Jihadist Fulani militias have killed even more Christians in Nigeria than Boko Haram. The total Christian deaths at the hands of Fulani Jihadist militias since June 2015 is more than 7,400. Fulani Jihadists have replaced Boko Haram as the deadliest terrorists in the world."[52]

The massive casualties are horrifying. And those casualty numbers don't include the traumatized survivors who endure agonizing injuries, intentionally mutilated bodies, and broken hearts and spirits.

In 2020, Christian Solidarity International (CSI) issued a genocide warning for Nigeria. "The conditions for genocide exist in Nigeria, with Christians, non-violent Muslims, and adherents of tribal religions being particularly vulnerable," CSI's John Eibner announced. "The increasingly violent attacks and the failure of the Nigerian government to prevent them and punish the perpetrators are alarming. CSI therefore calls on the permanent members of the U.N. Security Council to take swift action to uphold this commitment to genocide prevention in Nigeria."[53]

As we've seen, two primary factions of Islamist jihadis are responsible for much of the carnage. As Boko Haram—which is increasingly cooperating with ISWAP—continues to hold Leah Sharibu, the violence, abduction, and killing of other Christians continues.

The brutal Nigerian faction that has become even more deadly is often identified by the innocent-sounding name, "Fulani Herdsmen." Initially, their violence was attributed to attempts to confiscate grazing land for their animals. However, because of ever-increasing evidence of carnage, outrageous brutality, and shouts of *allahu akbar*, the Fulanis' jihadi intentions have been clearly exposed.

Generally, the horror stories involve rural villages with mostly Christian populations. And the reports are often much the same: well-armed jihadis suddenly appear in the dead of night. They attack house after house, breaking down doors, shouting *allahu akbar*. They shoot the elderly and able-bodied men. They rape, mutilate, and murder women. They kidnap young boys and girls. They torch houses, schools, and churches.

Sometimes they leave a handful of traumatized but grateful survivors. "Yes, I was shot in the head, but the bullet didn't enter. It's a miracle," said Rev. Canon Bayo Famonure, who is often called Uncle Bayo by his many friends at Messiah College in Nigeria's troubled Plateau State. Canon Famonure went on to say he was also grateful that bullets in his lower extremities had not broken any bones.

The three terrorists who attacked the Famonure family were Fulani jihadis. These so-called "herdsmen" who are said to be simply in search of pastures and water are usually armed with AK-47s and machetes. In the Famonure case, after targeting Canon they also shot his wife Naomi in the back, and his two children in the feet. The bullet that struck the clergyman's wife barely missed her spinal cord and lodged in less vulnerable tissue and following emergency surgery she was on the mend. In fact, quite miraculously, so was the entire family. But the trauma will never be forgotten.

A few weeks later CNN reported, "Uwaila Vera Omozuwa was attacked as she studied in church, according to Nigerian police. The 22-year-old died on May 30, just days after the brutal assault inside the church of the Redeemed Christian Church of God, or RCCG, in Benin city. . . . Omozuwa was a member of the choir who had studied privately at the church since lockdown measures due to the coronavirus pandemic were put in place in Nigeria in March."[54]

Week after week such stories appear, primarily in Christian publications. Often, but not always, the killers are identified. And unfortunately, no one really knows the precise numbers of Nigeria's victims either, thanks to mass graves, torched villages, chaotic aftermaths, and disappearances. Still, the numbers we've seen are shocking.

Nigeria's Christians are exhausted and distressed by their endless ordeal. They and their neighbors are also infuriated by the state and federal governments' inability or, worse, unwillingness to defend them. After reporting on the murderous attack on Canon Famonure and his family, an unnamed source wrote a few words about the incident: "Hapless residents are butchered in their sleep, their houses set ablaze and farmlands destroyed . . . and the government calls for calm. For many . . . it's a miracle to go to bed at night and wake up at the break of dawn."[55]

In short, there is a bloodbath in Nigeria. And those of us who track religious freedom violations and Christian persecution are alarmed, because it seems increasingly clear another genocide is already taking place. We know what happened in Rwanda. We saw what ISIS did in Iraq. And in recent decades, tens of thousands of Nigerians have been slaughtered. Yet their stories rarely appear in mainstream Western news reports, while virtually nothing is being done to stop the violence.

To make matters even more disturbing, there is mounting word-of-mouth and other evidence the present government of Nigeria is somehow complicit in the Islamist groups' assaults. While tens of thousands of Nigeria's Christians have been killed in recent decades, countless more have been mercilessly raped, maimed, disfigured, and disabled. And the displaced are innumerable.

As early as 2018, President Donald Trump raised this issue with Nigerian President Muhammadu Buhari. "We've had very serious problems with Christians who have been murdered, killed in Nigeria," Trump told reporters, with Buhari seated next to him. "We're going to be . . . working on that problem very, very hard because we can't allow that to happen."[56]

The remark fell on deaf ears.

However, religious freedom researchers and activists continue to pursue accurate fact-finding mechanisms, consistent documentation, and an official U.S. envoy to specifically address this travesty. More and more concerned voices—including USCIRF—are demanding accountability from Nigeria's leadership and are seeking an effective response from the U.S. government.

ATTACKS ON NIGERIAN CHRISTIANS: A TRAGIC BLIND SPOT

"Traveling by road into Maiduguri, the capital of Nigeria's northeast, has become one of the most dangerous journeys on earth." So begins an alarming and timely *Wall Street Journal* article by Joe Parkinson and Gbenga Akingbule about ever-encroaching violence in Nigeria,[57] Africa's largest country and most powerful financial center.[58]

Parkinson and Akingbule describe four primary highways leading into that northern Nigerian city, once known in happier days as "Home of Peace." Along those roads some 200 people have been murdered in the past six months. Today, Maiduguri is better known as the birthplace of Boko Haram, the brutal Islamist terrorist group.

"The attacks are conducted by militants fighting for Boko Haram and a splinter group loyal to Islamic State," Parkinson and Akingbule explain. "With each passing month they become more brazen, targeting civilians, aid workers, soldiers and even the state's most powerful politicians."

And unlike most Western reporters, Parkinson and Akingbule note that Christians are specifically targeted in these attacks. "Soldiers and Maiduguri residents who travel the roads say the extremists regularly erect mobile checkpoints, searching for Christians and government employees to kidnap for ransom or execute on the roadside."

Although violence against Christian communities by Muslim attackers was recognized well before the founding of Boko Haram, it became much more intense and frequent after 2009, when the group's founder, Mohammed Yusuf, was killed by Nigerian authorities. Subsequently the group—along with other smaller jihadi sects—became notably more deadly and dangerous.

With this acceleration in recent years, verified reports of murders, rapes, mutilations, and kidnappings of Christians in Nigeria have persistently increased. Yet—despite their obvious targeting of churches, Christian communities, pastors, and seminary students—some scholars, analysts, and, unfortunately, even U.S. authorities refuse to recognize the religious nature of numerous attacks and attackers. Paul Marshall, Senior Fellow for Religious Freedom at Hudson Institute, writes:

> In her July 17, 2019, confirmation hearing, U.S. Ambassador to Nigeria Mary Beth Leonard referred to the carnage in the Middle Belt of Nigeria as "banditry and inter-communal conflict" and "escalating farmer-herder and inter-communal conflict frequently based in resource competition, but enflamed by conflation of ethnic and religious overlays."
>
> Rabbi Abraham Cooper and Johnnie Moore, in their book *The Next Jihad: Stop the Christian Genocide in Africa* describe a meeting they had in February 2020 with Amb. Leonard in which they discussed the possible religious aspects of the violence wracking the country. "She denied that it was at all about religion and described the conflict as 'fundamentally a resource issue. . . . Religion was, according to Ambassador Leonard, only relevant as it served as a potential accelerant to conflict. She left us with the impression that people like us, by speaking up for victims of religious persecution, were part of the problem. We found this to be hugely alarming."[59]

Some years ago, Paul Marshall, Roberta Ahmanson, and Lela Gilbert co-authored a book called *Blind Spot: Why Journalists Don't Get Religion*. They had discovered that many—if not most—mainstream journalists are from very secular backgrounds, know little about faith, spiritual awareness, or devotion, and simply did not perceive how religion deeply shapes culture and conduct in most of the world beyond the West.

Sad to say, journalists are not the only experts suffering from that religious blind spot. A close look at diplomats, intelligence officers, politicians, and academics exposes many of them share that same handicap. It is quite remarkable, although self-proclaimed jihadis slaughter Christians in their homes, churches, and fields, beheading them and shouting *allahu akbar* as a victory cry, observers do not acknowledge the killers' Islamist intensions. As we've seen in Nigeria, Iraq, Syria, and far beyond, the truth about anti-Christian violence is often suppressed and rarely disclosed, understood, or reported. It's a blind spot for sure. And it's a deadly one.

NIGERIA—A COUNTRY OF PARTICULAR CONCERN

Near the end of 2020—a year when bad news seemed to be relentless and unstoppable—a good report emerged. The U.S. Department of State finally declared Nigeria a "Country of Particular Concern" (CPC). On Monday, December 7, Secretary of State Mike Pompeo said in a statement: "The United States is designating Burma, China, Eritrea, Iran, Nigeria, the DPRK, Pakistan, Saudi Arabia, Tajikistan, and Turkmenistan as Countries of Particular Concern under the International Religious Freedom Act of 1998, as amended, for engaging in or tolerating 'systematic, ongoing, egregious violations of religious freedom.'"[60]

The U.S. Commission on International Religious Freedom (USCIRF) praised the State Department's announcement that included Nigeria for the first time in its ten "Countries of Particular Concern" (CPCs), while also placing four countries on its "Special Watch List" (SWL) for severe violations.

"We are gratified that the State Department has named 10 countries as CPCs. We particularly welcome Nigeria's designation for the first time as a CPC for tolerating egregious violations of religious freedom, which USCIRF had been recommending since 2009. Nigeria is the first secular democracy that has been named a CPC, which demonstrates that we must be vigilant that all forms of governments respect religious freedom," said then-Chair Gayle Manchin.[61]

Unfortunately, however, less than a year after Sec. Pompeo's important decision, the new Biden administration removed the Country of Particular Concern designation in November 2021 without explanation. During Secretary of State Antony Blinken's first ambassadorial visit to Africa, he met with President Buhari and no mention of Christian persecution was reported in any coverage of discussions during Blinken's visit. In response to this, Family Research Council's President Tony Perkins said, "The CPC designation is the U.S. government's official 'worst of the worst' list regarding religious freedom violations. Nigeria's religious freedom problems are obvious and rapidly deteriorating even further. The Biden administration's removal of Nigeria from the CPC list defies logic and sound policymaking. This must be remedied, and Nigeria placed back on the CPC list so the full force of the federal government can be harnessed to address this crisis."[62]

Family Research Council subsequently delivered a letter to President Biden, signed by forty-seven concerned organizations and individuals of many religious backgrounds, decrying the de-listing of Nigeria as a Country of Particular Concern.[63]

Nigeria's President Buhari is himself a member of the Fulani ethnic group, which is responsible for a significant portion of the killing and has gone on unhindered during his presidency. Meanwhile, for decades, international authorities have turned a blind eye to Nigerian butchery perpetrated not only by Fulani jihadis, but by Boko Haram and Islamic State of West Africa Province (ISWAP). Making excuses for the violence and rarely addressing the religious nature of the conflict, even the American Embassy has seemed unwilling to do more than plead for useless and counter-productive "reconciliation" meetings.

Nigeria's designation as a CPC would lead not only to closer scrutiny and, presumably, additional pressure on all concerned in the violence, but also to financial measures. The U.S. State Department has stated: "Congress is notified, and where non-economic policy options designed to bring about cessation of the particularly severe violations of religious freedom have reasonably been exhausted, an economic measure generally must be imposed."[64] Economic measures might well diminish the hundreds of millions of aid dollars the U.S. has poured into Nigeria for many years.

Will there finally be a shift in the calculations of Nigeria's leadership and a crackdown on the surging violence of the jihadis? Or will the bloodbath increase until—as in Iraq during ISIS's devastating assaults on Christian and Yazidi communities—the world wakes up and takes action against the terrorists? Can the CPC designation really stop the vicious cycles of violence against Christians in Nigeria? Only time—and responsible international diplomacy—will tell. Tragically, however, it's already late in the game as the threat of another genocide looms larger every day.

On Friday, April 16, 2021, tens of thousands of Nigerians fled deadly attacks by armed groups. ABC News reported the shocking statement that "the latest rebel attack on Wednesday drove out as many as 80% of the population of Damasak, according to the U.N. refugee agency, who said up to 65,000 people were on the move. . . . Assailants looted and burned down private homes, warehouses of humanitarian agencies, a police station, a clinic, and also a UNHCR facility."[65]

Trying to verify this almost unbelievable story, FRC wrote to a Nigerian Christian friend (who must remain unnamed) who actively reports about the ongoing tragedy in his country. He replied, "Yes, the attack on Damasak and surrounding villages has been intense in the last two weeks. Most Christians have fled in the last four weeks as the intensity of the fight increased. Boko Haram has now taken over control of most of the region around Lake Chad up to the Cameroonian boarders. They are now moving in towards Mauduguri."

The bloodshed seems endless in Nigeria. But as we've seen from the beginning, it does not stop there. Nigeria represents what is presently the worst-case scenario for Christian persecution in Africa. Meanwhile, murderous incidents are acted out with accelerating frequency. Unfortunately, that picture is changing and worsening. The terrorist groups in Africa that enjoy major funding and notoriety are successfully reaching further into the continent, unifying their forces, absorbing other groups, and gaining greater power.

WHAT HAPPENS IN AFRICA WILL NOT STAY IN AFRICA

As American Christians, we often focus our attention solely on our own country and its increasingly anti-Christian leadership and legislation. However, as we watch, pray, and respond to opportunities to push back against ungodly forces in our homeland, let's also keep in mind there has never been a more dangerous and deadly time for Christians all across the world. As we reflect on America's present concerns, let's also remember to lift our eyes beyond our own borders. Let's pray for those who are endangered in faraway places—like long-suffering African nations, frontiers, towns, and villages—as if we were suffering with them.

It really is past time for the world to stop looking regretfully at Africa's tragedies in the rearview mirror. Instead, a determined coalition of nations needs to develop ways and means of extinguishing the surging jihadi violence. And it's essential our Christian communities continue not only to pray but to demand such action. Why? Because as the wildfire of terrorism continues to rage across that vast, violent continent, one thing seems certain: Africa's Christians will continue to pay the ultimate price for the world's inaction.

The stakes are exceptionally high for all of Africa, and the continuing upheaval is bound to increase. Thanks to both Sunni and Shiite radicals, African Christians will face massacres. Furthermore, heavily populated nations like Nigeria may well implode because of internal chaos and external negligence on the part of war-weary Western countries. This will send millions of refugees pouring into Europe and beyond. Clearly, what happens in Africa will not stay in Africa.

The increasingly worrisome reason innumerable African lives are so much at risk is because no nation or coalition appears to have a clear strategy for overcoming recurring Islamist invasions. And to make matters worse, the American military appears to be making plans to leave the region altogether. It is true there are many arguments about waning U.S. interest in protecting innocents abroad, or more succinctly, "being the policemen of the world." But in the face of genocidal activity, who will step in? Who will defend unarmed and defenseless Africans? They are experiencing unspeakable violence.

In late February 2021, the Jerusalem Center for Public Affairs (JCPA) published a startling article titled, "Africa Is a Jihadist Playground for the Resurgent Islamic State and al-Qaeda." The report explained that although the jihadi presence in Africa is nothing new, failure to remove it and neutralize its influence has "encouraged the extremists to penetrate shaky and unstable regimes hit by internal strife, poverty, and ethnic confrontations." As JCPA explains:

> Most of those jihadist groups are the offspring of either the Islamic State or of the al-Qaida organizations and have been active in the Sahel areas for many years . . . creating a vast web, interconnecting with other jihadist organizations, and extending their presence and destructive activities to Burkina Faso, Benin, the Central African Republic, the Ivory Coast, and Senegal. They have now reached the eastern parts of Africa (Kenya, Uganda, Ethiopia, Somalia, and Mozambique), thus creating a jihadist belt that begins in the Atlantic Ocean shores and reaches the Red Sea and the Indian Ocean.[66]

Will America step in as it has often done before to intervene in this surging danger? Due to the present draw-down of American troops in the region, there is little likelihood of the U.S. being involved. AEI's Margaret Zimmerman writes:

> West Africa is where the steepest drawdowns will probably occur. Already resource constrained, AFRICOM reported it had downgraded its

counterterrorism mission there. Despite the fact that regional security and stability have deteriorated rapidly over the past year, its new goal is only to contain the groups instead of degrading their ability to operate and stage terror attacks. West Africa is the only region where both al-Qaida and the Islamic State are expanding, coordinating, and getting deadlier. Allowing these groups to fester by further reducing resources could be costlier in the long run as they could begin to export their terror attacks—and thus require a more aggressive intervention.[67]

According to an August 2020 Pulitzer Center report, a U.S. counterterrorism effort is ongoing in northwest Africa, but only in the form of annual training exercises. One, for example, was conducted by Special Operations Command Africa, focused on enhancing the capability of nations in West Africa to plan and conduct counterterrorism missions. This involves eleven nations: Algeria, Burkina Faso, Cameroon, Chad, Mali, Mauritania, Morocco, Niger, Nigeria, Senegal, and Tunisia.[68]

At first that little news item might have sounded like a godsend to beleaguered African Christians. But the warriors involved will not be engaged in day-to-day protection or defense of terrorist targets. Thus, the vast majority of jihadi victims will remain utterly defenseless. Innumerable stories recount desperate calls for police or military assistance by frantic villagers—cries for help that result in at best an hour-long delay of deployed forces or, all too often, no response at all. A bloodbath inevitably takes place instead.

"From Mozambique on Africa's East Coast to Nigeria, Niger, Mali and Burkina Faso in West Africa, the region is under jihadi attack," Hudson Institute's Nina Shea has pointed out, "Islamic extremist militants are attacking the Christian presence there, and the young Sub-Sahara's Christian community is at risk of meeting the same fate, under the same pressures, as one of the oldest Christian communities, in Iraq's Nineveh. In fact, in recent years, Nigeria alone has seen more Christian martyrs than all the Middle East combined."[69]

In June 2021, Gen. Stephen J. Townsend, head of the U.S. Africa Command, praised the work accomplished in joint operations but painted a dark picture of threats besetting parts of Africa.

"I am concerned about the security situation across a band of Africa," from the Sahel region in the west to the Horn of Africa, Townsend told reporters. He noted deadly attacks by al-Qaeda and Islamic State-linked jihadis and al-Shabaab. "All of them are on the march," he said.[70]

"African neighbors are helping governments deal with the threat, but, he added, "all of that does not seem to be sufficient enough to stop what I call . . . (the) wildfire of terrorism that's sweeping that region."

Yet the problem of terrorism seems to be repeatedly ignored or dismissed by experts. Emily Estelle answers this question both sadly and succinctly in *Foreign Policy*:

> The blind spot over Africa's jihadi problem exists because policymakers are afraid to take on the intractable causes and difficult solutions to resolve insurgencies. For the countries in question, an enduring solution requires money and changes to their power structure that elites cannot or will not make. The international community is equally at

fault. It's time for those who profess to care about the continent to step up. There is a war going on.[71]

LTG (RET.) JERRY BOYKIN: AFRICA—AN EMERGING DANGER ZONE

Africa is a vast continent comprised of a complex array of sociological and ethnic parts and pieces. As we consider the multitude of issues related to the nations there, we see the differences in cultures, languages, religions, and traditions influence every aspect of life. It is also clear ethnic tribes play an enormous role in the formation of the countries we see on that African map. For example, Africa's largest country, Nigeria, is home to some 300 tribes, many of which have their own languages and traditions. The conflicts we see today—some of them deadly—often reflect those ethnic divisions. At the same time, religious differences—specifically Islam versus Christianity—continue to erupt in terrible violence and bloodshed.

Meanwhile, today there is another influential player in Africa—China. Overall, the Chinese probably understand Africans better than we Westerners do because they have done their homework on the various African countries and cultures. They've done so because they recognize the continent offers incredible possibilities, including massive natural resources and great human potential. The Chinese are now exploiting all that because they have taken a different and more subtle approach than the Americans. In Africa, the Chinese have no colonial history, unlike the French, the British, and the Belgians.

Today, the Chinese are reaping the benefits of their efforts. They are exploiting Africa's oil reserves and they're buying up other resources as fast as they can. In many cases, they're doing it by making loans on resource-based enterprises and then they're foreclosing on the loans, which gives them full rights to an oil, agricultural, or mineral operation. It could be coal or diamonds or anything else, but they'll go in and lend a lot of big money, knowing their debtors are never going to be able to pay it back. When the credit clock runs down, they foreclose and now own the diamond mine or the oil pipeline or whatever it might be. They're exploiting the locals, but they're doing it in a different way than the Western powers did.

When Westerners began to arrive in Africa, they called it the Dark Continent. There was no modernity. Much has been written about how they despicably wronged and abused the native populations. However, they also had something to offer—they brought with them technology, medicine, and education. They introduced a modern approach to things like agriculture, farming, and industry, and they also brought Christianity.

The truth is, there are more Christians on the African continent than any other religious group—including Muslims. And I think in many ways, Africans are a great model for Christianity, because once they come into the faith, they are passionate about it. They are similar to some of the black churches in America, where Sunday at church is an all-day affair. It's a celebration. People are coming to Christ with a great passion, with a great desire to know Christ better, with a great willingness to expend time and resources to serve Him.

And then there's Islam. In many cases, when Islam moves into an African country or region and begins to convert people, they claim that they're "bringing them back to their roots." Nothing could be further from the truth. Africans were pagan worshipers before anyone told them about Muhammad. And in many cases, conversion from their traditional religions to Islam took place at the edge of the sword as part of the Arab conquests. And the slavery that brought Africans to America in chains was often done by Muslim slave traders. In fact, slavery is still going on in Africa right now and it has nothing to do with America.

Unfortunately, Muslim conquest is surging again in Africa, acted out by militant Islamist groups like ISIS, Boko Haram, al-Shabaab, and others. We certainly see this in Nigeria, where tens of thousands of Christians have died for their faith. It is spreading across the Sahel and now in Mozambique, which is a largely Catholic country. Across Africa, radical Muslims are invading Christian communities—even going into Muslim communities that refuse to radicalize—and they're slaughtering, mutilating, and even beheading people by the dozens. This is an intensifying problem and a massive religious freedom crisis.

Both the Muslim Brotherhood and Iran are involved in these Islamization projects. But will terrorist-aligned groups dominate the continent of Africa? Certainly, Christians and others who refuse Islam will suffer. But when these terrorist groups can't find anybody else to fight, they always find a way to fight each other.

It is unfortunate that the military success America and our allies have had against radical Islamist groups like ISIS and al-Qaeda in Iraq, Afghanistan, and Syria has had an unintended secondary effect. It has increased the threat to Christians on the African continent. In Iraq and Syria, ISIS and al-Qaeda have not been destroyed, but they have been forced to relocate from their traditional safe havens and operational areas in the Middle East. And many of these terrorists have chosen Africa as their new home. While some have simply joined forces with existing jihadi groups—like al-Shabaab in Somalia or Boko Haram in Nigeria—others have remained intact entities carrying the name of their original terror group and have relocated to several African countries.

Does an Islamist threat in various African countries create a national security threat to the United States? While the Islamist aggression is increasing, at the same time U.S. interest in protecting African countries is waning. President Joe Biden's troop withdrawals from Afghanistan scheduled for August 31, 2021, reflected an American war-weariness that makes any future American military operations on the African continent to rescue or protect nationals—including Christians—very unlikely. At best, the U.S. may expend some diplomatic and economic capital to help threatened Christians or other non-Muslim populations. But it's questionable how effective that will be in reducing the threat from committed Islamic jihadi groups. Let's hope our intelligence community is able to foresee terrorist activities targeting the United States or U.S. interests before another September 11 tragedy transpires.

While it is unpleasant to consider, the reality is that Africa's struggle with radical Islamists may be a problem with no practical solution. The U.S. must consider what happens if Christians and other refugees start pouring out of Africa because of the atrocities being perpetrated against them. That scenario will signal a serious humanitarian crisis. The resulting death and misery will grab world attention—including an outcry for the U.S. to answer the call. Maybe that seems a bit unreasonable. Nonetheless, if history is indeed prologue, then there is a clear probability the United States will be under great pressure to react to the suffering—just as it has in the past.

However, I am personally more concerned about China's intentions than Islamist activities in Africa. The Chinese have set their sights on Africa because they recognize what great potential the continent has for providing them with the energy and the resources they need to maintain their industries, not to mention their military. We already know what China does to Christian believers—we've watched their kind of persecution unfold since 1948. They are persistent, technologically advanced, and ruthless in enforcing their ideology. I personally believe China is at least as great a threat to the continent of Africa as Islamist terrorists.

CHAPTER 3

MIDDLE EAST: WARS AND RUMORS OF WARS

Most Iranian Christians live quiet lives, wary of drawing unwelcome attention to themselves. This is especially true of converts from Islam—for them, keeping out of sight can be a matter of life and death. But not all Iranian Christians choose to keep a low profile, and Mary Mohammadi decided to walk a different and more difficult path.[1] Just twenty-three years old, she has been arrested and jailed on more than one occasion for reasons regarding her faith. For a time, she was held in Iran's infamous Qarchak women's prison, a germ-infested facility south of Tehran. She was ferociously abused in Vazara Detention Center by female authorities. She was also beaten so severely in Azadi Square by both male and female guards that her bruises could be seen for weeks.

Mary's courage and grace are noteworthy. Even President Donald Trump mentioned her by name during a National Prayer Breakfast speech, noting she was imprisoned because "she converted to Christianity and shared the Gospel with others."[2] Yet, despite the mistreatment she has endured, Mary refuses to be silenced about a number of injustices.

In personal correspondence, Lela Gilbert asked Mary about how her life changed after her confrontations with the authorities. Following Mary's arrests and detention, she lost not only a job that she loved, but also her ability to continue her university education. Clearly, the losses she lives with are distressing to a young, articulate, and intelligent woman. Mary is far from the only Christian who faces these deprivations. Iran is listed among the top ten persecutors of Christians in the world.[3] Mary wrote:

> The regime only formally recognizes certain Christian denominations—Assyrians and Armenians, and they have brutally killed some Christian leaders over the years like Mehdi Dibaj, Hosein Soodmand and Ravanbakhsh Yousefi. Furthermore, the regime prevents the rest of us from pursuing our education or finding work. Today they do not permit us to meet, to discuss, to worship, to talk about our faith, to have separate cemeteries, to hold funeral and marriage ceremony in a Christian way, to publish and sell the Bible in any language except in Armenian and Assyrian languages, to have any official churches, to adopt a child and more. To sum up, we don't have any rights. We are not citizens in our country. The government only provides us with a birth certificate and the "right to vote"—all to benefit itself.

Mary Mohammadi wants the world to know about the discrimination she and others experience. But her firm determination to speak so boldly seemed alarming. Gilbert cautioned her and tried to change the subject, asking more than once why Mary refused to be more careful.

Mary replied, "Why am I doing this? Because I am expected as a follower of Jesus to fight for justice. It is not just a choice but a command I have from Him. My primary objective is not to get rid of the regime but to gain justice for all Iranians. Yet that can never be done until the regime is gone, and until Iran has a government based on the rule of law."

Mary concluded by quoting a passage of Scripture, "He has shown you, O mortal, what is good. And what does the LORD require of you? To act justly and to love mercy and to walk humbly with your God" (Micah 6:8 NIV).

Mary Mohammadi is a brave woman who serves as but one example of the intense pressure endured daily by hundreds of thousands of courageous Christians in today's Middle East. Iran is certainly the source of much of this pressure, but there are other trouble spots as well. These issues and others will be discussed at greater length in the following pages. But for now, we'll take a quick look at the Middle East's cultural, ethnic, and religious composition and how those elements contribute to its volatile—even explosive—character that continues to threaten Christian believers.

SNAPSHOTS OF A MUSLIM—MAJORITY REGION

A stunning 2019 report in *The Guardian* stated that "In the Middle East the population of Christians used to be about 20%; now it's 5%." The article goes on to say:

Pervasive persecution of Christians, sometimes amounting to genocide, is ongoing in parts of the

Middle East, and has prompted an exodus in the past two decades, according to a report commissioned by the British foreign secretary, Jeremy Hunt. Millions of Christians in the region have been uprooted from their homes, and many have been killed, kidnapped, imprisoned and discriminated against, the report finds.[4]

A look at the history of Christians and Jews in the region provides useful background for the abuse and bloodshed that continue to make news today.

To begin, according to a Pew Research Center report on the future of world religions, "More than nine-in-ten people in the Middle East and North Africa were Muslim as of 2010 (93%)."[5] And, although there are many "moderate" Muslims, a major factor in the disturbing record of violence against Jews and Christians is found in historic Islamist ideology. Ever since the founding of Islam, Christians and Jews have been classified as a separate class of citizens. These "People of the Book" have long been known as *dhimmis*.

Under dhimmi status, Jews and Christians could not carry weapons, could not make converts, were not allowed to live in houses higher than those of Muslims, could not make a public display of their rituals, could only ride donkeys and not horses, could not build new churches or synagogues and had to pay a yearly poll tax. In addition, they had to wear distinctive clothing to differentiate them from Muslims.[6]

In practical terms, this historic discrimination against Jews and Christians has led to abuse and bloodshed.

Meanwhile, more recent developments have further aggravated the situation: the founding, growth, and military success of the Jewish State of Israel. Not only did Jews flood into Israel from Europe after the Holocaust, and more so following Israel's declaration as a nation in 1948, but as Arab armies repeatedly tried to attack the new state comprised of Jewish immigrants, Israeli fighters consistently repelled them. At the same time, within Muslim states, resentments grew. They were fed by antisemitic rumors and myths.

This, in turn, led to the great expulsion of Jews from Muslim lands. Many if not most of the Jewish populations had lived in their Middle Eastern homelands since antiquity. Israel's Ministry of Foreign Affairs reported in 2017:

> Current research estimates that the number of Jews living in Arab countries and Iran totaled more than 850,000 at the time of Israel's independence. Some scholars even think the number is closer to one million. In the North African region, 259,000 Jews fled from Morocco, 140,000 from Algeria, 100,000 from Tunisia, 75,000 from Egypt, and another 38,000 from Libya. In the Middle East, 135,000 Jews were exiled from Iraq, 55,000 from Yemen, 34,000 from Turkey, 20,000 from Lebanon and 18,000 from Syria. Iran forced out 25,000 Jews.[7]

But what about the Christians? They have also faced discrimination and violence in the Middle East for centuries. In fact, there is a slogan among jihadi fighters, which appeared on a flag confiscated in Israel during an Arab uprising. In Arabic it says:

"On Saturday we kill the Jews, On Sunday we kill the Christians."[8]

Following the expulsion of Jews from their ancient homelands, only a handful of elderly Jews remain today in several Arab countries such as Syria, Egypt, Libya, and Iraq. And now, in recent years, we have seen the massive displacement of Christians by Islamic State (ISIS) and other jihadi groups. In today's Middle East, Christians continue to flee many of the same countries that expelled the Jews in the mid-twentieth century, leaving behind plummeting populations and shuttered churches. Many continue to leave at their first realistic opportunity. Before we provide more detailed stories, here are a few glimpses of their current situations.

- **In Egypt,** although the current President al-Sisi has made both declarations and efforts to stop localized abuse of Christians in Egypt—the #20 worst persecutor on Open Doors' 2022 list—attacks still continue. Sisi's many big-picture gestures have been appreciated, but in numerous rural areas such as the Minya Governate in upper Egypt and in parts of the Sinai, anti-Christian abuses continue. Kidnappings, riots, and other violent attacks continue unabated, and no government agency, federal or local, has stopped them.[9]
- **In Iraq,** after the devastating ISIS attacks against Christians in 2014, the destruction of homes, towns, and villages has left untold numbers of displaced victims. And even those who manage to return to rebuild their homes must deal with Iran-sponsored militias that now occupy and

govern their villages and towns. These groups are dangerous to Christians and prohibit their attempts to return to normal life.[10]

- **In Syria**, the death toll (estimated at 606,000) and damage to the country following a devastating civil war has incapacitated the entire country.[11] In Northeast Syria, a de facto autonomous region, sometimes known as "Rojava," is working toward self-governance, offering equality for Muslims, Christians, Kurds, Yazidis, and others, as well as for women's rights. But Turkish aggression and resistance from the Bashar al-Assad regime continue to target Christians, Yazidis, and other minorities.

- **In Turkey**, President Recep Tayyip Erdogan's vision of a revived Neo-Ottoman Empire has taken a sinister turn in recent years. This has led to abuse and violence in his own country and Turkish military aggression in several others including Syria, Libya, Armenia, and Iraq. At the same time, Christians are under increasing pressure.[12] In 2016, American Christian pastor Andrew Brunson was arrested and imprisoned for two years by the Turkish government on false charges before his negotiated release. Since then, Christian refugees from Syria and elsewhere continue to be pressured to convert to Islam, non-Turkish Christian workers are being expelled, and Turkey continues to confiscate churches—including Hagia Sophia, an ancient Christian landmark.

- **In Saudi Arabia**, there are no churches whatsoever. Many of the millions of Christian foreign

workers suffer harsh abuse when they try to
gather for worship secretly, or are reported for
sharing their faith with their Muslim employ-
ers.[13] Many of them are essentially slave laborers.
Reforms, however, seems to be slowly moving
into the oil-rich kingdom. Will they lead to
positive change? No one is sure how powerfully
the radical Muslim Wahabi element will push
back against the forces of modernity. Meanwhile,
no churches exist in Saudi Arabia, and religious
freedom seems only to be a distant dream.

- **In Iran**, the country has been under the tight
  fist of a radical Shiite Muslim religious system
  since 1979, which anticipates the arrival of the
  12th Imam, an Islamic messianic figure.[14] Many
  Shiites around the world look for this appearance, but the eccentric Iranian cult—sometimes
  called "Twelvers"—believes that chaos and
  bloodshed must prepare the way for him. Under
  the authority of today's Supreme Leader, Grand
  Ayatollah Ali Khamenei, Iran's police, military,
  courts, and all relevant authorities actively pursue non-Shiite religious believers as threats to
  the country's security. Baha'is and Christians
  are particularly harassed, but the regime's most
  actively pursued targets are converts from Islam
  to Christianity, and particularly those whom we
  would call evangelicals or Pentecostals. They
  are seen as enemies of the state, agents of foreign subversion, "wrong cults," or are accused
  of "engaging in propaganda against the Islamic
  regimen," an oft-cited allegation.

- **In Israel**, according to the U.S. State Department's 2019 report, "[Israel's] laws and Supreme Court rulings protect the freedoms of conscience, faith, religion, and worship, regardless of an individual's religious affiliation, and the 1992 'Basic Law: Human Dignity and Liberty' protects additional individual rights."[15] Occasional religious tensions occur, triggering harassment and vandalism as a result of Israel's near 20 percent Muslim population, a tiny but deeply rooted Orthodox and Catholic Christian community, and numerous and sometimes hotly debated Jewish differences on faith and practice. But compared to the unrelieved violence in many of the surrounding nations, religious freedom in Israel is the rule, not the exception. Meanwhile, the incidents of violence in the disputed territories of Judea, Samaria, and Gaza—which sometimes spill over into Israel itself—are most often the result of terror activities and frequently result in a strong Israeli response to them.

THE BIG PICTURE—ENDANGERED CHRISTIANS IN CHRISTIANITY'S HEARTLAND

Since Iran's Islamic Revolution in 1979 and the Iraq wars in the early 2000s, the ancient communities of Christians across the Middle East have suffered increasing danger, abuse, and bloodshed. The spread of radical Islamist ideology—both Sunni and Shiite—has become the trigger for persecution, to varying degrees, in nearly every Middle Eastern country. The more radical the Islamist influences, the worse the treatment of Christians and other religious minorities. This was most painfully illustrated by the ISIS surge across Iraq and Syria in 2014, which led to a bloodbath of genocidal proportions, primarily directed at Yazidis (an ancient faith group) and Christians.

In the pages that follow, we'll look at several countries that have become hotspots for Christian abuse. Some regimes are growing more dangerous to minorities as their leadership intensifies its focus on religious enforcement, usually for reasons of ideological ambition. Along similar lines, some leaders become insecure about their capacity to control parts of the population that do not agree with their religious views. Still others seem to be moving in a more tolerant direction, although the road to religious toleration for Christian communities is inevitably rocky and uneven.

SLOWLY, SLOWLY: BETTER DAYS FOR EGYPT'S CHRISTIANS?

One of the oldest Christian communities in the world is Egypt's historic Coptic Christian Church, founded in Alexandria during the first century CE by the apostle Mark. These Christians, along with smaller Christian denominations, comprise between 8 and 10 percent of Egypt's 83 million citizens.[16]

The Copts' bloodlines are even more ancient than their Christian faith; they date back to the pharaohs, centuries before the Arab invasions in the seventh century CE. The Coptic language, still used in liturgy, is the existing language closest to that of ancient Egypt. However, despite their historical heritage, as a religious minority in a Muslim-majority state, the Copts have lived for centuries under the *dhimmi* status spelled out in Islamic Sharia law, and thus they are treated as inferior citizens.

Meanwhile, under some recent regimes, Copts have suffered escalating attacks, as Islamist extremists have specifically targeted them. Christians in Egypt suffered exceptional abuse during the brief regime of Muslim Brotherhood President Mohamed Morsi. Then, in July 2013, in response to millions of Egyptians taking to the streets in protest against the Brotherhood, Egypt's military removed Morsi from office.

This stunning turnaround offered some hope to Egyptians who were both wary and weary of the Brotherhood's efforts to seize control of all branches of government. But the military coup also unleashed greater violence against the Copts. After a litany of horrific incidents in 2011–2013, and after the brutal massacre of twenty-one Coptic Christian men on a Libyan beach in February 2015, reports of attacks on Christians have diminished, although isolated incidents have not ceased.

Meanwhile, since his election in May 2014, Egypt's President Abdel Fattah al-Sisi has taken several highly visible steps toward bettering state relations with the Coptic community, including his unprecedented move in attending a Coptic Christmas Mass, celebrated by Pope Tawadros. However, on May 25, 2015, the *Daily Telegraph* reported a horrendous attack on a village of Coptic Christians in El-Karm, located in Egypt's southern province of Minya.[17]

The trouble began—as anti-Christian attacks in Muslim-majority countries often do—with a salacious rumor. The story in this case was that a Christian man, Ashraf Thabet, was rumored to be having a sexual relationship with a Muslim woman. In an Islamic-oriented culture, this portends a death sentence—an honor killing—of the purported lovers.

Once the accused adulterer got wind of the local gossip, he ran for his life, with his wife and children in tow. Ashraf

Thabet's parents, knowing very well how vulnerable they also were, rushed to the police for protection. However, that was a wasted trip.

The next day, around 300 Muslim men set fire to and looted the parents' house. More horrifying, they stripped the elderly mother naked and paraded her on the street. They also set fire to and looted six other houses. "They burned the house and went in and dragged me out, threw me in front of the house and ripped my clothes. I was just as my mother gave birth to me and was screaming and crying," said Thabet's mother, later identified as Soaad Thabet; she was 70 years old at the time.[18] She was humiliated beyond description and feared for her life. It is difficult for Westerners to imagine the degree of cultural dishonor and disgrace to which she was subjected.

It wasn't until 2021 that five local thugs were found guilty and sentenced to five years in prison for torching the Thabet home along with burning and looting six others. And in June that same year, ten Muslim men were found guilty of sectarian violence and sentenced to five years for their vile abuse of Soaad Thabet. She finally saw justice served, although she later said, "if the defendants are sentenced to 100 years in prison, it does not compensate for the displacement of me and my family."[19]

Samuel Tadros—senior fellow at Hudson Institute's Center for Religious Freedom and the author of the critically-acclaimed book *Motherland Lost: The Egyptian and Coptic Quest for Modernity*[20]—was asked if there has been real progress in relations between the government and the Coptic community. Tadros explained,

> A spike in attacks came after the 2011 revolution
> for two reasons; collapse of security and rise of
> Islamists not just on national level, but on local

one, where they attempted to force their will on villages and small towns. Following the removal of President Morsi, these two factors have been somewhat contained. Policing is a bit better, not by much—they still ignore attacks on Copts—but there is somewhat better security in the streets; and Islamists are on the run. . . . But we have to remember, the president has changed, but the local security officer who won't protect the Copts is the same man, the local mayor or governor who will hold the reconciliation session is the same official, and most importantly the neighbors who hate the Copts are the same neighbors.[21]

One of the government's responses to such attacks is that of "reconciliation sessions" which are claimed to be of great importance. These sessions are in fact a disgraceful tactic, used again and again following incidents of Christian persecution. Such events essentially release violent perpetrators from all responsibility.

The idea of reconciliation may sound good on the surface: why not bring together the village's Christians and Muslims so they can work out their differences and get along with one another? What really happens, instead, is that an attitude of moral equivalency prevails. "Everyone" is responsible for the problem. Therefore, the Muslim radicals, who may already have been arrested and even indicted for their criminal behavior, are for all practical purposes "forgiven." The mob attack in El-Karm, Minya, was no exception to this scheme.

Bishop Macarius of Minya and Abu Qirqas, who was delegated by Coptic Pope Tawadros II to speak on behalf of the Coptic Orthodox Church on the Minya case, denounced the subsequent reconciliation meeting, stating it would prevent the perpetrators from being held accountable. "I refused to attend the meeting so as to deliver a message that enforcing the law should come before any meeting," he said in an official statement. Sam Tadros explains,

> There are several problems with the reconciliation programs that take place after every attack on Copts. First they are non-judicial practices that replace the courts. As such, no punishment is ever handed down to the attackers. By not punishing the attackers, the sessions create a culture of impunity. You can attack Copts and get away with it. Secondly, the sessions end up giving the attackers what they want: If they were objecting to a church being built, no church is built; if they were angry after a rumor about a Christian man insulting Islam or having a relationship with a Muslim woman, then he and his extended family are forced out of the village.[22]

Of course it's true that Christians are meant to forgive. We are also called to be peacemakers. But at the same time, while being gentle as doves, we are equally advised to be "wise as serpents." With that in mind, there seems to be much wisdom in the Coptic leaders' resistance to the phony peace and forgiveness promoted in Egypt's reconciliation sessions.

EGYPTIAN CHRISTIAN GIRLS AND WOMEN ARE TARGETED

"'We are the Church of Martyrs' is a phrase heard over and over in conversations with young Copts," writes Martin Mosebach, author of the profound and powerful book, *The*

21: A Journey into the Land of Coptic Martyrs. He provides a detailed portrait of each of the twenty-one men who died on a Libyan beach—all but one Egyptian, beheaded by ISIS on February 15, 2015. "It is the honorary title of the Coptic Church but has also been undeniably prophetic," Mosebach wrote. "For throughout history, the Copts have been given countless opportunities to maintain their status as just that: a fellowship of martyrs."[23]

So it was in 2015 for those faithful Christian men who refused to deny their faith at the cost of their lives, and so the threat remains today in their homeland.

Although some international observers, such as the U.S. Commission on International Religious Freedom (USCIRF), have noted that Christian persecution in Egypt seems to have diminished somewhat in recent years, they are also obliged to note it most certainly has not disappeared. And it is particularly evident in the abuse of females.

Egypt's Christian girls and women continue to face a silent epidemic of kidnapping, rape, beatings, and torture. Innumerable girls and women vanish forever, and even if they are somehow rescued, their stories are thought to be so shameful that they're hidden as dark family secrets. Sometimes doctors are able to quietly repair internal damage and "restore virginity" to the abused. Priests, if made aware of the situation, may try to protect family reputations when the girls return.[24]

But the devastated survivors will never be the same.

The attacks vary. Some happen randomly, when a vulnerable female is spotted walking alone on a sidewalk. Others are plotted by Islamist consortiums, who pay kidnappers as much $3,000 per captured girl. The assailants rape the victims, hold them in captivity, then demand the terrified young women convert to Islam—often violently abusing them until they surrender.

For more years than can be counted, it has remained true that Egypt's Copts belong to a "fellowship of martyrdom." Not all of them are murdered—like those beheaded on a distant beach, or blown apart in bombed churches, a tragic form of brutality which has happened all too often. But innumerable Christians have lost the life they once knew—whether it has been stolen by fanatical kidnappers, or violated by thugs, or simply reduced to a struggle for survival by constant threats of Islamist violence.

Describing President Sisi's religious freedom efforts, Hudson's religious freedom scholar Paul Marshall explains:

> Clearly, Egypt is not in the same category as highly restrictive countries such as Saudi Arabia, Iran or Afghanistan. Egyptian President Sisi has made repeated and important symbolic statements and appearances concerning Copts, the largest religious minority in the country and, at some 10 million, the largest Christian minority in the Middle East. He has emphasized the equality of Egyptians, visited the main Coptic cathedral at Christmas, and has assisted the construction of a Cathedral of the Nativity of Christ in Egypt's yet-to-be-named new administrative capital, 45 kilometers East of Cairo. A Parliamentary Committee has very slowly but steadily been giving official recognition to many already-built churches. But when examples of actual change are closely examined, by all accounts progress has been, at best, agonizingly slow. At worst, nothing has changed

at all. In some places like the Minya Governorate, the situation may have even worsened.[25]

For decades, the kidnapping of hundreds of Coptic girls has resulted in forced conversions to Islam and undesired marriages to Muslim men. Catholic news service *Terrasanta* reported, "The high number of missing girls and the repeating identical operating patterns have convinced lawyers, activists and priests—long engaged in the battle against the terrible practice—that there is an organized network behind the kidnappings. According to some, there are Islamic cells dedicated exclusively to the abduction of Coptic women."[26]

At the same time there are false imprisonments, such as that of Rami Kamel, a Coptic human rights campaigner and founder of the Maspero Youth Union. Egyptian state security arrested him for "membership in a terrorist organization" and for using social media to spread "false news threatening public order." Kamel remained in perpetual pre-trial detention for two years, spending much of that time in solitary confinement and suffering clearly declining health.[27]

Overall, there has been progress in Egypt during Sisi's presidency. But much more remains to be done. We need to pray and continue to speak up for the Copts and other Christians who live in what continues to be a hostile and dangerous country.

IRAQ'S SHATTERED CHRISTIAN COMMUNITIES

Beyond Egypt, the Middle East has many struggles with religious freedom and few as painful as Iraq. Wars, the demise of dictator Saddam Hussein, and the intrusion of Iranian militias have led to ceaseless upheaval and adversity. But in recent centuries, nothing has quite matched the ferocity of the ISIS uprising and invasion, primarily in Iraq and Syria, in 2014. In Erbil, Kurdistan in Northern Iraq, co-author Lela Gilbert interviewed a young Christian refugee in Iraq.[28]

"Miserable. We are miserable."

Faten confided her feelings with a shrug and a weak smile. Her English wasn't the greatest, so she made sure I understood that she wasn't criticizing the church that provides shelter for her and other family members. She was simply stating the facts.

I was visiting the Mar Yousef church compound in the Ankawa district of Erbil, Kurdistan. Ankawa is a Christian enclave in a mostly Muslim city, and it is packed to the rafters with refugees and their meager possessions.

In an odd way, it is rather colorful. The church's roofs and ramparts are strung with random items of laundry. Several classrooms have become sleeping quarters for 10 families each—40–50 women and children per room. During the day, the rooms are piled to the ceiling with brightly printed mats that serve as mattresses by night. A huge pot of rice simmers just inside each door.

Male refugees, even fathers and husbands, sleep in a different section of the compound. They mingle with their families during the day.

It was raining, and the air was damp and heavy with human smells—food, sweat and latrines. Bathing takes place in a cubicle with peeling paint, a rickety door and a cold water tap about three feet from the ground.

Two other cold taps on the grounds provide water for drinking, laundry and dishwashing. Beyond that, there is no running or hot water, no heat and the barest essentials to eat.

"We have no money to buy food," Faten, who was once a schoolteacher, told me. "Daesh took everything . . ."

Faten related that she has been a refugee twice. She grew up in Baghdad and lived there until after the U.S. invasion, when terrorist attacks on churches grew deadly. Around 2005, she fled Baghdad's anti-Christian violence. She left her teaching job and made her way to Qaraqosh.

Then, just three months ago, the Islamic State—commonly called Daesh in Kurdistan—swept into Qaraqosh after decimating Mosul's Christian community.

The invaders offered Qaraqosh's Christians the usual three options: Convert, pay the jizya tax, or get out.

Otherwise, they would face the Islamist's sword.

Needless to say, they fled. And they left with nothing. "They took everything," Faten said. "ID papers, money. They looted our houses, our shops. Everything."

An old woman, one eye obscured with the opaque whiteness of disease, interrupted us. She began to shout in Arabic or Kurdish—I wasn't sure which.

I thought she was angry about our intrusion into her broken world. But no, she just wanted us to know that she, too, had lost everything. Her brief outburst ended in bitter weeping.

In the months and years that followed that shocking invasion, the eyes of the world focused on the most blood-thirsty and openly barbaric group of Islamist radicals ever to bludgeon its way across the Middle East in modern history. The "Islamic State"—aka ISIS—a cult-like, burgeoning coalition of Sunni radicals led by a self-declared "caliph," horrified observers with their savage tactics and the bloodstained trail of rape, abduction, sex-trading, mutilation, beheading, and even crucifixion they leave behind.

After June 2014, ISIS became notorious for its wanton expulsion of Christians from Iraq's war-torn countryside. Neither were Yazidis, Kurds, and Shiite Muslims spared. The Islamic State's battalions of thugs forced "infidel" families from their homes, seizing all their material possessions as they drove them out. They murdered and sometimes beheaded resisters; raped women and children, and kidnapped young girls for sexual exploitation. They also proudly publicized their acts on social media—apparently for the sole purpose of terrifying all who stood against them.

And it wasn't as if the Christians they attacked were newcomers to their Middle Eastern neighborhood. Christians were in Iraq long before Mohammad, the founder of Islam, was born. Iraq's Christian community is far from a Western innovation or a colonial relic. It dates from the first century, when two of Jesus's disciples—St. Thomas and St. Thaddeus (also known as St. Jude)—preached the gospel in what was then Assyria. There has been a Christian presence in Iraq ever since.

The heartland of their community has always been in Mosul and the Nineveh Plain. There, in recent years, the Christian population swelled, as refugees from Basra and Baghdad sought protection there and then, over time, left the region altogether. According to *DW News*, "Around 1.4 million Christians in the country were counted in a 1987 Iraqi government census. But over the last three decades, their numbers have plummeted as Christians emigrated. Today, there are thought to be between 200,000 and 300,000 Christians left in Iraq."[29] Those Christians knew very well their days were numbered as long as Islamist radicals were free to target their homes and families.

Not long after the ISIS invasion of Iraq's Christian heartland, the cover of the Islamic State's English-language magazine *Dabiq* featured the Vatican on its front cover. Fluttering in the Italian breeze, atop the Egyptian obelisk at St. Peter's Square, is ISIS's notorious black flag with its characteristic white Arabic lettering. The lengthy article called on aspiring jihadists to target the Catholic Church and followers of the Christian faith. The Islamist organization claimed it would one day conquer Rome, threatening to "break [the] crosses" of infidels and sell and trade their women.[30]

Today, although the ISIS attacks of Iran and Syria were largely defeated, and their leader al-Baghdadi assassinated in late 2019, ruthless killers bearing the same ISIS flags are rapidly expanding in both East and West Africa, and little is being done to stop them.[31] *The Guardian* reported,

> Islamic State's affiliates in Africa are set for major expansion after a series of significant victories, new alliances and shifts in strategy reinforced their position

across much of the continent. Following recent gains in Nigeria, the Sahel, in Mozambique and the Democratic Republic of the Congo, Isis propaganda published by the group's leadership in its heartland in the Middle East is increasingly stressing sub-Saharan Africa as a new front which may compensate the group for significant setbacks elsewhere.[32]

IRAN'S FURTIVE OCCUPATION OF IRAQ'S CHRISTIAN COMMUNITIES[33]

Meanwhile, as if the ISIS invasion weren't enough, other forces are also arrayed against Iraq's shattered Christian villages, towns, and cities. ISIS's Sunni invaders and Iran's Shiite militias apply differing tactics, but their agenda is largely the same. Will Iraq's remaining Christians somehow find a way to retain their religious and cultural heritage, dating back to the first century?

No one knows for sure, but in the wake of ISIS and due to Iranian aspirations, the answer is far from encouraging. The story of Father Benham Benoka provides ample reason to doubt high hopes for Iraq's future—particularly the Christian communities there.

In an interview with Fr. Benoka, a Syriac Catholic priest from the Christian town of Bartella, he explained, "Bartella is liberated, but not free." Along with a handful of other displaced residents, he had recently managed to reenter Bartella, escorted by Iraqi soldiers. He explained that large portions of the town were beyond repair. ISIS had looted private residences, then demolished them with explosives. They had left building after building booby-trapped. Roadways were rife with IEDs.

"ISIS had excellent technology," Benoka said. "They mined everything. Even Bibles." During his visit, he made his way to St. George Assyrian Church, his spiritual home and a sizeable portion of Bartella's Christian community.

ISIS had all but destroyed St. George's interior. Bibles and New Testaments from the fourteenth, fifteenth, and sixteenth centuries were ripped up, burned, or otherwise desecrated. Perhaps most disturbing was a noose, hanging ominously in the church's courtyard, just inside the entryway. It bore mute witness to the demise of a Christian welcome center that had been transformed into an Islamist execution site.

When asked how he'd felt when he entered Bartella a few days before, Fr. Benoka paused. "I felt insecure," he finally replied. "I was so disappointed. I kept thinking, *What can we do?*" Clearly discouraged, he shook his head again and concluded, "And who will help us?"

This well-loved priest's concerns about his hometown's future have proved to be well-founded. One of his primary worries was about security for returning Christians. Today, although ISIS is no longer present, another formidable armed force occupies Bartella and the surrounding "liberated" communities. And those armed men are no friends of Christians.

Asia News reported, "There is no peace for Christians in northern Iraq. . . . The epicenter of this new chapter of anti-Christian persecution is Bartella, increasingly draped with banners depicting the militia battles against ISIS as well as saints and sacred figures of the Shia tradition."[34]

The major Christian towns of Qaraqosh, Bartella, and Karamles are now supposedly under the control of the Iraqi army, but the military force actually occupying them is an Iran-funded Shia militia. In fact, Michael Pregent, military intelligence analyst at Hudson Institute, reports it was initially under the command of Iran's Quds extraterritorial force and its infamous general, the late Qasem Soleimani.

The tentacles of the Iranian ayatollahs' acolytes are coiled around the Christian communities in Iraq's Nineveh Plains and well beyond, and they continue to tighten their grip. Flags bearing Shia religious slogans and photos of Supreme Leader Ayatollah Khamenei flutter and sway in plain view.

A British priest, Fr. Benedict Kiely—founder of Nasarean. org, a charity assisting persecuted Christians—was asked about the militia that the Christian community faces there. He replied, "They are certainly intimidating Christians. The most notorious incident was a shooting at St. George's Church in Bartella before Christmas. In that case, a pistol was put in the face of the pastor, Fr. Benoka. He has said that the Shia militia are 'the new ISIS,' although thankfully, there's been no killing yet."

Iranian Supreme Leader Ali Khamenei's expansive agenda couldn't be clearer. And the Iranian Revolutionary Guard Corps (IRGC) is actively pursuing it—not only in Iraq, but also in Yemen, Afghanistan, Syria, Lebanon, and Gaza. For years, Israel's Prime Minister Benjamin Netanyahu tirelessly warned the world about Iran's global ambitions and nuclear intentions.

Meanwhile, the future of Iraq's Christian communities hangs precariously in the balance. In reality, by most accounts, the once-bright hope of their continuing presence in the Middle East grows dimmer every day. As Benoka aptly asked, "Who will help us?" When it comes to security for Iraqi Christians, an uneasy silence is the answer.

Unfortunately, Iraqi Christians are not the only ones facing upheaval, uncertainty, and danger. Syria is a largely Muslim country, and its religious minorities have been shattered by more than a decade of civil war and all the death and destruction that has caused.

SYRIA'S DEADLY CIVIL WAR

When reflecting on today's uncertainties in the Middle East, no one should forget the so-called Arab Spring, which ripped the region apart and sowed seeds of terrorism and radical groups that have never altogether disbanded. The uprisings began in December 2010 in the little town of Sidi Bouzid, Tunisia. There a desperate young street vendor, Mohammed Bouazizi, set himself aflame in protest of a cruel police action—they had confiscated his vegetable stand because of Bouazizi's failure to obtain a proper permit.

Bouazizi's dramatic self-immolation (he later died of his wounds) literally ignited the "Jasmine Revolution" in Tunisia. Street protests in Tunis eventually escalated, and ultimately drove president Zine El Abidine Ben Ali out of the country.

Activists who were weary of their iron-fisted governments were inspired by Bouazizi's self-sacrifice, and across the Middle East they stirred up protests large and small—some far more influential than others. But three countries were gripped by anti-regime violence that erupted into full-scale civil wars: Libya, Yemen, and Syria.

The Syrian conflict being in March 2011. At that time, some fifteen teenagers from Daraa—now known as "the birthplace of the revolution" against President Bashar al-Assad—were arrested for scribbling anti-regime graffiti on the wall of their school. According to locals, when the families and friends of the young men protested their arrest and demanded their release, security forces opened fire and killed three people.

As protests continued, the population's rage increased exponentially. Before long buildings were torched, including one owned by one of Assad's cousins. In April, the Syrian army launched a massive crackdown and by May, more than 240 protestors had been killed.

Thus began the horrific Syrian civil war. And it quickly spread like wildfire across the country.

Bashar Assad is far from the only brutal dictator in the region; however he is loathed by many. And as the violence swelled in Syria, calls for military intervention—seeking Assad's removal from power—began to resound across the region as well as in the West.

Over a decade later, the Council on Foreign Relations summed up the resulting state of affairs:

> Ten years since protesters in Syria first demonstrated against the four-decade rule of the Assad family, hundreds of thousands of Syrians have been killed and some twelve million people—more than half the country's prewar population—have been displaced. The country has descended into an ever more complex civil war: jihadis promoting a Sunni theocracy have eclipsed opposition forces fighting for a democratic and pluralistic Syria, and regional powers have backed various local forces to advance their geopolitical interests on Syrian battlefields. The Turks have pushed Kurdish forces, the United States' main local partner in the fight against the Islamic State, from border areas. Russia, too, has carried out air strikes in Syria, coming to the Assad regime's defense, while Iranian forces and their Hezbollah allies have done the same on the ground.[35]

The dream of regime change in Syria has diminished and for one clear reason—there is no alternative leaders that promise to be any better than Assad. The terror groups that seized large portions of Syria are still entrenched there, and would be joyfully energized by the possibility of seizing authority of a decapitated state. Meanwhile, Turkey remains embedded in Syria's north, Russia continues to maintain a presence in the country, Iran has implanted itself in proximity of Israel's border and—thanks to the COVID pandemic and relentless international sanctions, Syria remains unstable. And, of course, its people suffer the most.

INSIDE AN OASIS OF RELIGIOUS FREEDOM IN NORTHEAST SYRIA

Syria has struggled for years—even before its devastating civil war—with human rights abuses and inadequate protection for freedom of religion under Bashar al-Assad's national government. However, the Syrian civil war gave birth to a new regional government in the country's Northeast that is widely viewed as a rare defender of religious freedom and equality in the Middle East—the Autonomous Administration of North and East Syria (AANES). Unfortunately, this new regional government is under constant threat.[36]

In 2019, Turkey launched a military incursion against the region of Northeast Syria, which is controlled by the Kurds, who were staunch U.S. allies in the fight against ISIS. Heartbroken religious freedom advocates watched Turkey's authoritarian President Tayyip Erdogan invade the region governed by the AANES. Today, Turkey still controls some of the areas in Northeast Syria that it invaded.

The AANES administration not only respects religious minorities but also has placed women in leadership positions, a defining characteristic that sets Northeast Syria apart from much of the Middle East. Elizabeth Kourie is one such woman, a Syriac Christian who represents her communities and others in Northeast Syria. Kourie's native tongue is Aramaic—the language spoken by Jesus.

Kourie's work started during the Syrian civil war, an agonizing conflict that cost some half a million lives. Violence continues, due to al-Assad's brutal dictatorship and the emergence of countless terrorist groups—including ISIS—and power moves by Russia, Iran, Turkey, and other competing nations.

But against all odds, the region Kourie represents in Northeast Syria has continued to offer a thriving democracy, religious freedom, and women's rights. Of course, AANES has suffered along with the rest of war-torn Syria—in their case, suffering that is often the result of relentless attacks by neighboring Turkey.

Kourie described her experience during one such assault:

> One of the first bombs that came from Turkey struck a Syriac Christian house in Qamishli, severely injuring parents and their children. Our people were very much afraid. We knew that Turkey was coming with its Sunni jihadist mercenaries. We faced them a year ago in Afrin. We faced them in the history of the Ottoman Empire. We have had experience with Turkey with a couple of genocides, the largest being 1915. We know that if Turkey is coming, it's coming with jihadists. And we know that we Christians will be targeted more than anyone else.[37]

As a result of Erdogan's repeated assaults, thousands of Christians in Northeast Syria have had to run for their lives. This situation was aggravated by the withdrawal of U.S. military troops in late 2019.[38]

On October 7, 2019, the *New York Times* reported, "In a major shift in United States military policy in Syria, the White House said on Sunday that President Trump had given his endorsement for a Turkish military operation that would sweep away American-backed Kurdish forces near the border in Syria."[39]

It was a stunning declaration. And, sadly, more than one American expressed regretful sentiments such as, "I'm ashamed of my country today." Why? Because Turkish President Recep Tayyip Erdogan was attacking Kurds, as well as Christians, Arabs, and others, who fought valiantly alongside American forces against Islamic State. Unsurprisingly, more than a few U.S. soldiers—past and present—who've served with the Kurds were infuriated by Trump's decision.

On October 13 came the infamous phone call to the White House from Erdogan announcing the Turkish army would imminently launch a military operation into northern Syria, and Trump should immediately withdraw its U.S. forces from the area. A twenty-mile wide swath along the Syria-Turkey border is the centerpiece of Erdogan's plan for what he calls a "safe zone," meant to protect Turkey from Kurdistan Workers Party (PKK) affiliated terrorists, and to resettle millions of Syrian refugees living in Turkey.

Trump's flash decision seems to have been made during that phone call with Erdogan, and interpretations of the conversation vary. But it seems to have boiled down to a green light for a Turkish incursion, perhaps motivated by Trump's weariness with America's "endless wars" and wariness about U.S. military casualties. Whatever the case, the results have become chaotic.

It didn't take long for more than a few human rights observers to warn that a program of ethnic cleansing was about to take place. And they were right. Tens of thousands began to flee their homes. The "ceasefire" quickly failed, and reports have proliferated—supported by videos and photographs—of bloodshed at the hands of Turkish fighters, brutalizing Kurds, Christians, Yazidis, and Arabs, all the while blocking ambulances and relief efforts and targeting others who have done nothing more than seek a safe haven.

The Times of London spoke to Bassam Gabro, an Assyrian Christian, who was standing outside his church in Syria, eight kilometers from the Turkish border. He was terrified.

"'I hope to God the Turks don't come,' he said, eyes filling with tears. 'They are monsters.'"

The Times continued, "Memories of the massacres of Assyrians by Ottoman forces more than a century ago are close to the surface. The Seyfo, or Year of the Sword, came at the same time as the mass killings of Armenians in 1915. 'These people have no mercy,' said Gabro. 'We remember the Seyfo. We know what they're like. They don't care if we're Kurdish, Assyrian or Arab. They'll kill everyone.'"[40]

The frantic departure of refugees, many on foot or hitching rides with strangers, is all too reminiscent of ISIS's 2014 assault on Iraq's Christian towns and cities. Residents ran for their lives to escape explosions, gunfire, and air assaults, not to mention widely reported rapes, beheadings, and other atrocities. In fact, the Turkish aggressors' tactics seem eerily similar to those of Islamic State.

The U.S. Congress condemned Turkey's invasion, with the House passing a resolution, 354-60, opposing the president's decision to withdraw from northeast Syria and demanding that Turkey stop the invasion.

During the subsequent Turkish incursion, few defenders remained to assist the people of Northeast Syria. Free Burma Rangers stands apart, along with a handful of others, as a Christian organization that provided humanitarian aid on the frontlines of the conflict.

Since that time, USCIRF has repeatedly urged the U.S. to elevate its engagement with AANES, recognize it as a legitimate local government, and lift sanctions from all areas it governs. In order to give the religious freedom found in Northeast Syria a chance to flourish, the U.S. government should exempt the AANES regional government from broader sanctions placed on Assad's regime in Syria.

USCIRF also believes "the U.S. should pressure Turkey to provide a timeline for its withdrawal from Syria, particularly given the disastrous consequences that its presence in northeastern Syria could precipitate: the tragic disappearance—and feared religious and ethnic cleansing, if not worse—of Yazidis, Christians and other marginalized communities."[41]

However, unfortunately, Turkey and its terrorists have not posed the only threat against Northeast Syria. The COVID pandemic is also a danger. On April 2, 2020, an urgent appeal was sent to the director-general of the World Health Organization (WHO). It was signed by Bassam Said Ishak, co-chief of the U.S. Mission of the Syrian Democratic Council (SDC) and two colleagues, pleading for COVID test kits to detect coronavirus infections in war-torn northeastern Syria.[42]

Meanwhile, across northeastern Syria, warnings about the virus were distributed and shelter-in-place guidance was issued. Anxiety was intense, in large part thanks to the massive numbers of displaced persons in the region, many of them crowded into ramshackle camps. Survival is difficult enough there, without the threat of the viral infection.

Of course, topping the list of instructions for COVID prevention is hand washing and personal cleanliness—number one priorities in preventing infection. But that simple act became increasingly difficult in the communities of Hassake and Tal Tamer, where Turkish-backed forces controlled the main source of the water supply and attacked the water lines to the cities.

The local population repeatedly struggled to find clean water simply for drinking and cooking—much less for hand washing. The situation is worse for the internally displaced persons (IDPs) in collective shelters and in the camps. According to a Kurdish source, these shelters accommodate about 1.5 million IDPs from inside Syria, and about 300,000 who fled from the last Turkish invasion.

The AANES report explained that the health system infrastructure in north and east Syria (NES) "has deteriorated as a result of the ongoing crisis in Syria, which started more than nine years ago. The health situation worsened after the closure of al-Yaroubiah border crossing with Iraq, which was used by the UN to deliver medical and humanitarian aid to NES. The medical supplies in NES have continued to be insufficient to confront the coronavirus pandemic . . . which requires huge resources."[43]

Now, with the spread of the pandemic across the Middle East, those communities are facing double jeopardy: Turkish terror and attacks on non-Islamist religious groups and a pandemic for which—through no fault of their own—they are almost completely unprepared.

Both of these dangers threaten life in northeastern Syria. Those who become sick enough to need medical care—and especially the critically ill—will face nearly insurmountable obstacles. A few may be transferred to Damascus, but there will be many fatalities.

In the meantime, Turkey's President Recep Tayyip Erdogan is far from likely to cease his aggression against Christians and Kurds in the region—or elsewhere. He will continue to maim, kill, and destroy. And he will do so until he is powerfully and permanently stopped in his tracks.

TURKEY'S INCREASING HOSTILITY TO CHRISTIANS

Once upon a time, tourists in Turkey eagerly made their way to Hagia Sophia—a historic architectural marvel shimmering with the golden light of ancient mosaics. Although marred by many centuries, images of Jesus, Mary, and John the Baptist reflect the spirit of a fledgling Christian world. In fact, Turkey's earliest churches are recalled in the New Testament itself—in Antioch, where St. Paul began his missionary journeys, and in the Seven Churches portrayed by St. John in his Book of Revelation.44

Christians were a significant part of the population in Turkey, until the Ottoman Empire's 1915 genocide of Armenians, Assyrians, Greeks, and other Christians. And today, the Islamist regime of President Recep Tayyip Erdogan and his neo-Ottoman agenda has magnified Turkey's anti-Christian hostility. Since an alleged coup attempt in 2016, the regime has intensified its scapegoating of Christians, while occasionally making deceptively amiable gestures toward them.[45]

In July 2020, Erdogan officially declared that Istanbul's Hagia Sophia—beautiful mosaics and all—would once again become a mosque. Erdogan announced this would gratify "the spirit of conquest" of Mehmet II, the Ottoman sultan who captured Constantinople from the Christian Byzantines in 1453, and turned the church of Hagia Sophia into a mosque. That, and the transformation of Istanbul's beautiful Chora Church of the Holy Savior, merged into a swelling stream of Turkish Christian churches being confiscated, shuttered, torn down, or converted into mosques.[46]

Troubles within the Greek Orthodox patriarchate and a disputed election of the Armenian Orthodox patriarch have also sounded international alarms. But even more troubling are the enmity and abuse displayed by the regime toward Christians themselves, both as faith groups and individuals.

During the genocidal ISIS invasion of Syria and Iraq, floods of refugees poured into Turkey. Most were Muslim, but a considerable number of them were Christians representing venerable Middle Eastern churches. As a bloc, the refugees were useful to Erdogan who, if his political demands weren't met, periodically threatened to release millions of them into Europe.

Meanwhile, according to numerous sources, Christian refugees in Turkey have been treated with contempt, consigned to remote locations, far removed from existing churches or co-religionists. Neither Turkish speakers nor Muslims, the Christian men could not legally find employment, while language and religious issues sidelined women and children struggling to work or attend school.

Unwarranted confrontations with authorities have become commonplace.

Charmaine Hedding is founder of Shai Fund, a Christian charity. After the ISIS invasion in Iraq, she visited Turkish refugee centers across the country several times in order to provide food vouchers for destitute Christian families. On one visit, quite unexpectedly, she and two colleagues were roughly taken aside by a local government official. He ordered them into a room, locked the door, and then angrily slammed a Koran onto the table in front of them. He pointed a finger at each of them, demanding they convert to Islam. This angry radical lectured them for several hours before their release. They were terrified.

One beloved Christian, who selflessly assists refugees who fled ISIS, is a Chaldean Catholic priest named Father Remzi Diril, who visits and comforts Christian families, providing religious services, sacraments, infant baptisms, and charitable assistance. He "logs thousands of miles tending his flock, the community of Iraqi Christian refugees in Turkey. Their exact number is unknown, but it is estimated to be 40,000."[47] Unsurprisingly, Father Diril has also faced harassment.

Ominously, Father Diril's elderly parents—ages seventy-one and sixty-five, residing in a tiny Christian community—were kidnapped from their home in 2020.

AsiaNews reported in March 2021, "Turkey's human rights agency has rejected the request by Fr. Remzi Diril for an investigation. Nothing is known about his father who went missing over a year ago while his mother's body was found naked, with signs of torture." This horrific crime remains unresolved.[48]

As Father Diril prays and waits, we're reminded of the arrest and imprisonment of American Pastor Andrew Brunson. After serving as a Christian clergyman in Turkey for twenty-three years, he was suddenly locked up in solitary confinement in October 2016 under ridiculously false charges. Brunson's case became a top news story in the U.S. while former President Donald Trump repeatedly demanded his release. Brunson, who struggled with intense anxiety and depression during his imprisonment, finally walked free in July 2018.

In the meantime, friends inside Turkey report, since 2019, some seventy-three foreign Christians have been expelled from the country, including spouses of Turkish pastors, thus tearing innocent families apart. Some of these workers are denied re-entry at passport control upon arrival. Others receive N82 visa stamps on their travel documents, falsely labeling them as a threat to public health, safety and/or order and making their return to Turkey impossible.

Morning Star News reported, "A German pastor fighting expulsion from Turkey is hopeful that he may be the exception to a wave of foreign Christian leaders expelled from the country as 'threats to national security.'" And a Syriac Orthodox monk was accused of terrorism, tried, and sentenced to more than two years in prison for providing bread and water to hungry monastery visitors.[49]

It is noteworthy that Erdogan's government—particularly since the Egyptian coup in 2013—has increasingly been embraced by the Muslim Brotherhood. A 2020 report on the Turkish-Brotherhood relationship recounted,

> In April 2016, Arab Islamists close to the Brotherhood held a major event in Istanbul that they called "Thank You, Turkey." The three-day event was dedicated to extending the Brotherhood's gratitude to the Turkish leadership for hosting Islamist politicians and opposition leaders from different Arab countries. Keynote speakers described Erdogan as a "sultan," and Turkey as the house of the "caliphate." The acting supreme guide of the Muslim Brotherhood, Ibrahim Mounir, was present. Khalid Meshaal, the

former leader of Hamas, attended and said that "Turkey presented the best example of political Islam in democracy, governance, and economy.[50]

Violations of religious freedom against Turkey's Christians are increasingly rampant. Former Turkish parliamentarian and Foundation for Defense of Democracies Aykan Erdemir explains, "The Erdogan government's glorification of the Ottoman 'spirit of conquest,' and references to the 'right of the sword' in converting Hagia Sophia and other churches, have relegated Turkey's Christian citizens to an inferior rank of conquered minorities. Such supremacist policy and rhetoric will exacerbate precarious conditions for Christians. They will be at the mercy of a repressive government that swings back and forth between outbreaks of persecution and spectacles of tolerance."[51]

Hagia Sophia—No Longer a Church

In 2020, when a Turkish court announced the decision, permitting Turkey's President Recep Tayip Erdogan's regime to convert the ancient Christian church Hagia Sophia—the Church of the Holy Wisdom—into a mosque, there was an outcry from all around the world.

That revered Christian historical site had served as a museum after the overthrow of the Ottoman Empire following WWI and the subsequent secular presidency of Kemal Ataturk. The magnificent building—an architectural marvel—contains some of the most beautiful Christian frescos and mosaics in the world. Hagia Sophia was long the most popular tourist site in Turkey and was regularly visited by millions of Christian pilgrims.

The existing structure, located in the heart of Istanbul, has for centuries been a sacred space for Christians worldwide. It stands intact as one of the most ancient artifacts of early Christian history. "The first church was built at the same location where there had been a pagan temple before. It was Constantius II who inaugurated Hagia Sophia on 15 February 360. From the chronicles of Socrates of Constantinople, we know that the church was built by the orders of Constantine the Great."[52]

That earliest church was torched during rioting; a second Hagia Sophia was inaugurated in 532. Again, violence led to the church's damage and destruction.

Today's Hagia Sophia was completed and inaugurated in by Emperor Justinian the Great in 537; the magnificent mosaics—some of the finest in the world—were completed later in the sixth century. It is for both historic and sacred reasons that voices are protesting the Islamization of the holy site.

On July 10, 2020, USCIRF decried the declaration that the ancient church would be converted into a mosque. USCIRF Vice Chair Tony Perkins explained:

> USCIRF condemns the unequivocal politicization of the Hagia Sophia, an architectural wonder that has for so long stood as a cherished testament to a complex history and rich diversity. Both Christians and Muslims alike ascribe great cultural and spiritual importance to the Hagia Sophia, whose universal value to humankind was reaffirmed with its inclusion in the United Nations Educational, Scientific, and Cultural Organization (UNESCO) World Heritage List in 1985.[53]

Earlier that year, Erdogan—well-known as an aggressive Islamist—celebrated the fifteenth-century conquest of Constantinople with festivities centered on Hagia Sophia. It was converted into a mosque when the Byzantine (Christian) army was defeated by the armies of Sultan Mehmed II of the Ottoman Empire on May 29, 1453. Turkey's *Hurriyat Daily News* reported:

> The program was followed with the recitation of the 48th chapter of the Quran, surah Al-Fath. . . . Erdogan expressed gratitude to all those who did not abandon Hagia Sophia, the heirloom of the conquest. He stressed it was important to remember the 567th anniversary with prayers and surah Al-Fath. Erdogan said he had dedicated his life to his beloved Istanbul and noted that if the city was somehow removed from Earth, world history would have to be rewritten. A presentation with the theme of the conquest of Istanbul was performed on a platform in front of the museum.[54]

For years, Hagia Sophia persisted as a coveted trophy for Erdogan, who publicly cherishes neo-Ottoman Islamist sentiments. His dream came true in July 2020. It was certainly a step in the right direction as far as he was concerned. But it was far from his only ambition. His eyes were focused on several dream conquests, and his motives were cloaked in radical religious terms. This became clear in late 2019, when in Turkish and Arabic tweets, Erdogan described his forces as "the heroes of the Mohammadian army"—a term dating back to the Ottoman Empire.

TURKEY, ERDOGAN, AND THE "MOHAMMADIAN ARMY"

Voice of America reported, "While announcing Erdogan's operation into Northeast Syria, he tweeted in English that the operation by the Turkish army and its allied Syrian militants was to neutralize terror threats against Turkey by the Kurds and to establish a safe zone for the return of Syrian refugees." The VoA article went on to say that during public speeches preceding the invasion of Turkish violence, Erdogan claimed that it was "to protect the dignity of the ummah," meaning the Muslim world. He went so far as to praise the Turkey-backed rebels as "jihadists who even intimidate and kill death itself."[55]

Observers in Israel have long been aware of the rancorous nature of Turkey's president, whose animosity toward the Jewish state increasingly knows no bounds. And of course Jews have a very long history of dealing with sudden pogroms against their people in the Middle East. To this day, there are only handfuls of Jews left in Syria, Lebanon, Egypt, Libya, or Iraq. And Turkey's regime has become increasingly worrisome to its shrinking Jewish population.

So it came as no surprise to Israelis that Turkey's Muslim strongman unleashed his troops on the Israel-friendly Kurds—and their Christian neighbors.

What did come as a shock to millions—including U.S. military personnel who fought alongside courageous Kurdish fighters during operations to destroy ISIS—was U.S. President Donald Trump's thumbs-up to the attacks and its inevitable results: Turkish forces displaced some 400,000 residents, while killing and wounding hundreds. This took place along an approximately twenty-mile wide strip of northeastern Syrian land, which Erdogan claimed as his own.

An ancient Christian community had quietly survived in that area of Syria since the first century. But now thousands of them have urgently fled—thanks to Erdogan's "heroes of the Mohammadian army." Though less large and dramatic, the flight of those Christians bore a strong resemblance to ISIS's overnight assault on Iraq's ancient Christian communities in the Nineveh Plains in August 2014. They, too, left with little more than the shirts on their backs, and tens of thousands of them remain virtually homeless to this day.

In an interview with Lela Gilbert, Elizabeth Kourie commented on the Turkish assault. "Following Trump's phone call with Erdogan, within three days, Turkish troops began to move south across the Turkey-Syria border. They bombed all along the border. They were attacking anybody who was there; their targets were not military. Civilians were killed and wounded." She went on to say,

> One of the first bombs that came from Turkey struck a Syriac Christian house in Qamishli, severely injuring parents and their children. Our people were very much afraid. We knew that Turkey was coming with its Sunni jihadist mercenaries. We faced them in Afrin. We faced them in the history of the Ottoman Empire. We have had experience with Turkey with a couple of genocides, the largest being 1915. We know that if Turkey is coming, it's coming with jihadists. And we know that we Christians will be targeted more than anyone else. Today, we estimate that 100,000 Syriac Christians are still somewhere in the area. A hundred thousand already fled in 2015.

By June 2020, Turkish aggression was reported in at least five countries. Erdogan made power moves in Israel, Libya, Iraq, Syria, and Greece.[56]

And it remains well known that whenever Turkey moves in, religious freedom moves out. Only Turkey's Islamist practices are respected by Erdogan's henchmen. Among the countries in which Turkey has ambitions for conquest: Israel.

The Jerusalem Center for Public Affairs (JCPA) wrote in June 2020, "Turkey is working diligently to deepen its involvement and influence on the Temple Mount, in the Old City of Jerusalem, and in east Jerusalem neighborhoods." In these locations, there is evidence that the activists involved are ideologically linked to the Muslim Brotherhood movement in east Jerusalem. Of course, Israelis know very well what the Muslim Brotherhood and its cohorts think about Jews and Judaism—on the Temple Mount and elsewhere. And it is worth noting that Erdogan is a loyal supporter of the Muslim Brotherhood.[57]

That same June, *the Jerusalem Post* reported Egypt and Turkey might come to blows over Libya's civil war. Egypt, the UAE, Saudi Arabia, and Russia, along with others, back General Khalifa Haftar in the conflict. Turkey and Qatar back the Government of the National Accord (GNA), and Turkey has been aggressively involved, providing aircraft, militias, and arms. Notably, GNA is also rooted in the Muslim Brotherhood movement.[58]

In Iraq, Turkey bombed Sinjar Mountain, where countless Yazidi refugees have taken shelter. Michael Rubin, a scholar and expert on the Middle East, has explained Erdogan's primary goal is his continued ethnic cleansing of Kurdish groups. Rubin went on to say that many Yazidis have returned to live on Sinjar Mountain, ". . . the refugees, the women, the girls who have been returning from Syria, liberated from ISIS. They're trying to get their life together."[59]

He went on: "And it's not clear why the Turks are insisting on bombarding them. . . . It raises questions about whether Turkey is waging counter-terrorism, and it's clear they're not—or whether they're pursuing a religious agenda—an intolerant religious agenda." *The Jerusalem Post* also reported that Turkish attacks put Christian villages in jeopardy in the same area.[60]

About Syria, The Washington Kurdish Institute reported, "During the first days of June 2020, around 20 different human rights organizations signed a petition to raise awareness on crimes carried on by the many Turkish-backed militias in Afrin, Syria and asked for international intervention."[61]

It is well known and widely reported that Afrin's religious minorities have been violently abused by the Turks and their militias. Thousands of Christians fled the invasion of Afrin; few remain. And today, Christian and other minority communities in the Rojava region, where many fled Afrin, are again living in fear because of ongoing Turkish threats, attacks on resources, and occasional shelling.

Arab News reported regarding Greece, "In an escalating war of nerves between Athens and Ankara, bilateral relations have deteriorated, sparking fears of a military confrontation between the two NATO allies. Greek Defense Minister Nikolaos Panagiotopoulos recently highlighted the country's 'readiness for military conflict with Turkey.'" Even rumors of an impending Turkish invasion of Greece have been reported, although unverified.[62]

As for Greece, a historic perspective reveals widespread Turkish killings of Greek and Assyrian Christians in the early twentieth century, with more than a million dead. Even today,

Greek Orthodox properties in Turkey are confiscated and desecrated. Christian refugees from Syria and Iraq—Syriac, Protestant, and Orthodox alike—who fled to Turkey from ISIS have been deprived of their ability to support themselves and dare not practice their faith. Kidnappings and murders have been reported.

In its 2021 report, USCIRF recommended the U.S. government "Include Turkey on the U.S. Department of State's Special Watch List for engaging in or tolerating severe violations of religious freedom pursuant to the International Religious Freedom Act (IRFA)."[63]

Turkey's treatment of its own Christians and its reckless, ruthless intrusion into country after country is believed by some observers to reflect Erdogan's vision of a glorious, Neo-Ottoman Empire. Other scholars are more inclined to view his motivation as strictly religious, demanding pan-Islamist conquest. Certainly the two intentions are not mutually exclusive.

The Turkish and Azeri Invasion of Nagorno-Karabakh

How familiar are most Americans with the ancient country of Armenia? It's probably best recalled because of the great tragedy in the early twentieth century—the Armenian Genocide. That massacre of some 1,500,000 Armenian Christians (along with the murder of around 750,000 Greek Christians) took place between 1914 and 1922.

In 2021, President Joe Biden was the first U.S. President to formally acknowledge the systematic murder of more than a million Armenian Christians by the Ottoman Empire was, in fact, a genocide.

"The American people honor all those Armenians who perished in the genocide that began 106 years ago today," Biden explained. "Let us renew our shared resolve to prevent future atrocities from occurring anywhere in the world. And let us pursue healing and reconciliation for all the people of the world."[64]

Although Joe Biden was the first American president to recognize the genocide, he was not the first world leader to do so. During a Sunday sermon in April 2015, Pope Francis referred to the 1915 Turkish mass killings of Armenians as the "first genocide of the 20th century."[65] At the time, his papal declaration exploded into a diplomatic uproar. It infuriated Turkey's Islamist President Recep Tayyip Erdogan, who "warned" the Pope against repeating his "mistaken" statement. But in fact, Pope Francis spoke for many if not most Christians around the world.

Those massacres cost 1.5 million Armenian Christians their lives, along with hundreds of thousands of Assyrian and Greek believers. The heartbreaking story began on April 24, 1915, when Turkish authorities arrested thousands of Armenian professors, lawyers, doctors, clergymen, and other elites in Constantinople (now Istanbul). Revered members of the community were jailed, tortured, and viciously murdered in cold blood.

In fact, the abuses had begun earlier in April.[67] But on the 24th of that month, house searches were launched in earnest. The Ottomans claimed they were looking for weapons, accusing the Christians of arming themselves for a revolution. In those days, since most Turkish citizens kept firearms for hunting and self-defense, of course the Turks found many guns in Armenian homes. This served as their pretext for mass arrests.

Unspeakable terrors followed. The family members who helplessly watched these home invasions—mostly women, children, the ill and the elderly—were then rounded up and informed they would be "relocated." Instead, they were herded like animals with whips and cudgels. At gunpoint, they were sent on a death march to nowhere.

The captives were provided with little or no food or water. Old people and babies were the first to die. Women were openly and repeatedly raped; mothers were gripped with insanity, helplessly watching their little ones suffer and succumb; more than a few took their own lives. Eyewitness accounts and photographs remain in circulation today, and they are heart wrenching. Corpses littered the roads; nude women were crucified; dozens of bodies floated in rivers.

On January 5, 2015, Raffi Khatchadourian published a personal essay in the *New Yorker* about his Armenian grandfather, who somehow survived the genocide. He described the brutality:

> Whenever one of them lagged behind, a gendarme would beat her with the butt of his rifle, throwing her on her face till she rose terrified and rejoined her companions. If one lagged from sickness, she was either abandoned, alone in the wilderness, without help or comfort, to be a prey to wild beasts, or a gendarme ended her life by a bullet.[68]

In numerous accounts, the Armenian Genocide has been described not only as a genocide—which continued well past 1915—but also as a jihad.[69] Some Armenian women were even told they would be spared if they would convert to Islam. It is noteworthy that less than a year before the genocide's beginning, on November 13, 1914, a call to jihad—a holy war against Christian "infidels" was officially announced: "The Ottoman Sultan Mehmed V, in his role as Caliph, along with his Sheikh-ul-Islam, issued a call for *jihad* against the Allied powers of Britain, France, Russia, Serbia, and Montenegro."[70]

On October 1, 2020, Armenia was once again the site of violence. Another violent and dangerous war erupted in a tiny Armenian Christian enclave—a spot on the globe few Americans can probably find. And it bears a name that even fewer know how to pronounce: Nagorno-Karabakh (also known as Artsakh). This area has been populated by Armenian Christians for centuries, but in 1991 Muslim Azerbaijan disputed Armenia's rights to the land following the collapse of the U.S.S.R and a deadly conflict ensued.[71]

In late 2020, as the latest fighting began, the *New York Times* reported:

> The three-week-old conflict between Azerbaijan and Armenia over a disputed territory in the Caucasus Mountains, where Europe meets Asia, has settled into a brutal war of attrition, soldiers and civilians said in interviews here on the ground in recent days. Azerbaijan is sacrificing columns of fighters, Armenians say, to eke out small territorial gains in the treacherous terrain of Nagorno-Karabakh, an ethnic Armenian enclave that is part of Azerbaijan under international law. . . .
>
> Azerbaijan, an oil and gas hub on the Caspian Sea, has deployed superior firepower, using advanced drones and artillery systems. . . . But three weeks into the conflict, Azerbaijan has failed to convert that advantage into broad territorial gains,

indicating that a long and punishing war looms. It could morph into a wider crisis.[72]

Before long, besides being a confrontation with between Armenia and Azerbaijan, Turkey's ambitious Islamist President Tayyip Erdogan entered the fray. On September 28, Germany's *Deutsche Welle* (DW) News reported:

Armenia and Azerbaijan have accused each other of reigniting their decades-long conflict in the enclave of Nagorno-Karabakh after fresh violence erupted in the breakaway region. The two sides resumed open conflict again on Monday morning with the use of heavy artillery. Outbreaks of violence had continued through the night, according to the Armenian Defense Ministry spokesperson Shushan Stepanyan. During night battles continued with different intensity. Early in morning, Azerbaijan resumed its offensive operations, using artillery, armored vehicles, TOS heavy artillery system," Stepanyan wrote on Twitter.[73]

Family Research Council learned, in a conversation with a friend in Yerevan, that Azerbaijan's 2020 invasion was perceived by most Armenian Christians as the continuation of the 1914 Islamist jihad against Armenia's Christians, and the desire for genocide continues even today.

Armenia was the first country in the world to convert to Christianity—in AD 301. Its Armenian Orthodox Church is rooted in the earliest Christian history. In fact, the biblical record of Armenia's land stretches back to the book of Genesis, when Noah's ark came to rest after the Great Flood on what came to be known as Mt. Ararat. But although that beloved mountain was for centuries the symbol of the Armenian nation, along with the lives of millions of Armenians, it also fell into the hands of the Turks. Following the Treaty of Kars in 1923, the area was divided between Turkey and the USSR, and the new border, which became internationally recognized, placed Ararat on the Turkish side. Even after this, most Armenians still claim the mountain as their own.

Mt. Ararat has remained a potent symbol both of Armenia's spiritual heritage and her terrible losses. The threats against her never seem to end. And, even until today, the most virulent aggression against Armenia emanates from Turkey. During the 2020 incursion, Turkey's Islamist President Erdogan declared that Armenia was "the biggest threat to peace in the region."[74] His posturing directly threatened Armenia and Karabakh, both of which are almost entirely Armenian Orthodox Christian.

Turkish aggression in at least five countries was headlined in international news reports in June 2020. Those accounts focused on President Recep Tayyip Erdogan's intrusions into Israel, Libya, Iraq, Syria, and Greece.[75]

Meanwhile, it is noteworthy to those who focus on international religious freedom that whenever Turkey moves in, religious freedom moves out. There can be no lasting freedom of worship for any faith unless it conforms with Turkey's Islamic practices.

Thus, Armenia was added to the list of Erdogan's Islamist ambitions. Based on his anti-Christian hostilities, his transformation of Istanbul's Hagia Sophia and Chora Church into mosques, and his frequent expressions of triumphalism, a couple of serious questions arise:

Does Turkey, led by its Islamist President Erdogan think that Armenia and Nagorno-Karabakh, which are ancient Christian historical heritage sites, represent yet another

Hagia Sophia-type landmark? Does he feel driven to seize, Islamize, and declare them as yet more trophies for his neo-Ottoman Empire?

Those questions seemed to be clearly answered in a report from *Asia News*:

> Turkey sent 4,000 Syrian Isis mercenaries from Afrin to fight against the Armenians of Nagorno Karabakh. A few days ago land convoys reached Turkey and then Azerbaijan by air. The salary is 1,800 US dollars a month, for a duration of three months. A leader of the Syrian terrorist group said: "Thanks to Allah, from September 27 until the end of the month another 1,000 Syrian mercenaries will be transferred to Azerbaijan."[76]

Azerbaijan was more than happy to have Turkey's support—some say instigation—to continue religiously and ethnically cleansing Nagorno-Karabakh of Armenians. That enabled the Azeris, supported by their Turkish allies, to reclaim Nagorno-Karabakh's disputed cities, towns, and villages for itself.

Turkey's firepower is formidable. But besides placing Turkish soldiers in harm's way alongside the Azeris, Erdogan also financed Syrian jihadi mercenaries—reportedly thousands of them—to augment the attack on the Armenian enclave. *Foreign Policy* headlined one story, "Syrians Make Up Turkey's Proxy Army in Nagorno-Karabakh: After fighting Turkey's battles in Libya, the Syrian National Army is caught in the conflict between Armenia and Azerbaijan—and dozens are dying."[77]

A ceasefire took place on November 10, 2020. The death toll has remained unclear, but the devastation and destruction have continued even since the official end of the conflict.

Not long after the initial 1994 conflict, co-author Lela Gilbert traveled to Nagorno-Karabakh and Armenia with Baroness Cox, Lifetime Peer in the U.K.'s House of Lords. There she learned firsthand about the deeply held religious significance the conflict had for combatants and civilians alike. Meanwhile, she was struck by Baroness Cox's deep concern for the local Christians, their churches, and their charities. During the October 2020 conflict, Baroness Cox was again actively involved and, speaking for her organization HART, published her response:

> We strongly condemn Turkey's provocative actions and demand the immediate withdrawal of the Turkish armed forces, including the air force and jihadi terrorist mercenaries from the conflict zone. The direct involvement of Turkey and the scale and ferocity of this offensive raises the genuine fear of an attempt at the genocide of the Armenian people which Turkey's highest leadership has declared in so many ways, especially since the July aggression by Azerbaijan. The revival of Ottoman rhetoric by the Turkish Government reinforces the possibility/danger of realisation of this evil intent. In the previous attempt by Turkey to achieve the genocide of the Armenians in 1915, the UK stood firmly against this genocide.
>
> The historic and recent acts of ethnic cleansing committed by Turkey and Azerbaijan mean that for the Armenians, the preservation of Artsakh is a question of survival of their people and of their spiritual, cultural and political heritage. As the Nobel Prize Sakharov put it at the outset of this conflict:

"The Nagorno-Karabakh conflict is a territory for Baku whereas for the Armenians of Artsakh it is fighting for their home and very existence!"[78]

HART also published personal accounts of the grief and courage described by some who were caught in the conflict:[79]

Knar Avanisyan Varangatagh, age 30:

My husband, a firefighter, was killed on 30 September during Azeri attacks in the North, in the Mataghis region of Martakert. His body was so destroyed that we needed DNA to identify him. I don't know what to say to my four children. They asked me this morning about him, and why he has stopped sending money. What can I say? We hid under trees to escape the UAVs and aerial bombardments, running so fast that I didn't even have time to get my phone.

We escaped in a car, first to the village of Drmbon, then Shushi, then Sevan. The church has been a life-saver, providing us with food and shelter. But my home is in ruins and I have nothing left. My brother-in-law told me that everything in the village has been stolen or demolished. He was attacked by mercenaries—small groups of special units—who want to take over the soil. I pray for peace, that I would see my husband again, and for my children to be able to lay flowers on his grave. [I know a] family whose son, an Armenian soldier, was captured by Azeri forces. His phone was stolen by his captors and they posted an image of his beheaded body and sent this to his own social media account for his own family and friends to see.

Angelina, age 23:

On 26 September we had a family party in Stepanakert. The next morning, we woke up to the sound of bombs. I told Aram (aged 13) to get up immediately. My husband (a military doctor) put on his uniform and left the house. This city was built so beautifully we couldn't believe they would attack such a beautiful city. The building next to our home was hit with Smerch. We hid in the basement for four days. We then escaped by car and asked a random house if we could stay with them. I have health issues so they don't tell me the truth about what is happening at home. I don't know. I am worried sick. We just want peace and recognition of Artsakh [Nagorno-Karabakh]. We don't want big houses. We can live in small houses. We just want to return to our homes.

Armenian Human Rights Ombudsman, Arman Tatoyan:

Atrocities committed by Azerbaijan and Turkey must no longer remain hidden from the world. For weeks, their military forces engaged in targeted attacks against peaceful populations, including with illegal cluster munitions and chemical weapons. They have destroyed, on purpose, infrastructural objects vital to civilians: gas and water supplies; schools and kindergartens; religion and cultural heritage sites. As many as 100,000 people have been forced to flee—and still, there appears to be little-to-no concern from the international community.

Every family is affected. I know of one mother who has lost all of her sons. Initiating this war during a pandemic was a crime against humanity. COVID cases have increased because of the escalation of conflict. Doctors now have to treat patients with injuries and with the virus. But Turkey blocked aid to Armenia from the USA (by forbidding air transit across Turkey) which is yet another crime against humanity. Humanitarian assistance eventually came via Qatar, but two days late. We have video evidence of torture and mutilations. Civilians and POWs are humiliated by their captors. Azerbaijan have returned 29 military bodies and few civilians—DNA was needed to identify four bodies. . . .

It is no exaggeration to describe the methods of Azerbaijan and Turkey as "terroristic" in nature. It is a campaign of ethnic cleansing—a genocidal policy—against the people of Artsakh. Their hatred of Armenians runs deep. Hate speech is organised by the Azeri state and promoted in schools, curriculums and textbooks.

In an unpleasant postscript to the late 2020 Nagorno-Karabakh conflict, on September 11, 2021, a brief and ominous news item was published by *Radio Free Europe* announcing new activities that clearly reflect President Tayyip Erdogan's insatiable appetite for intrusion into the Caucasus arena. It was headlined, "Turkey and Azerbaijan strengthening their military alliance":

Azerbaijan's Defense Ministry has said that Baku will host joint military drills in the days ahead with troops from Turkey and Pakistan—the first such drills involving the three countries. The ministry said in a statement that the goal of the so-called Three Brothers-2021 exercise is to improve the combat interoperability of the special forces from the three countries, to "prepare for operations in peacetime and wartime," and to exchange "knowledge and experience."[80]

IRAN—A HOTBED OF RELIGIOUS PERSECUTION

In February 1979, the dramatic overthrow of Iran's ruling monarch—Shah Mohammad Reza Pahlavi—culminated in the triumph of the Islamic Revolution. This downfall of a Western-backed monarchy placed Iran's government in the hands of an anti-Western religious leader—Ayatollah Ruhollah Khomeini, who launched a specifically anti-Western, and anti-Israel Shiite theocracy that continues until today. The once-warm relationship between the U.S. and Iran has been cold as ice ever since. Following Khomeini's death in 1989, he was replaced by Ayatollah Ali Khamenei. Both share the same apocalyptic beliefs and ideological perspectives, which are based on scenarios that lead to the triumph of Shiite Islam across the world at the end of days.

For example, the MEMRI news site—which translates and broadcasts speeches, sermons, or other pronouncements by sheikhs, imams, and mullahs—reported the words of senior Iranian Ayatollah Mohammad Mehdi Mirbagheri: "In Order for the Hidden Imam to Reappear We Must Engage in Widespread Fighting with the West."[81]

Some observers are aware of the deeply religious nature of
Iran's regime. However, particularly in the U.S. and Western
Europe, references to religious influences in international
affairs are either disregarded or find their way into an editor's
trash can. Yet some declarations should not be overlooked,
and that includes references—particularly among Iran's highest levels of leadership—to the Hidden Imam.

The Hidden (or Twelfth) Imam plays a dominant role in
one specific form of Shiite Islamic theology, called "Twel-
verism," which happens to be the primary belief system of
Iran's leadership. There is a messianic belief that at the end
of days, the Hidden Imam will appear; in the eyes of the
more radical, this will take place in the midst of a violent
apocalyptic scenario played out on a battleground stained
with infidels' blood.[82]

Saeed Ghasseminejad is a fellow at Washington, D.C.'s
Foundation for Defense of Democracies (FDD). In 2013,
he penned an article titled "Iran's Apocalyptic Policy Makers." He wrote,

> Two of the most lunatic and apocalyptic high-
> ranking figures in Iran are Ayatollah Ali Khamenei
> himself and his now disgraced one-time protégé,
> Mahmoud Ahmadinejad. While Khamenei deeply
> believes his task is to prepare for Mahdi's appear-
> ance, Ahmadinejad takes the apocalyptic narrative
> to an unprecedented level of lunacy and weird-
> ness, even by the Islamic republic's measures. He
> believes, for example, that the real reason behind
> the US invasion of Iraq was to search for the Hid-
> den Imam and to postpone his appearance. Many
> observers believe Khamenei chose Ahmadinejad as

president mainly because of their shared belief in this apocalyptic version of Islam.

While many experts tell us Iran is a rational, pragmatic regime like any other in the world, all the facts shout that it is not. A large number of Iranian officials and decision makers have deeply rooted apocalyptic beliefs. Underestimating this radical ideology even as the Iranian regime is on its way to building a nuclear bomb can lead to dangerously wrong conclusions. The suggestion taking hold of late that a nuclear armed Iran is not the end of the world may unfortunately be dead wrong.[83]

Although policymakers in the West rarely seem to take this apocalyptic vision seriously, it is one of the elements that drives Tehran's decision-making process. Preparing the ground for the reappearance of the Hidden Imam is the Islamic Republic's *raison d'etre*. Ignoring it leads to misinterpretation of Tehran's actions and miscalculation by Western policymakers.

Meanwhile, hostility to Israel—often heard in the official chant "Death to Israel!"—is related in the minds of many observers to the thinly disguised Iranian nuclear weapon program. One thing is certain: although much of the Islamic Republic's malicious activity is concealed, Israel takes seriously the threats Iran makes against her.

For instance, in recent years, Israeli agents exposed an Iranian warehouse overflowing with undeniable evidence of deadly intentions. They somehow managed to seize and export thousands of notes, reports, and graphs, documenting comprehensive development of nuclear weaponry. It had all been carefully hidden—until it wasn't.[84]

Meanwhile, Iran's bloody fingerprints continue to appear in various conflicts in Syria, Lebanon, Iraq, Yemen, and beyond. And its tireless attempts to assault Israel continue, primarily acted out through proxies like Hamas and Islamic Jihad—not to mention Hezbollah, whose secret tunnels between Lebanon and Israel were recently exposed and destroyed.

On the other hand, there's little to hide when Iran boasts of new weaponry, flashy military exercises, or battlefield triumphs. In fact, the late Quds Force Commander Qasem Soleimani has proudly proclaimed Iran's intentions, "We are witnessing the export of the Islamic Revolution throughout the region. From Bahrain and Iraq to Syria, Yemen and North Africa."[85]

Indeed, during celebrations of the Islamic Republic's 40th anniversary, Ayatollah Khamenei, Iran's supreme leader, declared the Islamic Revolution had entered its "Second Phase": a time "of self-development, society-processing and civilization-building of the Islamic Revolution." This second phase was affirmed by a Qom University spokesman as "the cornerstone of major policy makings in the country."

In other words, the worst may be yet to come.

Take, for example, Iraq, where Iran's strategy is one of creeping hegemony. So far it is working well through such tactics as political intimidation, shady financial transactions, and armed intrusion.

As we've seen, Iran-backed militias, under the command of the Quds Force, are tormenting minorities attempting to return to their homes—Christian and Yazidi genocide victims. A campaign of intimidation, threats at gunpoint, and cruelty at checkpoints continues unabated. Some who've tried to return and resettle in their towns and villages have fled yet again, too traumatized to remain.

Fear and stealth are also wielded like weapons inside Iran itself. Sudden arrests, fierce interrogations, and mass executions of political and religious "enemies of the state" are mostly concealed from the world's eyes. Baha'is are the largest religious minority in Iran, described by the regime as a "deviant sect," whose members are "de facto apostates." According to USCIRF, "Iran's government has systematically persecuted the Baha'i community for decades. Baha'is are restricted from pursuing education in Iran and security forces regularly close down Baha'i businesses, raid Baha'i homes, and conduct mass arrests of Baha'is. In December 2020, the U.S. House of Representatives passed H.Res. 823, a bipartisan bill that cited USCIRF's reporting and condemned religious freedom violations against Baha'is in Iran."[86] It is noteworthy that the Baha'i World Centre is located in Haifa.

By Iran's definition, the term "Evangelical Christians" usually identifies converts from Islam to Christianity. According to Western experts, there are potentially hundreds of thousands of these converts. They are variously accused of "acting against the regime," "threatening national security," and, interestingly, "promoting Zionist Christianity."

"Zionist Christianity" was explained in a conversation with a former Iranian house church leader. New converts from Islam treasure the Bible—a book most of them have never seen before, and they read it voraciously. There they discover its accounts of the Jews—of the Patriarchs, the Exodus, and the journey to the Promised Land. They begin to understand Israel's existence as a God-given miracle. For these converts, Islamist chants of "Death to Israel" stir feelings of solidarity with the Jewish people. This sounds like dangerous subversion to the devotees of the Supreme Leader's apocalyptic cult. And with that in mind, it's unsurprising, according to Open Doors 2021 World Watch List, Iran is the world's ninth worst persecutor of Christians.[87]

Among Iran's many transgressions—including its hatred of Christians and other religious minorities—surely the most egregious has been its clandestine project to produce a deliverable nuclear weapon—no doubt meant to undergird its ruthless efforts to "export the revolution" and to annihilate Israel. For this and innumerable other reasons, the international community's most urgent and pressing tasks in the Middle East should be to expose the ayatollahs' deception, to further intensify financial pressure on the regime, and above all else, to ban the Iranian bomb.

Yet in the midst of all this, there are astonishing reports from unexpected sources affirming some amazing rumors we have heard in recent years. In June 2021, Jewish Middle East scholar Daniel Pipes wrote a *Newsweek* article titled "Iran's Christian Boom" in which he described something remarkable:

> Something religiously astonishing is taking place in Iran, where an Islamist government has ruled since 1979: Christianity is flourishing. The implications are potentially profound. Consider some testimonials: David Yeghnazar of Elam Ministries stated in 2018 that "Iranians have become the most open people to the gospel." The Christian Broadcast Network found, also in 2018, that "Christianity is growing faster in the Islamic Republic of Iran than in any other country." Shay Khatiri of Johns Hopkins University wrote last year about Iran that "Islam is the fastest shrinking religion there, while Christianity is growing the fastest."

This trend results from the extreme form of Shi'ite Islam imposed by the theocratic regime. An Iranian church leader explained in 2019: "What if I told you the mosques are empty inside Iran? What if I told you no one follows Islam inside of Iran? . . . What if I told you the best evangelist for Jesus was the Ayatollah Khomeini [the founder of the Islamic Republic]?" An evangelical pastor, formerly an Iranian Muslim, concurred as far back as 2008: "We find ourselves facing what is more than a conversion to the Christian faith. It's a mass exodus from Islam."[88]

Meanwhile, those conversions are unfolding across Iran against a backdrop of apostasy. Atheism is surging. There are numerous anecdotal reports of mosques sitting nearly empty in major Iranian cities, and religious practices are rapidly diminishing. The more Iranians turn their backs on the brand of Shiite Islam ruling the country with an iron fist, the more dangerous and potentially deadly Christian conversion becomes.

Iran is a religious dictatorship, and a cruel one. As we've seen, at its core is an apocalyptic cult, preparing for the emergence of a Shiite messianic figure, the Imam Mahdi. Those preparations involve not only persecution of other faiths, but attacks on individuals, states, and movements that stand in the way of what the regime calls "exporting the Revolution." The dangers of such a belief system are self-evident, and the trail of blood is well-documented.[89]

Yet, despite that perilous bulwark, the bold and brave witness of untold numbers of new Christians is inspiring hope across the world. Mary Mohammadi, whom we introduced early in this section, serves as one of many thousands of

Muslim background believers who are beginning to illuminate the Middle East and beyond. These converts embody the zeal of New Testament believers. They are willing to pay the price in ways Western Christians can barely fathom. And their light shines brightly among the shadows of today's increasingly troubled world.

ISRAEL—A MIDDLE EAST MELTING POT

As Iranian and various antisemitic fanatics continue to chant "Death to Israel," and while leftist radicals demand the world seek to disgrace Israel by labeling it an "apartheid state," most visitors to Israel experience an entirely different impression. In Jerusalem, for example, daily life looks very different from the false "apartheid" categorization. A walk around the city is marked by bustling crowds. Some of them wend their way along the Mamilla Mall's lively pedestrian shopping street, ascending and descending a flight of stairs to the Old City's Jaffa Gate.

In addition to the mall's very appealing collection of shops and boutiques, one of Mamilla's most colorful attractions is the exceptionally varied array of shoppers. And that array demonstrates like nothing else the religious freedom existing in Jerusalem, perhaps one of the most religious cities in the Middle East. Even the casual observer can make a fairly accurate guess about what people believe in, based on the first impression of what they wear.

The shopping throngs at Mamilla Mall comprise a casually defined religious mixture, with Muslim women in hijab shopping shoulder-to-shoulder with traditionally-clad Orthodox Jewish mothers, fathers, and children. At the same time, Christian clergy in clerical frocks representing the most venerable church traditions mingle with American evangelical retirees and foreign youth groups wearing matching T-shirts.

The absurd accusation that Israel is an "apartheid state" was first popularized in Jimmy Carter's infamous book *Palestine: Peace Not Apartheid.* Carter's accusation was particularly ridiculous to South Africans who have actually experienced apartheid. Even the notorious South African judge Richard Goldstone, who trashed Israel's 2009 "Operation Cast Lead" in Gaza in a United Nations report, later decried the "apartheid" accusation in a *New York Times* op-ed. He wrote:

> In Israel, there is no apartheid. Nothing there comes close. Israeli Arabs—20 percent of Israel's population—vote, have political parties and representatives in the Knesset and occupy positions of acclaim, including in its supreme court. Arab patients lie alongside Jewish patients in Israeli hospitals, receiving identical treatment.[90]

Goldstone was correct (at least about that). Israeli Arabs are judges, army officers, lawyers, and business people—even diplomats.

Take, for example, Arab-Israeli diplomat George Deek, the Jewish State's first Orthodox Christian Ambassador. An outspoken critic of what he describes as a "culture of victimhood," Deek claims this perspective robs Israeli Arabs of their dignity. Of his own upbringing, he has said, "I was a Christian Orthodox kid in a French Catholic school with a majority of Muslim students, in the Jewish country in the Arab Middle East. And nothing seemed more normal."[91]

Deek has also pointed out that, while Arabs in Israel experience one of the "best qualities of life for Arabs in the region," these people are surrounded by the ever-growing persecution of Christians in the Middle East. "Outside Israel, Easter celebrations have become a rare sight. Christians were driven out of Mosul in Iraq. [They were] put to flight in Syria. The last church in Afghanistan was destroyed in 2010. [Twenty-one] Christians were beheaded in Libya. And in Gaza, bishops are beaten up and Christian symbols are forbidden."

It is all too true that the Middle East—the cradle of Christianity—is all but going up in flames. Israel is the only country in the Middle East in which the Christian population is growing. It is no wonder some Arabic-speaking Christians in Israel have noted they live in the region's sole safe haven for their faith. And they have decided to do more than give thanks.

An increasing number of Greek Orthodox, Maronite, Assyrian, and other Christian communities want to defend their homeland—and more than a few have chosen to take action.[92] Not only are they choosing to enlist in the Israeli Defense Forces, but they are also forming political parties and seeking reforms in Israel's educational system, insisting the country's officially sanctioned curriculum includes Christian history alongside Judaism and Islam.

As Goldstone pointed out, Arab-Israelis—both Christian and Muslim—serve essential roles in the country's leadership. For instance, Judge George Karra, an Arab from Jaffa, presided over the judicial panel that sentenced former Israeli President Moshe Katsav to a seven-year prison term for rape. Meanwhile, another leading Israeli jurist, Salim Joubran from Haifa, was the first Arab judge to receive a permanent appointment to the Israeli Supreme Court.

None of this should imply the relationship between Arab and Jewish Israelis is trouble-free. It is not. There are debates, declarations and discussions, public and private, which include everything from infinitesimal woes to hugely significant issues affecting both populations. These involve matters like income and educational equality, construction permits, trash collection, bureaucratic impartiality, and innumerable other issues involving alleged discrimination.

Of course, anyone who follows international news realizes that, although Israelis live in relative peace, random attacks of various intensity intrude with diverse forms of violence. These vary from occasional and sometimes deadly attacks on individual Jews in Judea and Samaria (West Bank), to rockets from Gaza and attacks on Israeli ships at sea. More than a little of this disturbance can be traced to the influence of Iran—Israel's arch enemy—or to the Muslim Brotherhood's funding of anti-Israel activities. Meanwhile, the United Nations and its disgraceful Human Rights Council piles on the accusations against Israel while overlooking the horrific abuses in China, North Korea, Sub-Saharan Africa, and beyond.

Above all else, innovative and patriotic Israelis are the beating pulse of the country. Like people everywhere, they have their problems, and they struggle and worry and fret. But they are exceptionally courageous—insolent in the face of danger, and mockers of death. As a people they are quick to laugh, sing, and applaud. And when life goes wrong, they weep their tears, sweep up the remains of the day, and go out to face tomorrow.

In large part, this remains true because the people of Israel—despite all that threatens them—embody an ancient commandment: "I have set before you life and death, blessings and curses. Now choose life, so that you and your children may live" (Deut. 30:19 NIV).

That's exactly what the Israelis have done. And, in fact, they do far more than choose life. They celebrate it. Unfortunately, that choice is not so readily available to many of their Arab Christian neighbors.

THE SILENT STRUGGLE OF CHRISTIANS IN BETHLEHEM

The difficulties faced by Christians in the West Bank—what Israelis call the biblical lands of Judea and Samaria—have intensified in recent years, mostly thanks to the radicalization of Muslim communities, and more specifically, the incursion of Hamas into their communities.

Hamas, which was launched in the 1980s, is designated as a terrorist organization by the United States, the European Union, Canada, and Israel; its military wing is separately categorized as such by Australia, New Zealand, Paraguay, and the United Kingdom.

A Counter-Terrorism report explains that Hamas's ideology "blends Islamism and Palestinian nationalism and seeks the destruction of Israel and the creation of an Islamic state between the Mediterranean Sea and the Jordan River. Since 2017, Hamas claims to have severed its ties to the Brotherhood. The group also receives financial and military support from Iran. Qatar has also provided significant funding for the group."[93]

West Bank Christian communities find themselves threatened by Hamas both directly and indirectly. But it's difficult to hear the details of their concerns without having heart-to-heart conversations with them.

Co-author Lela Gilbert describes a visit to Bethlehem and the far-reaching concerns that were raised in her conversations there:[94]

It's a surprisingly short drive from West Jerusalem to Bethlehem—10 or 15 minutes, at the most. But on a hot summer night, it felt like traveling light-years, setting out from a bustling city-center Jerusalem neighborhood and arriving at a poverty-marred home in a quiet Bethlehem village.

In my mind, the leafy, well-lit street from which I departed was quickly juxtaposed with my gloomy, poor-lit destination. I flashed back to a journey I had made from West to East Berlin in the late 1980s. Back then, the Stasi (East German secret police) were the threat. Today, in Bethlehem, it's the Islamists.

After the Israeli border guards glanced at our United States passports, my American friends and I were waved through the checkpoint that separates Israel from King David's ancient hometown.

Upon our arrival at a Christian family's home, the wariness of our hosts also felt eerily familiar to me. They did not want to speak except in very low tones; they feared that somehow their apartment conversations could be heard beyond their four walls. I could almost read their minds: "Who saw them come into our house? Who might be listening? Can we trust these friends-of-friends?" For me, having visited Berlin before its infamous wall came down, the mood was reminiscent of the bad old days: Life behind the Iron Curtain.

I wish I could use real names when I write about Bethlehem's Christians. Why can't I do so? Because the slightest hint that Bethlehem's Christians are "informing outsiders" about the troubles they face would likely endanger not only them, but also their friends and family members.

In international news reports, the tension in Bethlehem and elsewhere in the West Bank is blamed on the "Israeli occupation" and the security fence. In some places, including Bethlehem, there is indeed a formidable military wall—also reminiscent of Berlin—officially called the "West Bank Barrier." It divides Arab communities from the Israeli population.

It is true that the wall is an encumbrance to those who live behind it. It is an eyesore and, in some places, has taken a heavy toll on business and commerce. And the checkpoints into Israel can also be a nuisance. This is particularly so since, in years gone by, Arabs and Israelis alike were able to come and go without restrictions. This was so until the ill-starred Oslo Peace Accords robbed all concerned with of their freedom of movement.

But the security wall has also saved lives. It was erected in 2002 during the Second Intifada, at a time that felt like an endless barrage of exploding buses, pizza shops, cafes and other public venues devastated Israel for well over three years. That uprising cost more than 1,000 Israeli deaths. It is widely reported that after the West Bank Barrier was constructed, the number of suicide bombings decreased by more than 90 percent.

Meanwhile, story after story I heard confirmed that among other discomforts, Christian women are sexually harassed, threatened and even raped for not following Islamic dress codes. I was told about one young Christian woman from a village near Bethlehem who was walking home from school, and she was not "covered." That meant she did not wear an Arab-style headscarf or a long skirt.

When a gang of local Muslim males cruised past her, they made obscene remarks and tried to force her into their car. She escaped and ran home, where she tearfully poured out her terrifying experience to her brother "Habib."

It didn't take Habib long to figure out who the Arabs were.

He knocked on the door where the ringleader and his friends hung out. When Habib demanded that they leave his sister alone, they laughed at him. They were, however, not amused. In the days that followed, they began to track Habib.

One afternoon, Habib and his cousin went to a nearby forest to walk and talk and relax. Suddenly 13 young men, who had arrived in cars and on motorbikes, surrounded them. At first, they seemed only to be armed with sticks and a billy club. Then the knives appeared.

While his cousin was beaten and held back from interfering, Habib was stabbed 28 times. He was knifed on the head, neck, hands and the inner thighs (the attackers were trying to sever a main artery) and left for dead. Once the assailants fled and the cousin was released, he frantically drove Habib to the hospital before he bled out. Habib received massive blood transfusions; his wounds were repaired, and his life was spared. But he required extensive surgery.

I also learned about a Christian property owner who had rented an apartment to a Muslim family. When the rent came due, the new tenants refused to pay. This continued for months. The local authorities were alerted, but they simply shrugged. "Nothing we can do about that," they said. "Our hands are tied."

Following my visits to Bethlehem, I learned that in recent years, several church properties in Bethlehem have been vandalized, set ablaze or invaded by violent intruders during celebrations or worship services. PA law enforcement usually arrives long after the emergency call is made—if at all.

In short, life for Christians in Bethlehem is a continuous challenge. Many have quiet dreams of departing for places where their faith is not a handicap to a safe and sane existence.

Over the years, the Christian population of Judea and Samaria, including Bethlehem, continues to shrink. In 2020, *Christianity Today* reported that specifically in Bethlehem, only one in five residents today are Christians (22 percent). A decade earlier, more than four in five were believers (84 percent).[95] This plummeting Christian population is invariably blamed on the "Israeli occupation." But if this is so, why hasn't the Muslim population diminished too? The fact is, along with inconveniences and economic deprivations, Christians are escaping the West Bank because of anti-Christian persecution.

In *Providence Magazine*, Philos Project's Executive Director Robert Nicholson authored a persuasive article, "Why Are Palestinian Christians Fleeing?" He explained "the Palestinian Authority—the government created by the PLO to manage the West Bank and Gaza—is, by its own constitution, an Islamic state that embodies the principles of sharia."[96]

Christians living under the Palestinian Authority (PA) are "accorded sanctity and respect," but, as is the case under all Sharia-based systems, Christians are relegated to the status of second-class citizens. Of course, it is illegal to convert from Islam to Christianity. And the sale of land to Jews is a crime punishable by death.

Discrimination against Christians under the PA isn't just legal—it's also social. Bethlehem's Christians are at risk of being detained by authorities based on vague accusations. An "interview" with local officials may lead to stern threats or, even more frightening, to an arrest on trumped-up charges.

For years, the late Justus Weiner, a legal scholar at the Jerusalem Center for Public Affairs, wrote extensively about the condition of Christians under the Palestinian Authority.

"Under that regime," Weiner explained in an interview, "Christian Arabs have been victims of frequent human rights abuses by Muslims. There are many examples of intimidation, beatings, land theft, firebombing of churches and other Christian institutions, denial of employment, economic boycotts, torture, kidnapping, forced marriage, sexual harassment, and extortion. PA officials are directly responsible for many of the human rights violations."[97]

Weiner went on to say that Muslims who have converted to Christianity are in the greatest danger. They are defenseless against abuse by Muslim fundamentalists. Some have been murdered. Many Christians are subject to various fees and fines, which amount to bureaucratic extortion or protection money—a thinly disguised *jizya* tax.

Numerous Palestinian Christians have described how, during times of conflict, Muslim terrorists have commandeered Christian homes and used them to direct sniper fire on Israeli soldiers. Others speak of systematic discrimination in hiring, housing, and education. Of course, all of these conversations take place in private meetings and hushed tones.

Christians in Bethlehem rarely interact with Muslims beyond the marketplace, and are, in fact, very much afraid. But in public, Palestinian Christians equate their situation with that of their Muslim neighbors and laud the happy coexistence between the two groups.

They don't have a choice. They are hostages inside their own city.

GAZA: "STAY SILENT. IT'S SAFER."

Much has been written about the near-continuous conflict between Israel and the infamous Gaza Strip. Life for Gaza's Christian communities was never ideal under the rule of the PA, but for some years those Christians were more or less tolerated. However, in 2007, Hamas staged a violent takeover of PA government installations in the Gaza Strip; the terrorist group has since maintained a de facto government in the territory. Although the area technically falls under PA jurisdiction, Hamas rules there with an iron fist.

"Every year I pray they will give me a permit so I can celebrate Christmas and see my family," Randa El-Amash, age fifty, told Reuters. "It will be more joyful to celebrate in

Bethlehem and in Jerusalem." Thankfully, in 2019, Randa's family was able to welcome her once again to Bethlehem, the birthplace of Jesus, where the Christmas story began.[98]

One of the outspoken voices in support of Gaza's Christians is Nina Shea, at the Hudson Institute's Center for Religious Freedom. She has explained the general reaction to the ban:

> Israel maintains that its government protects access for all religious groups to the religious sites that are under its control. In keeping with this, it is incumbent that it provide permits to all Gaza's Christians to visit Christian holy sites in Jerusalem and the West Bank, especially during the great feast of Christmas, one of Christianity's holiest celebrations. These Christians pose no terror threat, as Israel fully acknowledges by giving permits to travel abroad at this time.

Thanks to myriad prayers and protests, the Israeli Christmas-ban story in 2019 had a happy ending. Families and friends were reunited, feasting flourished, and Christmas hymns resounded in Bethlehem, Jerusalem, and beyond. However, in 2020, Hamas declared a lockdown due to COVID concerns. Meanwhile, pandemic or not, continuous injustices and provocations faced by Gaza's Christians carry on day in and day out during the rest of the year. It's no wonder they want to flee the scrutiny of Hamas and other radical Islamists. Gazan Christian Khalil Sayegh described what life is like for Christians in Gaza.[99]

"Like all Palestinians in Gaza," he began, "the Christians are suffering from the current situation in Hamas-controlled

Gaza. They struggle with unemployment, lack of freedom of travel. They cannot hold government jobs. But, in addition to that, the Christians of Gaza are facing religious discrimination in various ways. Christians in Gaza have to tolerate being harassed in the streets just for being Christians. Their school children have to listen to all kinds of bad things about Christians in their classrooms, because Hamas controls their education, teachers, and schools."

Khalil continued: "And while Hamas claims to protect Christians, its presence in Gaza has empowered Islamist radicals who harass Christians and even physically attack them in some instances. Violence occurred a few years ago, when a Salafist jihadist murdered Rami Ayyad [a Christian bookstore manager who was shot and stabbed to death in 2007]. And since then there have been several attempts to bomb Gazan churches."

Khalil went on to say even secular Gazans can't work in the government. A man who wears a cross will be harassed. And in some parts of Gaza it is unsafe for women who do not fully cover themselves and wear a hijab.

When asked whether there are Christmas decorations in Gaza, Khalil Sayegh explained that a YMCA facility is decorated, but only inside the building. Otherwise, there's no sign of holiday festivity in the streets. He recalled a Muslim merchant who donned a Santa hat one year, trying to inspire a little holiday spending. Angry authorities confronted the shopkeeper and demanded that he take off the Santa hat immediately.

"They reject any indication of Christian celebration," Khalil explained. And why do Americans and perhaps even Israelis know so little about all this?

"Nobody wants to talk about it," he concluded. "Stay silent. It's safer."

IS RELIGIOUS FREEDOM POSSIBLE IN THE MIDDLE EAST?

On August 13, 2020, *World Israel News* reported the United Arab Emirates and Israel had "agreed to establish full diplomatic ties as part of a deal to halt Israel's extension of sovereignty over Judea and Samaria. The announcement makes the UAE the first Gulf Arab state to do so and only the third Arab nation to have active diplomatic ties to Israel."[100]

There was, of course, debate in Israel and beyond about whether the agreement had cast aside annexation of biblical Judea and Samaria for the sake of an elusive peace gesture. At the same time, there was celebration among young Israelis, embracing new hopes for harmony with the Arab world.

For several years, the United Arab Emirates sought to depict itself not only as a super-wealthy Arab state, but also as a haven of religious freedom. And since Pope Francis's dramatic visit there in February 2019, much has been said to affirm that these efforts amount to more than a photo-op.[101]

Deutsche Welle (DW) described the Pope's visit as an historic milestone, reporting, "More than 130,000 worshipers flocked to the Zayed Sports City Stadium in the UAE capital, Abu Dhabi, on Tuesday to celebrate a Mass with Pope Francis. . . . He is the first leader of the Catholic Church ever to set foot on the Arabian Peninsula, the birthplace of Islam."[102]

If peace between Jews, Muslims, and Christians is possible in one small Arab country, why couldn't it extend further? Reflecting on this possibility, prayerful optimists have lifted their eyes heavenward while world-weary cynics continue to shake their heads.

On the optimistic side, DW explained at the start of his papal visit, Pope Francis met with Crown Prince Mohamed bin Zayed Al Nahyan and other UAE leaders at the presidential palace. "He also signed a document promoting 'human fraternity' with Sheikh Ahmed el-Tayeb, the grand imam of Egypt's Al-Azhar, the seat of Sunni Muslim learning. During an address to a gathering of interfaith leaders, he called for an end to wars in the Middle East, including in Yemen and Syria. All religious leaders had a 'duty to reject every nuance of approval from the word war,' he said."

But, as less-than-upbeat observers will quickly note, religious freedom in the Middle East often ends where radical Islam begins, whether that dangerous version of ideology is rooted in Shiite or Sunni tradition. In fact, in its 2021 Country Report, USCIRF declared Egypt, Iraq, and Turkey were included on its "Special Watch List," while Iran and Saudi Arabia continue to be "Countries of Particular Concern" (CPC).[103]

Still, efforts for peace—whether motivated by economic promise or intended to create a bulwark against Iranian and Turkish aggression—should not be disregarded. It is a region where churches are sometimes bombed or torched and surviving synagogues are broken relics of happier days—before the wholesale expulsion of entire Jewish communities.

Nonetheless, the UAE has begun a unique project intended to transform the marred image of Muslim, Jewish, and Christian relations: a Multi-Faith Complex—including the first official synagogue in the country's history.

"A church, mosque and synagogue will share a collective space for the first time, serving as a community for inter-religious dialogue and exchange, and nurturing the values of peaceful co-existence and acceptance among different beliefs, nationalities and cultures," the committee overseeing construction of the complex said in a statement.[104]

For years, Israel and the UAE had been holding clandestine meetings. Now their newly revealed projects include both economic and defense opportunities to which both have contributed expertise and funding. And since that initial breakthrough with UAE, Bahrain signed a similar accord on September 11, 2020;[105] Sudan on October 23, 2020,[106] and Morocco on December 10, 2020.[107]

Hopeful regional conversations about peace and prosperity should never be silenced. Nevertheless, wary eyes keep their watch as Turkey's President Tayyip Erdogan and Iran's Supreme Leader Ali Khamenei rage and rant about the Israeli-Emirati agreement as a betrayal of Islamic empire-building. And while Abu-Dhabi's construction of the Multi-Faith Complex prepares for its 2022 opening, deadly gunfire shatters quiet nights in Iraq, Syria, and Lebanon, while rockets and explosive balloons continue to darken the sunlit skies above Israel.

The future of the Middle East remains both unsettled and unsettling. Nonetheless, conversations about peace, freedom, and positive possibilities ought never be mocked or silenced. Prayerful candles should always be lit by people of faith who yearn for religious liberty. At the same time, wary eyes must surely keep their watch.

> LTG (RET.) JERRY BOYKIN:
> WHAT DO AMERICANS NEED TO KNOW
> ABOUT THE MIDDLE EAST?

Most Americans realize that the Middle East is a pivotal region of the world. And many present concerns about global politics and controversies about resources, conflicts, and international relations emanate from there. For Jews and Christians, the Middle East—both ancient and modern—is central to biblical history as well as exposition of Scripture and prophetic interpretation.

Much of this centers on the Jewish people God chose as His own, and Israel, the land God promised to the Jews in the beginning of the Bible. Today, we can still find on the map the countries we read about in both the Old and New Testaments. Some of them have different names, and some have grown more powerful or become less important than they once were. But the Middle East region has been ground zero for biblical understanding ever since the beginning of the Jewish and Christian faiths. Islam came along several centuries later, of course, but it also finds its roots in that ancient map.

New Hope for Christians in Egypt

For example, Egypt was a Christian nation before it was an Islamic nation. It had a strong Christian culture for centuries. Then, after Mohammad started spreading his notion of Islam, the Christians were persecuted and many of them were killed along with Jews. Nonetheless, even today, strong Coptic, Orthodox, Evangelical, and Pentecostal churches continue to thrive in Egypt.

As for the political face of Egypt, in recent years some familiar names come to mind, particularly familiar to those concerned about Christian persecution and religious freedom in the Middle East. For example, President Hosni Mubarak came into power in Egypt after Anwar Sadat was murdered. Sadat seems to have tolerated Christians more than the historic precedent set by some of the earlier Egyptian rulers.

Once Sadat was assassinated, the persecution of Christians increased under Hosni Mubarak. However, Mubarak wasn't necessarily directly involved.

Those were the days when Islamist groups were gaining strength in Egypt and beyond—groups like the Muslim Brotherhood. They targeted Christian enclaves, and Mubarak did nothing about it. It's my view that he didn't go after the Christians himself—he just let it happen. Although he wasn't a big fan of the Muslim Brotherhood, which was causing a good deal of the violence, he still just let the persecution continue.

Then, Mubarak was overthrown and Mohamed Morsi came into power. I'm convinced that since Morsi was the head of the Muslim Brotherhood, that created an opportunity for the Brotherhood to do what hardcore jihadists always do—go after the People of the Book. There were only about a dozen Jews left in Egypt by then, so Morsi allowed and encouraged the killing of Christians, along with running them out of the country. But in the meantime, he made a crucial mistake: he appointed Abdel Fattah al-Sisi to be his defense minister.

Sisi had an unusual history. He had been to America and studied at the American Army War College. And he had a high level of education and sophistication that Morsi thought was going to be very useful to him, since Morsi didn't have a military background. By choosing Sisi, Morsi had also brought in a guy who was one of the most respected men in the country in terms of his military experience. But there was a side of Sisi that Mohamed Morsi didn't understand. Sisi was a Sufi, which is a mystical and often peaceable sect. And Sisi saw that Islamic Sharia law was being implemented by the Muslim Brotherhood. He also noted there was a tremendous amount of unrest.

Maybe he didn't act sooner than he did because the Obama administration was providing him with substantial amounts of top-end military hardware, aircraft, and M1 Abrams tanks. And, of course, as the defense minister and as a guy who had just come out of the military, Sisi wanted all that. He knew it was important for Egypt to be able to defend itself. But when the time was right, he overthrew Morsi in a military coup and took over as Egypt's president.

Along with other concerns, Sisi knew he had to reverse what Morsi had done to Egypt's Christian population. So he reached out to the different Christian denominations. In fact, in 2017 a group of us met with Sisi and with Christian representatives from all across Egypt. Evangelicals such as Tony Perkins, Joel Rosenberg, Michele Bachmann, along with myself and others were included. We were introduced to a number of dignitaries; we even met with Anwar Sadat's widow.

We soon came to understand that Sisi genuinely recognized the importance of religious freedom. During his time at the U.S. Army War College, he had traveled all over the country and had gained an appreciation for U.S. culture. He realized we supported religious freedom as a nation. Of course, there were Muslims here, and some of them wanted to do us harm. But there were also many Muslims who were worshiping peacefully and without bad intentions.

When we met with him, it quickly became clear Sisi had done more for Christians than any Egyptian leader before him. Yes, he could have been doing this because he thought it would be in his own best interest. But I sensed an attitude of justice in him. In any case, the situation for Christians in Egypt is much better than it has been in the past. The one place where things are not so good is in the Sinai, probably just across the canal, because there have been several terror attacks against the Christian enclaves there. And some attacks also persist in remote rural areas like the Minya Governate. Generally, though, Egypt's Christians are living in relative peace.

Egypt can also take credit for having led the way in terms of its relationship with Israel. Anwar Sadat went to Israel himself to try and bring peace to that part of the world. It was an important moment in history when he visited Israel Prime Minister Menachem Begin and addressed the Knesset. Keep in mind this was in November 1977. Israel had only been a country since 1948, and there was Sadat trying to make peace with her. That was one of the reasons that he was assassinated.

Egypt's influence in the Middle East has always been significant. I'd have to say that if Anwar Sadat had not made that trip to Israel, there wouldn't be any Abraham Accords today. Nowadays, Israel is the big dog on the block. Egypt is working quietly and very closely with Israel, particularly with regard to the terrorist supply chain that comes out of Egypt and passes across the desert into the Gaza Strip. I think Egypt is concerned about terror threats that would threaten Sisi's regime. So, there is a substantial cooperation between the two countries. In fact, if you want to put it in the context of biblical prophecy, Egypt is really not one of those countries prophesied to attack Israel in Ezekiel 38 and 39.

Meanwhile, Sisi is a sincere man who continues to make a concerted effort to help Egypt's Christians rebuild their churches. He had a cathedral constructed to serve as a shrine honoring the twenty Christians from Egypt (the twenty-first was from Ghana) who were beheaded by the Islamic State in Libya. He has also helped individual churches rebuild after the destruction that occurred while Mohamed Morsi was president.

When our delegation met with Christian leaders, we asked them, "What message do you want us to take back to our president?" They said, "Tell President Trump to support al-Sisi because he's done more for us than any Egyptian leader ever has done."

So today in Egypt, Sisi—a Sufi—is in charge. And he's actually going after the more radical elements remaining in the country. He has also protected the Christians to the extent that he can. Of course, there are still attacks on Christians. But Sisi's good intentions toward Christians are demonstrated not only in what he has said but also in what he has done.

SHOULD AMERICA HAVE INVADED IRAQ?

After 9/11, the United States quickly deployed U.S. forces in Afghanistan. Then we built a coalition there—a coalition of the willing. A lot of NATO nations ponied up, because according to NATO's charter, an attack on one country is an attack on all and other members must respond. I think even those who were really reluctant to do so wound up putting personnel on the ground in Afghanistan. We essentially drove al-Qaeda out the country, and the coalition was doing pretty well.

And then, in my view, the U.S. made a very bad decision.

President George W. Bush decided to go into Iraq, while turning over Afghanistan to NATO. The first thing you have to understand is there are probably only three countries that will really fight in a situation like that: the Americans, the British, and the Canadians. The rest of the countries don't actually fight. They go in there and they hunker down. They bide their time until they can go home. And then they rotate somebody else in that hunkers down the same way.

They don't get out and engage the enemy. But, generally, the Canadians, the British, and the Americans do.

So we turned everything in Afghanistan over to NATO and instead we went into Iraq. To be honest, we went with some very sketchy intelligence, and with what I think were some questionable motivations. It appears our entry into Iraq had a lot to do with the fact there had been a plot against George W. Bush's father, George H. W. Bush. There were other debatable reasons as well.

But once we left Afghanistan, all of a sudden, the Taliban and even al-Qaeda started a resurgence in the area. All at once, the war in Afghanistan wasn't going so well. But now we were in Iraq on a different mission.

At the same time, Christian suffering in Iraq began to surge.

Today, as we reflect on how badly Christians were affected by our decision, keep in mind one of Saddam Hussein's top officials—his foreign minister Tariq Aziz—was a Christian. And there were a significant number of Christians scattered in little enclaves around the country. But as soon as the fighting started against the Americans, those Christians started to get pushed around.

Iraq was estimated to have nearly 1.5 million Christians before the 2003 U.S.-led invasion that toppled dictator Saddam Hussein. That community dated back to the first centuries of the faith and included Chaldean, Syriac, Assyrian, and Armenian churches. Today, only about 250,000 Christians remain from that million and a half. And it's not only a matter of them being killed. Many fled the country because the threat against them was so intense.

So what should the U.S. have done when we went into Iraq? One of the things we clearly didn't do was carefully protect the Iraqi Christians. We simply didn't put a lot of thought into questions like, who needed protection? Who was vulnerable? This carelessness is reflected in our recent concern about who we needed to protect and rescue in Afghanistan when we abruptly pulled our troops out in August 2021. During the twenty years of fighting there, we had employed thousands of interpreters for our military. Now they need our protection. From a moral perspective, we remain indebted to them. But at the time of this writing, we have not managed to get all of them and their families out of there.

I think by taking Saddam Hussein out, we opened the door to the radicals. Saddam was not anti-Christian; he was pro-Saddam. We didn't understand the environment there. In fact, I think he saw Christians as far less of a threat to his regime than the Muslims or the Kurds. Keep in mind the majority of the Muslims in Iraq were Shias. I think Saddam was actually more comfortable with Christians for one good reason: there were not enough Christians in Iraq to overthrow the government.

After Iraq's success in the eight-year Iran-Iraq war in 1988, Saddam was emboldened. In August 1990, he invaded Kuwait hoping to gain access to the oil supply there. When he refused to pull out, the U.S. led a coalition of more than thirty nations to force his withdrawal. This war was called Operation Desert Storm and it was successful: Saddam pulled out of Kuwait.

Saddam Hussein was again defeated by America's forces in late 2003. But once he was sidelined, other dangers had materialized—not only for Shia Muslims but for Christians. Al-Qaeda, which was launched in 1989 by Osama bin Laden, was gaining attention and traction after the first World Trade Center bombing in 1993. It didn't take long for that terror organization to be seen as a global threat.

Al-Qaeda first appeared as a separate entity in Iraq in 2004. Then, Abu Musab al-Zarqawi, a Jordanian-born radical Islamist, formed an alliance with bin Laden's al-Qaeda. He agreed to become "al-Qaeda in Iraq" and thus became the larger al-Qaeda's little brother, if you will. He was determined to do his own thing. But I think he saw franchising was in his best interest because it gave him a certain level of credibility and legitimacy he did not have before. Through the use of suicide bombings, he and his radicals successfully attacked Iraqi government and military sites.

Zarqawi was killed in a U.S. bombing attack in 2006. Osama bin Laden was killed by U.S. Special Forces in 2011. At that time, Ayman al-Zawahiri, an Egyptian-born terrorist who had been second-in-command to bin Laden, took over al-Qaeda.

Three years later, in 2014, Abu Bakr al-Baghdadi, a cleric who had risen in power within al-Qaeda in Iraq, renamed his organization "Islamic State in Iraq and Syria," better known today as ISIS. From the Great Mosque of al-Nuri in the Iraqi city of Mosul, Baghdadi declared his newly-minted terror group a "caliphate," and announced himself as its caliph.

In 2014, when ISIS surged through the Nineveh Plains, thousands of uprooted Christians fled into Erbil with nothing but the shirts on their backs. Then ISIS went after the Christians in Syria.

BASHAR AL-ASSAD AND CONTROVERSIES ABOUT SYRIA

When the Arab Spring caught fire in 2010, the U.S. did not carefully think through our policy in Syria. Instead, we had a stated policy of wanting to remove Syrian President Bashar al-Assad from power. That began under the Obama administration—they said Assad should go. It's important to note here that Assad was never a threat to Christians.

Meanwhile, that policy raised some key questions: Who's the replacement going to be? Where's the next leadership going to come from? Is it going to come out of one of those various Sunni groups? Or maybe the Alawite groups operating in cooperation with the Muslim Brotherhood? What kind of leadership will that produce? Will some terrorist organization be running the whole country?

Christians serve in the legislature in Syria. Assad has never targeted Christians, and in fact is said to have assisted them on some occasions. The U.S. had a foolish policy in Syria. Why? Because Obama wanted to get rid of a leader who was never a threat to Christians and never a threat to Israel.

Meanwhile, ISIS devastated Syria's Christians, raping nuns, beheading priests, killing kids. They went after Christians, all Christians, destroying old monasteries and many ancient shrines. They even devastated Palmyra. It wasn't until Donald Trump came into office that there appeared to be a change of course. But no matter who is president, you can't just go into Syria and take out Assad, expecting that everything's going to go back to "normal."

It's just unbelievable to me we ever had such a foreign policy.

Iran and Its Never-Ending Threats

As turmoil surged in the Sunni Muslim world, Iran continued on its own radical Shiite path of expansion and violence. Iran is about 50 percent Persian, and the rest are a mixture of all kinds of ethnicities and cultures—including Arabs, Tajiks, and millions of Kurds. It's a hodgepodge, but most Iranians are Shiite Muslim.

Now, an interesting thing has happened in Iran, and to some extent it has been inspired because of the repression and the brutality of the Iranian government. What they have today is a far cry from what they thought they'd gain from the original Supreme Leader Ayatollah Ruhollah Khomeini. They expected great economic benefits from him, but what they actually got was one huge disappointment: the loss of freedom, economic disasters, and the strict enforcement of a radical form of Shiite Islam that Khomeini and his henchmen promoted. The beliefs that dominate the regime are focused on the appearance of the 12th Imam—the Shiite Messianic figure who will introduce a time of global peace and prosperity—something like the Christian millennium. Those who follow this radical apocalyptic teaching are often called "Twelvers."

The regime's particular interpretation of this belief dictates that Twelvers have to stoke a period of bloodshed and chaos to usher in the 12th Imam's appearance. That's why people like Mahmoud Ahmadinejad and General Qasem Soleimani were so dangerous. They believed that they were personally going to bring forth the reign of the Messiah. Let's not forget the two key slogans accompanying that quest: "Death to Israel" and "Death to America."

Meanwhile, what are the Iranians facing today? Right now, they can no longer deny there's a growing Christian community in Iran. More and more Shias are converting to Christianity. The mullahs can't pretend it isn't true anymore. So they're in all-out assault mode trying to ferret these people out and deal with them. Part of what they're discovering is these new believers are willing to die for their newfound faith.

That's really frightening to everybody from the Supreme Leader right on down the line, not because Muslims aren't willing to die for their faith, but because they have had to realize this growing Christian movement is a force to be reckoned with. So how do they stop it? Are they going to go door to door and kill them all? They would have to kill more than a million people.

To make matters worse for the regime, these Christian converts from Islam are proselytizing in their own country. They're converting their own people, and it is apparently driving the authorities crazy. It's interesting, because at the same time, the youth in that country are fed up with Islam. They realize it is oppressive. In fact, it's more dictatorial than their parents accused the Shah of being.

Meanwhile, the people in the community have banned the imams' call to prayer from the minarets. They call it noise pollution there. This is in Tehran! And the people there hate their government. We now know the government's response: Soleimani killed about 15,000 Iranian citizens for marching and protesting against government policies. Now stop and think about this—not so long ago, Christians were run out of Iraq. Now you look at Iran and you see the church is bursting at the seams. I talked to a pastor who's been underground in Iran for about twelve years. He told me four years ago that the Iranian church was probably about four million strong and still growing. He said the church growth is unbelievable.

But let's bear in mind these Christians are facing the most extreme form of Shia Islam, extreme in the context of the Twelvers' apocalyptic beliefs. When he was the Iranian President, Mahmoud Ahmadinejad openly declared he had been ordained by God to usher in the reign of the 12th Imam. He was convinced it would be his task to do that. However, he would have to create global bloodshed and chaos. Now, how is Iran going to create bloodshed and chaos? Would they go so far as to use a nuclear weapon against Israel?

It is possible it could come to that because I believe their ambition is very serious. They can justify attacking Israel according to their theology. They've given the world full warning with the rhetoric they've espoused: "Imagine a world without Israel!" and "Wipe Israel off the map!" Verbiage like that is a very serious threat, and I don't think the American government or the rest of the world is taking it seriously.

At this point, we don't know precisely how close the Iranians are to their objective, but we know they are working and making progress on their nuclear program. They are not only developing the warhead, but also working diligently on the delivery system. I believe, had it not been for Israeli covert action, we'd already be on the threshold of an Iranian nuclear weapon.

DREAMS OF A NEW OTTOMAN CALIPHATE IN TURKEY

Turkey's President, Recep Tayyip Erdogan, is a Sunni Islamist who is growing more tyrannical with every passing day. Although there's all kind of talk about a "coup" supposedly intended to overthrow him in 2016, I don't believe there was a coup at all. I think it was staged.

A Turkish friend of mine, a very smart guy who ran his own company here in America for years, was pretty clear about the whole thing. At the time, he had only been in America about five years, but he had grown up and been through school in Turkey. One day he said to me, "Let me ask you something. You know anything about coups in Turkey?"

I said, "Well, I know a little bit about coups, so . . ."

He said, "What time of the day do they happen?"

"Oh, well, actually, not during the day," I answered. "Coups normally take place at something like two or three o'clock in the morning."

"Yeah, that's right. So what time did the one in Turkey occur? What time was that?"

"I don't know."

"It happened at eight o'clock at night," he told me, "when everybody was out on the street."

You don't do a coup when everybody's on the street, not if you're serious about it. My Turkish friend said it was not a legitimate coup. That was just another excuse for Erdogan to lock up more military leaders, more journalists, and more judges and to consolidate his power. So, this was all about Erdogan increasing his power and influence over the nation of Turkey.

Today, Turkey has the second largest military in NATO and everybody knows that very well. That means Erdogan's military is larger than any other in the Middle East. He has made it clear in any number of ways he is seeking to create a neo-Ottoman Empire—a caliphate—and he, of course, will be the caliph. Turkish activists have been working since 1924 to make the caliphate a reality. Now, all of a sudden, you've got Erdogan, who has the potential to actually recreate this global super state. That's why ISIS claims they had so many recruits—young dreamers they developed into killers.

I believe Erdogan will continue to fund Sunni groups who are trying to recreate this caliphate. What he's going to do is alienate himself from NATO, because the two requirements for being a NATO nation are being a representative government and having a market economy. He misses on one count—he does not have a representative government.

At some point—although it may be another decade—somebody in NATO is going to face up to the fact Turkey does not technically belong in NATO.

In 2019, Erdogan marched his army into northern Syria, and Donald Trump started pulling American forces out of there. That was a great win for Erdogan in the eyes of the Arab world. It showed him standing up to Donald Trump and to the American military. Meanwhile, NATO didn't do anything about it. First of all, it was a terrible decision on Trump's part. But I also think it demonstrated how feckless NATO is today. Someday they'll have to come to grips with the fact that Erdogan is an evil man.

At the moment, I seriously believe Erdogan is the number one threat in that part of the world in terms of his ambitions and his capabilities to back up his agenda. He's going to continue working on his caliphate dream, and if it doesn't work one way, he'll try it a different way, which is what we've seen as his pattern. As a result, there's likely to be increasing unrest in Turkey in the next four or five years. In fact, just look at what Erdogan has done to the Christians there. Look at what he's done to Hagia Sophia and other churches—both ancient and modern. He is strangling Christianity. The Turks are kicking out all non-Turkish Christian workers. Erdogan is also shattering the hopes of the Christian refugees who fled there from Syria by making life miserable for them.

That being said, I'm unsure Erdogan will succeed in his Ottoman dream because of modern communications. Today, with the transparency of the entire world in which people can see how other cultures live, nobody but an Islamist fanatic wants to go back to the sixteenth century. There's just too much information out there today for any specific people group to accept abuse and repression without doing something about it. Most of us want the best for our children and grandchildren. However, I think Erdogan is going to keep pushing. He's going to keep trying. He's going to keep looking for that golden opportunity.

This raises another question. Are the Abraham Accords frustrating Erdogan's ambitions? He is deeply opposed to Israel, and yet several Arab countries have signed agreements with Jerusalem—countries that would logically be part of a restored Ottoman Empire. This includes Sudan, which is now in a pact with the Israelis.

THE ABRAHAM ACCORDS AND ISRAEL

At the time I write this, four countries have signed Abraham Accords with Israel: Bahrain, Morocco, Sudan, and the United Arab Emirates. The question arises whether these accords will weaken Turkey, but more significantly Iran. To begin with, the accords are making a psychological difference because the Iranians are watching this process very closely. What they're seeing is Sunni brothers aligning themselves with their mortal enemy. That's not a positive for them in any way.

Why is it a threat to them? These Sunni nations are aligning themselves not only with Iran's number one enemy, but they're also putting themselves in a situation in which they can draw upon the military capabilities of the Israelis. And clearly, the Israelis are going to do what they can against Iran because it's in their best interests. This is incredible. It could only have been orchestrated by God Himself that these nations should align themselves with Israel at a time when Iran is becoming more and more belligerent. A well-informed friend once told me, "Don't think for a minute these Twelvers are not serious about what they espouse and don't think for a minute they wouldn't use a nuclear weapon."

I think these Abraham Accords are miraculous. I believe these nations are being motivated by the power of the Holy Spirit to become friends with people they've considered their number one enemy for who knows how long. At this point, we don't know precisely how close the Iranians are to producing that nuclear weapon, but we know they are making progress. In fact, there are some reports they already have a nuclear warhead. Now they need a reliable delivery system.

But the truth is that Israel has much to offer in terms of technology, medical research, and certainly intelligence and covert activities. Israel brings quite a bit to the table. It's not difficult to see why the Abraham Accords might be very appealing.

As we've seen, Israel's number one enemy right now is Iran. Today, there are elements of Iran in the form of Hezbollah poised both in south Lebanon and Syria. Those are very serious threats because they've been armed with multiple weapons—a lot of missiles and a lot of rockets—and they're sitting right on Israel's border. At any time, they can wipe out a kibbutz or a moshav in northern Israel. They are a huge threat. The same thing is happening in Gaza, where Hamas and Islamic Jihad—funded by Iran and the Muslim Brotherhood—regularly launch rockets, incendiary devices, or gunfire in order to instigate short-term warfare.

The rest of the world needs to understand Israel lives in an environment where at any moment they could be on the receiving end of rockets and missiles from their enemies next door. Mexico and Canada are on America's southern and northern borders, but we have no existential threats from either one of those places. However, Iran extends its deadly intentions all the way to Israel's borders. If Iran manages to get a nuclear warhead, which they will, you have to ask the question: Would Iran then move it into one of those Hezbollah strongholds or a Hamas stronghold in the Gaza Strip and use that as a tactical nuclear weapon against the Israelis?

You don't need an intercontinental ballistic missile to deliver that kind of a weapon across a border—it's a very short distance. You can do it with something a little more conventional. As Americans, as non-Israelis, as non-Jews, it is important for us to understand what our Jewish brothers are living with every day. Why? Because biblically, we have a mandate to support them. We need to understand their environment and the threat against them. Unfortunately, I don't think most people do.

An additional important concern is rarely mentioned. Another conflict in Israel, whether conventional or nuclear, will endanger nearly seven million Jewish people. But there is also a small Christian population in Israel as well. Interestingly, it is the only Christian population in the entire Middle East that is growing and not radically shrinking. Those Christians in Israel will also be at grave risk if an Iranian attack on Israel transpires.

Of course, it is well known that Israel has nuclear weapons. Sometimes the question is asked whether they would actually use them. Why would they have them simply as a deterrent? If it were an existential threat they were responding to, of course they would use them. Sure, nukes provide good deterrence. But we need to understand the Twelver leadership in Iran have their own way of looking at a nuclear weapon. It would be fine with them to nuke Israel because, in their view, all the Jews they kill are going straight to hell. And if there was a retaliatory strike on Iran, all the Iranians killed would be martyrs and they would go straight to heaven. That's their theology, as warped as it is.

But as far as conventional weapons are concerned, let's hope Israel's leadership has learned something from their 2006 conflict in Lebanon. Instead of thinking they can win it with air power, they're going to have to make a decision right up front that air power is only going to be used to support ground forces; otherwise, they're not going to be able to control territory. They're not going to be able to ferret enemies out of their strongholds without a ground force. It's a painful reality because it means there'll be more casualties.

Sometimes people ask me what the future holds for Israel. Prophetically speaking, the Christian community has differing views about Israel. I generally don't discuss that, although I have my own beliefs. I don't share those with a lot of people simply because there is so much disagreement on the subject.

What I can say is the Bible gives a significant amount of attention to Israel and Israel's future, as well as the future of the Jewish people. I think that's all I need to say about that.

CHAPTER 4

AFGHANISTAN: SNAPSHOT OF A RELIGIOUS FREEDOM DISASTER

FTER DAYS OF CONFLICTED NEWS REPORTING, America watched in near disbelief on August 16, 2021, as President Joe Biden officially abandoned the country of Afghanistan. Many Americans were troubled as they listened to their president's awkward speech publicly dismissing a twenty-year war—a vast American investment in blood and treasure—while putting at risk untold thousands of Afghan lives. And few were more at risk than those who do not share the Taliban's radical Islamist religious ideology.

Perhaps *The Economist* summed up the big picture best:

America has spent $2 trillion dollars in Afghanistan; more than 2,000 American lives have been lost, not to mention countless Afghan ones. And yet, even if Afghans are more prosperous now than when America invaded, Afghanistan is back to square one. The Taliban control more of the country than they did when they lost power, they are better armed, having seized the weapons America showered on the Afghan army, and they have now won the ultimate affirmation: defeating a superpower.[1]

Afghans Face a Taliban Reign of Terror[2]

That "defeat" was not the only result of the U.S. pull-out. More than a few viewers walked away from Biden's broadcast feeling stunned, well aware of their country's international disgrace. Even worse, they also knew that for many Afghans—including a little-known community of Christian converts—the worst was yet to come.

By hastily fleeing Afghanistan's notoriously difficult battlefield after twenty years—where thousands of American fighters had sacrificed their lives and countless more were permanently disabled—millions of Afghans now faced denunciation, personal disaster, and death for their loyalty to America and its military efforts.

In the meantime, *Business Insider* reported the Afghan health care system was near collapse. "To make matters worse, Afghanistan's acting health minister has told *Insider* that roughly one-third of all COVID-19 tests carried out on September 7 were positive. The country—which is struggling to get COVID-19 PCR tests—is facing the potential of a surge of the virus alongside the political and economic turmoil resulting from the Taliban takeover."[3]

Still other innocents were soon being terrorized by religious persecution in its most vicious form—ISIS-like violence against non-observant Muslims and, worse, secret converts from Islam. Those at risk include thousands of underground Christian believers.

First in line for impending abuse are the most obvious: girls and women. Even those who are already covered by robe-and-hijab were soon scurrying to locate burkas to fully hide their faces and bodies altogether from the Taliban's vicious scrutiny. Christine Rosen wrote for *Commentary Magazine*:

> Since Kabul fell, reports have poured in of women and girls being beaten by Taliban forces. Some footage shows horrific images of Taliban soldiers beating a woman and her child unconscious. Those attempting to flee are being forcibly turned away at Taliban checkpoints. Girls are being turned away from schools and women's health clinics shut down in places like Kandahar and Herat. Women report being refused service in stores and told to return only with a male relative as an escort.[4]

Taliban commanders quickly demanded that communities turn over unmarried women to become "wives" for their fighters. And fears will continue to grow along with the likelihood that young girls will be kidnapped for marriage or enslavement. "What is happening in Afghanistan today is going to put this country 200 years back," says Mahbouba Seraj, the founder of the Afghan Women's Network. Considering the view of women among radical Islamist males, feminist fears in Afghanistan of rape, torture, and death are reasonable and, indeed, urgent.[5]

A less recognized danger is to Afghan Christians, who are also very much at risk. And until recently, only few were aware they even existed. For one, Open Doors, and their annual "World Watch List" has listed Afghanistan as the second-worst persecutor of Christians for several years, second only to North Korea. At first this seemed rather unlikely, and it raised a few questioning eyebrows. But other reports began to appear, such as Landinfo's 2021 report from Norway, "Afghanistan: The Situation of Christian Converts."[6]

However, in January 2022, Open Doors placed Afghanistan on its Watch List as the world's worst persecutor of Christians.[7] And after learning more about the horrific abuses and murders of Christians and other religious minorities that have since been reported by refugees and their rescuers, this is undoubtedly correct.

It is well known that under strict Sharia law, apostasy from Islam is a capital crime, so secret Christian worship among converts is literally a matter of life and death. Voice of the Martyrs describes the situation concisely:

> Afghan Christians cannot worship openly. They must worship in homes or other small venues, and evangelism is forbidden. Christians and seekers are highly secretive about their faith or interest in Christianity, especially following a surge of arrests in the past decade. Beatings, torture and kidnappings are routine. . . . Afghan house churches continue to grow. A small number of Christians are martyred every year in Afghanistan, but their deaths generally occur without public knowledge. A few are also in prison, but . . . Christian converts from Islam are often killed by family members or other radicalized Muslims before any legal proceedings can begin.[8]

The actual number of Christians in Afghanistan is generally said to be unknown—various suggestions vary from hundreds to thousands. However, Catholic News Service recently reported Afghanistan's Christian community is estimated to be between 10,000 and 12,000 people and is the country's largest religious minority group.[9] Meanwhile, International Christian Concern writes, "Some known Christians are already receiving threatening phone calls. In these phone calls, unknown people say, 'We are coming for you.'"[10]

As the Afghanistan story continues to unfold, many Americans are experiencing something like *déjà vu*. In the summer of 2014, they watched as Islamic State/ISIS rampaged across Iraq and committed genocide against Christian and Yazidi communities in the Nineveh Plains and Sinjar. Thousands were killed; untold tens of thousands remain displaced in miserable refugee camps. ISIS was more or less defeated, thanks to U.S. military assistance.

However, it is essential to note that although Islamic State and the Taliban have fought against each other for territorial and other reasons, they share most radical Islamist beliefs. And they both practice the same deadly tactics against "infidels" who reject their severe interpretation of Sunni Islam. In short, they are terrorists. They kidnap, enslave, and forcibly marry women and girls. They viciously torture and kill those who disagree with their ideology or resist their control. They take pride in publicizing their most atrocious killings, such as the Taliban's amputation and execution of "convicts" in a Kabul soccer stadium[11] and the ISIS beheadings of Christians on a Libyan beach.[12] These similarities are not difficult to recognize, and they raise a disturbing question:

Why has the United States of America handed over the country of Afghanistan to an ISIS-like terrorist organization?

MORE QUESTIONS, NO GOOD ANSWERS

Meanwhile, another significant question arises among skeptical American observers: Why are rescue efforts intended to assist endangered Afghans being blocked? That question is being raised widely in daily emails, WhatsApp messages, or texts from people on the ground in Afghanistan. It is also repeatedly voiced by NGOs, philanthropists, and everyone else who is trying to help thousands of would-be Afghan refugees. Why are these refugees becoming *refuseniks*—those refused permission to leave?[13]

We also hear the "why" question impatiently asked, if you speak to former U.S. military service members about what's being said and done on the ground in Afghanistan. Or if you seek information about refugees from American and European Christian organizations. Or if you interview humanitarian workers who have long labored in Afghanistan, inquiring about the status of at-risk Afghans who are on the run.

Two big questions have emerged: Who is hindering or blocking evacuation operations? And when people groups are finally approved to depart, why is the final permission process so unpredictable, unnerving, and complicated?

The answer continues to be the same: The U.S. State Department appears to be obstructing numerous passageways out of Afghanistan. For example, after days of dithering with authorities, one charter flight was cleared for departure on a Thursday. But it apparently still required Taliban approval.[14] That meant it could be delayed for days, or worse, might never happen. At the time, *RealClearPolitics* reported, "Several other planes in the same group—each carrying at least a dozen American citizens—are still awaiting an okay from U.S. officials to leave, the source said."[15]

Meanwhile, borders are closed to anybody who tries to flee Afghanistan on foot, and the rules for evacuee documentation continue to be changed arbitrarily and without explanation. For far too many, this has made departure impossible.

On September 1, Mindy Belz wrote in *WORLD* that President Biden promised to "ensure safe passage for any American, Afghan partner, or foreign national who wants to leave Afghanistan." However, she added, "Experts involved in ongoing extractions say the State Department is actually making the process more difficult by imposing new requirements on countries in the region that process Afghan refugees."[16]

On August 30, the Federal Aviation Administration said Kabul airport was without air-traffic control and civilian aircraft were barred from landing in Afghanistan without prior approval.[17] In fact, a *Becker News* story claimed, "Amid widespread reports of rescue efforts from groups like Task Force Pineapple, Task Force Dunkirk, and Team America, the U.S. State Department has issued an advisory to nations surrounding Afghanistan to deny support to aircraft conducting such operations in Afghanistan."[18]

Conservative writer John Cardillo tweeted, "Now being told that State Dept. is telling nations surrounding Afghanistan not to allow private jets handling the private extractions to land and/or refuel. This is inexplicable and evil."[19]

Charmaine Hedding is president of Shai Fund, a privately funded international charity that is providing logistical support for Glenn Beck's Mercury One rescue flights. Shai Fund is assisting, among others, at-risk religious minorities who are seeking to escape danger posed by Taliban threats.

Hedding explained:

> This is a privately funded initiative, and we have permission from several countries willing to welcome our refugees. But, from time to time, Mercury One's aircraft have been grounded and unable to leave Afghan airspace due to U.S. scrutiny and shifting

regulations. Our passengers have included those
under severe risk of religious persecution including Hazara converts to Christianity, who recently
had their IDs changed from Muslim to Christian,
which sent the Taliban door-to-door looking for
them. We also listed Ahmadiyya Muslims who have
been victims of the most heinous crimes, forcing
most of the population to flee in recent years. But
despite our best efforts and the very real dangers at
hand, frustration meets us at every turn. Thankfully,
however, in spite of everything, we've managed to
rescue several hundred people.[20]

Others involved in refugee efforts, who have asked not to
be identified, are deeply concerned about the level of authority
the Taliban has been granted with respect to the approval of
passage for American citizens. Despite appeals through U.S.
senators and military leaders, the State Department has largely
remained intractable. How is it that our government's cooperation with the Taliban has taken priority over America's tradi-
tionally compassionate and generous humanitarian activities?

At the time of this writing, official help is not on the way
for thousands of at-risk American passport or green card
holders, military translators, religious minorities representing several religions, and thousands of others whose lives
are at risk. Of course, those risks are due to the Taliban's
arcane edicts. But even more disturbing is the U.S. State
Department's acquiescence to them.

WOMEN IN AFGHANISTAN

In the face of these challenges, and in a bold act of defiance against the Taliban, hundreds of Afghan women took

to the streets of Kabul one Tuesday morning after the American withdrawal, demanding the Taliban respect their rights.[21] Taliban fighters beat them with sticks and rifles in response. Validating the fears of Afghan women's rights activists, the Taliban seemed to show its true colors after initially attempting to reassure the world it would respect human rights.[22]

In the 1990s, the Taliban regime was notoriously oppressive to women and girls. With President Biden's ineptly managed withdrawal and the Taliban's sudden return, women have been sent back to the dark ages of Taliban rule. Many young women and girls who grew up in a democratic Afghanistan are suddenly faced with those dark ages for the first time.

Physical danger to Afghan women is intense. Taliban spokesman Zabiullah Mujahid recently warned women should stay inside their homes since Taliban fighters "have not been yet trained" to respect women. And the targeting of women has already begun.[23]

Well-known Afghan journalist Beheshta Arghand has already fled the country, afraid for her life. She said, "When a group of people don't accept you as a human, they have some picture in their mind of you, it's very difficult."[24] At the same time, the Taliban were accused of murdering a pregnant policewoman.[25] For good reason, other Afghan women who had achieved career success continue to be afraid of being similarly punished by the Taliban.[26]

The Taliban promised that women "will be given all their rights within Sharia 'the Islamic laws.'" Unfortunately, the Taliban's interpretation of Sharia law in the 1990s meant women could not leave their homes without a male guardian, most women could not work outside the home, and girls could not even go to school or play sports.[27]

Knowing the risks after the U.S. withdrawal, many Afghan women stopped going to work, even though the Taliban promised they could continue. Reportedly, recent measures which sent women home from work in parts of Afghanistan were temporary. However, twenty-five years ago, the Taliban instructed women to stay home after they seized power, and those orders were also said to be temporary. But they weren't temporary at all; it was the new reality.[28]

The Taliban's lightning takeover of Afghanistan dramatically demonstrates what an assault on women's rights really looks like. It serves as a worst-case scenario for Afghan women, and they are understandably devastated. True, small groups of women have staged protests demanding basic rights. But a diminishing number will be so bold, and most will mourn silently.

Particularly heartbreaking for some brave and talented female athletes, women's sports will no longer exist in Afghanistan under the Taliban regime, according to the deputy head of their cultural commission. Ahmadullah Wasiq told an Australian reporter that it was "not necessary" that women play cricket or other sports. "In cricket, they might face a situation where their face and body will not be covered. Islam does not allow women to be seen like this," he said. For the liberated women who blazed the trail that led to the development of women's sports—an opportunity that did not previously exist in Afghanistan—the announcement confirmed their worst fears about Taliban rule.[29]

The State Department has responded to apprehensions about women's rights by expressing its own concern the acting government "consists exclusively of individuals who are members of the Taliban or their close associates and no women."[30] The lack of female representation is indeed worrisome. But more disturbing are the brutal attacks on women already being committed by the Taliban. Nor does the resurrection of the notorious Ministry for Propagation of Virtue and Prevention of Vice bode well.[31]

In reality, the Taliban has no desire to permit the basic rights of women or to see women participate in the public sphere at all. While explaining why women would no longer play cricket, Wasiq said, "It is the media era, and there will be photos and videos, and then people watch it. Islam and the Islamic Emirate [Afghanistan] do not allow women to play cricket or play the kind of sports where they get exposed."[32]

For many Afghan female athletes, the Taliban's crackdown is no surprise. Twenty-five members of the Afghan girls' cycling team were able to flee to the United Arab Emirates. One of the girls told CNN, "It's really difficult because the main reason, specific reason, that I leave Afghanistan was because I was not secure as an athlete. I was doing sports in Afghanistan, but nowadays, that is not safe . . . I was forced to leave my country."[33]

The simple act of playing a sport as a girl should not be a dangerous activity anywhere in the world. However, under the Taliban, it now is.

To the Western eye, it is puzzling to see photos of rooms full of only men as the Taliban pronounces their decisions. For Afghan women who have no advocate in the room, it is tragic. At the very least, the Biden administration should use their international platform to speak up for the women who are no longer free to speak for themselves. At home, President Biden has no problem positioning himself as a women's rights advocate. So why hesitate to speak up for Afghan women who face suppression, punishments, or even death?

The State Department's statement on the interim government warned, "The world is watching closely."[34] At a protest held following the announcement, one woman held up a sign in English. It asked, "Why is the world watching us silently and cruelly?" That's a question that should be taken seriously.[35]

Yet even as the front pages of newspapers have noticeably shifted away from focusing on Afghanistan, the reports we see trickling in from that country are increasingly troubling. The Taliban's new acting government is comprised of many of the same characters the United States and our allies kicked out of power in 2001.[36] At the same time, countless women and girls in Afghanistan are facing an impossible future, with reports surfacing that women must be segregated in universities, women may no longer work alongside men, and, again, are prevented from playing sports. These are disastrous steps backward for women's rights in a country that made a lot of progress in the past twenty years.[37]

When asked about the future of women's rights in Afghanistan during a Senate hearing, Secretary of State Antony Blinken said ever since the Taliban takeover, the U.S. government has "worked to rally the international community to set very clear expectations going forward to include the expectation that it will uphold the rights of women and girls as well as minorities."[38]

Presumably, the "minorities" Blinken referred to include religious minorities, such as Christians, Hazara Muslims, Hindus, and Sikhs. Those minorities who have not managed to flee are in great danger.

CHRISTIANS IN TODAY'S AFGHANISTAN

Eric Patterson wrote in *Providence* that "Christians and other religious minorities are fearful of venturing out in public, despite their needs for groceries, medical assistance, and other basic necessities." Patterson also heard reports of Taliban spies collecting the names of possible Christians by infiltrating crowds of people outside the Kabul airport even while they hoped to escape.[39]

Instead of working to help vulnerable Christians, the Biden administration has made it more difficult for believers to flee. Private charities are still trying to help rescue endangered religious minorities and other at-risk Afghans with their own flights out of Afghanistan. As we've seen, those involved in private rescue efforts are convinced the State Department has hindered efforts to rescue threatened Afghans.[40]

In addition, the State Department also neglected to make religious minorities eligible for the Priority 2 (P-2) designation granting them access to the U.S. Refugee Admissions Program. Conversion from Islam is a crime punishable by death under the Taliban's interpretation of Sharia law, and exposed Christian converts face almost certain death for their religious views. Even though there were only a small number of Afghan Christians to begin with (several thousand), they have not been prioritized by the Biden administration.[41]

President Joe Biden's disastrous withdrawal from Afghanistan will also forever affect the families of the thirteen U.S. military members who died in a suicide attack from ISIS-K at the Kabul airport in the chaotic last days of the evacuation. The grief of their families will not soon subside. Although they volunteered to serve our country knowing the risks, ill-conceived strategic decisions unnecessarily put them in harm's way.[42]

Some commentators have noted the news cycle devoted to the Afghanistan withdrawal is "over." But ongoing dangers and tragic disasters continue for those whose lives have been forever affected by America's hasty withdrawal from Afghanistan. The suffering of millions of people will far outlast the news cycle, and so should our collective American memory.[43]

RELIGION IS ESSENTIAL TO UNDERSTANDING THE TALIBAN[44]

Stranded U.S. citizens, Afghans with green cards, and thousands who assisted the U.S. military during twenty years of war still continue to face bewildering U.S. government demands. Meanwhile, heroic rescuers carry on their searches for thousands who remain endangered, left behind by America to the Taliban's devices. As we've seen, trapped individuals and families—some are calling them hostages—include American citizens, those with U.S. green cards, military translators, and other experts who assisted the American military. Women's rights activists have been left behind, too, having risked their lives to seek equal rights for women and girls in Afghanistan's profoundly patriarchal society.

Nor should the risks faced by religious minorities in Afghanistan be overlooked. Innumerable dangers are posed by the radical Islamist beliefs of the Taliban. And yet, in more than a few reports and discussions, terrorism is noted while the profoundly religious nature of the new Afghan government remains unaddressed. A quick look in history's rearview mirror offers some perspective.

The final 9/11 Commission Report stated the aftermath of the September 11, 2001, attacks were not best described as a "War on Terror" but rather as a war with terrorists who harbored a specific origin and agenda, deriving from "a radical ideological movement (commonly known as Islamism or radical Islam) in the Islamic world . . . which has spawned terrorist groups and violence across the globe."[45]

The Taliban, although not formally recognized as a terrorist group, are allied with al-Qaeda even today. In an April Congressional Research Service report, United Nations monitors assessed al-Qaeda and the Taliban continue to maintain strong ties:

> The Taliban reportedly issued orders in February 2021 barring their members from sheltering foreign fighters, but otherwise do not appear to have taken tangible steps that might constitute a break in ties with Al Qaeda. AQ sympathizers have celebrated the Taliban's takeover and the Taliban have reportedly freed prisoners, including AQ members.[46]

THE TALIBAN, RELIGION, AND TERRORISM

A look at Afghanistan's new caretaker government, as reported by the *New York Times*, provides

> . . . the clearest indication yet that the group sees power as something to be shared exclusively among the victors, rather than fulfilling their promise of an inclusive government that factored in the reality of a changed Afghanistan where women and ethnic minorities were represented in decision making.[47]

For example, Sirajuddin Haqqani, the new interior minister, is the son of the mujahedeen commander and Haqqani
network founder Jalaluddin Haqqani. "His (Sirajuddin's)
Haqqani network, known for its close ties to the Pakistani
intelligence service, was the most dogged opponent of the
U.S. presence in Afghanistan. It was responsible for hostage-
taking, targeted assassinations and suicide bombings, including some of the huge truck bombings that killed civilians in
Kabul," the New York Times reported.[48]

"The Haqqanis sit at the nexus between the Taliban
and Al Qaeda—they are one of the key bridges," Thomas
Joscelyn, a senior fellow at the Foundation for Defense of
Democracies and senior editor of the group's Long War
Journal, told the Times.

Abdul Haq Wasiq, the Taliban's new intelligence
minister, was one of the five Guantanamo Bay prisoners
released in exchange for the last U.S. prisoner of war, Sgt.
Bowe Bergdahl.[49] According to The New York Times report,
Wasiq's interrogation files from his time in Guantanamo
revealed his close ties to al-Qaeda, including arranging for
the terrorist group to provide training for intelligence agents
of the Taliban government.[50]

The Taliban's religious views are based on a Deobandi
brand of Islamic thought. According to Indiana University
scholars Sohel Rana and Sumit Ganguly:

> [They] adhere to orthodox Islamism, insisting that
> the adherence to Sunni Islamic law, or sharia, is the
> path of salvation. It insists on the revival of Islamic
> practices that go back to the 7th century—the time
> of the Prophet Muhammad. It upholds the notion
> of global jihad as a sacred duty to protect Muslims

across the world, and it is opposed to any non-Islamic ideas.[51]

The Taliban are well remembered for their earlier oppressive rule. Following their recent seizure of power as the self-declared Islamic Emirate of Afghanistan, terror struck the hearts of many Afghans who were aware the same Islamist ideology would immediately be enforced. This led to panicked efforts to flee the country and resulted, in part, to the deadly chaos at the Kabul airport.[52]

The Islamic State group's Afghanistan affiliate and the Taliban continue to be at war, and the former is said to have sponsored the suicide bombing that killed thirteen U.S. military personnel in Kabul. What is the primary difference between them? ISIS groups are focused on a global caliphate—a traditional form of Islamic rule—while at this time, the Taliban's full attention appears to be on ruling Afghanistan. However, it bears noting these two radical Islamic groups share a large number of beliefs, and they practice the same deadly tactics against those who reject their severe interpretation of Sunni Islam.

Both groups kidnap, enslave, and forcibly marry women and girls. Both viciously torture and kill those who disagree with their ideology or resist their control. Both take pride in publicizing their most atrocious killings. This was evident in ISIS's carefully produced videos of assassinations and the Taliban's public amputations and executions. Those same practices are reappearing today.[53]

As we assess the failures of the U.S., the bleak future of Afghanistan, and the very real risks that lie ahead, it is essential we remain focused on the religious nature of America's present threats. According to Osama bin Laden,

America was attacked on 9/11 because of radical Islamic ideology.[54] Likewise, today's circumstances in Afghanistan are not primarily based on territorial disputes or political disagreements. Instead, they are deeply rooted in religious dogmas. Those dogmas inspire and motivate Islamist organizations like al-Qaeda, ISIS, and the Taliban. Their fanatical Islamist belief systems utterly reject the concept and practice of religious freedom. Christians and other religious minorities in Afghanistan will be the primary victims of this debacle.

LTG (RET.) Jerry Boykin summed up the situation succinctly on a Fox News broadcast:

> After 20 years, we pulled out of Afghanistan in a dishonorable way. This was not an honorable departure, and we have now lost a lot of allies. But more importantly, we have encouraged the terror networks around the world. Because the message they're getting is that Islam wins, the U.S.—the "Great Satan"—has been brought down after 20 years of persistence. That makes us and the rest of the world far more vulnerable.[55]

CONCLUSION:
HOW WE CAN MAKE
A DIFFERENCE

H AVING READ THIS FAR, YOU KNOW HOW PERSE-
cution is affecting people across the globe. You
have some context to explain the forces that drive
religious persecution. But why is it our responsibility to care
and take action?

For Christians, the answer is rooted in Scripture. The
New Testament makes it clear the universal church is linked:
"If one member suffers, all suffer together; if one member
is honored, all rejoice together" (1 Cor. 12:26).

Writing to the early church which was already beginning
to experience persecution, the writer of Hebrews admonishes
Christians, "Remember those who are in prison, as though
in prison with them, and those who are mistreated, since
you also are in the body" (Heb. 13:3). And so, Christians
have an obligation to learn the stories and care about the
plight of the persecuted church.

Jesus said, "Truly, I say to you, as you did it to one of the
least of these my brothers, you did it to me" (Matt. 25:40).

From this, we learn we are not meant solely to pray and express concern for the persecuted. There is also a practical element of caring and providing physical aid for those in need.

Religious freedom is not just for Christians, and we are called to care for the oppressed and downtrodden beyond fellow believers in the persecuted church. Likewise, Christians ought to care not only for our own religious freedom but for the freedom of people of all faiths to seek after God as they see fit.

Attacks on religious freedom target the human conscience—the very core of our being. This makes religious freedom a unique and essential right. Tom Farr, a well-known advocate for religious freedom, says, "Our nature impels us to seek answers to profound questions about ultimate things. If we are not free to pursue those answers, and to live according to the truths we discover, we cannot live a fully human life."[1] Recognizing each individual's right to practice their faith is essential to respecting their human dignity and treating them with respect.

Religious freedom is not merely the right to attend church and practice our religion within the walls of a church, synagogue, or mosque. Rather, it is the ability to live out our faith, including in the public square. For Americans, this broad conception of religious freedom is enshrined in the United States Constitution. The First Amendment protects this basic right, often called our "first freedom." The First Amendment states, "Congress shall make no law respecting an establishment of religion, or prohibiting the free exercise thereof."[2]

Beyond America's borders, religious freedom is also a fundamental human right owed to all people. Religious freedom is widely recognized by international resolutions and treaties, including the Universal Declaration of Human Rights adopted by the United Nations in 1948.[3] However, although the right to religious freedom is widely recognized, laws in many countries put qualifiers on the legal right to religious freedom, empowering governments to crack down when the beliefs of a community or an individual are perceived to oppose the government. The failure to secure religious freedom is deeply harmful for any society.

Societies that embrace religious freedom and pluralism tend to be more prosperous and secure. This makes sense. Societies that embrace the freedom of individuals to express their own viewpoints and live according to their beliefs are going to attract, rather than repel, talented people abroad as well as global economic engagement. Pluralistic societies that value human dignity and do not view religious groups or beliefs as a problem to be marginalized or eliminated will not suffer from the violence fostered by religious discrimination.

Religious freedom corresponds with and affirms other basic freedoms, including freedom of speech and freedom of assembly. The right to openly express your most deeply held beliefs is essential to religious freedom, as is the right to peacefully assemble in houses of worship and elsewhere.

Unfortunately, the concept of religious freedom is often misunderstood. This is seen with increasing frequency with activists who pit religious freedom against the demands of the moral revolution. For example, those whose beliefs about gender and sexuality are influenced by their faith are caricatured as intolerant and their beliefs are perceived as subversive. The resulting tension threatens to erode support for religious freedom as a freedom that benefits everyone—religious and non-religious.

VIOLATIONS OF RELIGIOUS FREEDOM LEAD TO OTHER HUMAN RIGHTS VIOLATIONS

Religious freedom fosters human flourishing, while a lack of religious freedom can lead to human suffering. This book bears witness to that. When religious freedom is violated, it has countless additional consequences that affect more than simply religious practice. Such violations tend to lead to increasing human rights abuses. One example of this is the relationship between a lack of religious freedom for some religious minorities in Asia and human trafficking.

One brave survivor of human trafficking shared her story at a State Department event titled, "Trafficking of Women and Girls in China via Forced and Fraudulent Marriage."[4] A Kachin girl from Burma (Myanmar) said, "My friend asked me to go work with her in China . . . I agreed to go with her as long as the work there would be good." This is how she ended up as a victim of human trafficking and forced marriage in China. Soon after her arrival in China, the friends she came with left her with a Chinese man to live as his wife.

Forced to stay at his house, she was afraid and unsure of where to go for help. Before long, she gave birth to twins. Finally, she determined one day to wake up before her captor and flee to seek help from the authorities in a nearby city. She spent two months in a Chinese jail before being transferred to Burmese authorities who took her back to Burma, where a humanitarian organization provided her with shelter and support.

She is just one of many Kachin girls—as well as women from other countries neighboring China—who have been deceived into crossing the border into China with offers of work or tales of a legitimate marriage, which turns out to be sexual exploitation.

The Kachin ethnic group, like many ethnic minorities in Burma, receive little support from the Burmese government. Insurgencies in the Kachin state are among several across Burma which are collectively referred to as participants in the Burmese civil war, a conflict that has been ongoing for decades and the source of multiple humanitarian crises. Some estimate that more than 90 percent of the Kachin people are Christian—mostly Baptist and Roman Catholic. The ongoing conflict and lack of support from the government makes Kachin girls and women vulnerable to manipulation by traffickers and brokers. In 2019, Human Rights Watch published a heart-wrenching, exhaustive report on the trafficking of Kachin "brides" from Burma to China.[5]

Other countries that surround China also deal with widespread bride trafficking issues, including Pakistan, Vietnam, and North Korea. China's former "one-child policy," imposed from 1979 to 2015, along with a cultural preference for sons, has created a skewed male-female ratio and a significant shortage of women. This imbalance fuels human trafficking and prostitution within China.

Bride trafficking in Pakistan earned international attention last year when Pakistani authorities compiled a list of 629 Pakistani women and girls sold as brides to Chinese men and taken to China.[6] The investigation was soon shut down due to Pakistani officials' fear that the inquiry would ire China and threaten Chinese investments into the cash-strapped country.

During the Pakistani investigations, Christian women were found to be particular targets because the pervasive social marginalization of Christian communities makes them easy targets for foreign traffickers. Many Christians in Pakistan are uneducated and impoverished, exacerbating the problem. Christian women from poor households lack the agency in society to protect or advocate for themselves.

Corrupt pastors in Pakistan—abusing their trusted role in the community—have been found to work with Chinese brokers to identify prospective female targets for trafficking and orchestrate fake marriages.

At the State Department event, Saleem Iqbal, a Christian activist who has helped rescue several girls from China, described how brokers, sometimes cooperating with a pastor who receives a cut of the profit, convince their victims to go to China: "The promises that were made were not just that the man is a Christian man who is from China and is just looking for a wife and will provide a good life in China, but also that the [woman's] family will be taken care of when the woman is taken to China. And since they come from a poor household, they did not want to turn down these offers . . ."[7]

The cases discussed at the State Department's event are troubling. As Ambassador-at-Large for Global Women's Issues Kelley Currie noted, human trafficking may not be the first thing that comes to mind when thinking about China's many human rights violations, but this significant trend deserves global attention and action.

Former Ambassador-at-Large for International Religious Freedom Sam Brownback has highlighted the connection between religious freedom issues in Burma, Pakistan, and elsewhere and the issue of human trafficking, saying, "Often religious minorities, not exclusively because they're religious minorities, but because they're vulnerable" are targeted, "and it's incumbent upon us, as the international community, to aggressively push back against both ends of this problem," which are religious freedom violations and human trafficking.

In many devastating cases, human trafficking and religious freedom violations assist each other. Each of these is a serious human rights issue, and together they create even more tragic scenarios. Activists that work on human trafficking issues—and other human rights issues—have a lot to gain by working with religious freedom advocates.

WHY RELIGIOUS FREEDOM MUST BE A PART OF AMERICAN FOREIGN POLICY

International religious freedom started to emerge as a prominent American foreign policy issue in the 1980s and '90s. The U.S. International Religious Freedom Act (IRFA) of 1998 sought to prioritize religious freedom and define what constitutes a violation in U.S. foreign policy. IRFA defines violations of religious freedom to include arbitrary prohibitions on, restrictions of, or punishment for assembling for religious activities, speaking about religious beliefs, changing religions, possessing and distributing religious literature, and raising children according to religious teachings.

Religious freedom is connected to national security and economic growth.[8] We cannot afford to ignore or misunderstand that connection any longer. Yet religious freedom cannot exist alone; it is tied to other freedoms. The freedom to truly live in accordance with one's faith requires, at a minimum, freedom of speech and assembly. When a country embraces religious freedom, other basic human rights come along with it. The pluralism and tolerance fostered by religious freedom policies have been linked to more prosperous and stable societies.

Thus, promoting religious freedom is in the United States' national interest and has, to varying degrees, played a role in American diplomatic interactions since the passage of IRFA.

U.S. officials have successfully advocated for the release of political prisoners such as American pastor Andrew Brunson, who spent two years in a Turkish prison on bogus charges of aiding a coup attempt. Brunson was finally released after the U.S. put economic pressure on individual Turkish officials. As former U.S. Ambassador-at-Large for International Religious Freedom Sam Brownback has said, "If you can sell agricultural products to other countries, you can sell religious freedom." When religious freedom is prioritized in U.S. diplomacy, it signals to our friends and foes that we value this human right and notice when it is being abused. The U.S. has a significant role to play in advocating for religious freedom.

While foreign policy is the responsibility of the executive branch, Congress also has a role to play in promoting international religious freedom, and there are several good reasons they should do so.

1. AMERICANS CARE ABOUT RELIGIOUS FREEDOM.

Even as legal challenges to religious freedom have mounted in this country, Americans continue to value this basic right. One poll conducted in 2020 by The University of Chicago Divinity School and The Associated Press-NORC Center for Public Affairs Research found that eight in ten Americans say religious freedom issues are at least somewhat important to them, and 55 percent say they are very important.[9]

Members of Congress often understandably keep one eye on their next election. Support for religious freedom may actually help candidates in the voting booth. The 2020 Becket Religious Freedom Index found that more than six in ten registered voters say a candidate's stance on religious liberty is important to them.[10] Supporting the expansion of religious freedom as the universal standard around the world, in addition to the U.S., is an effective way for politicians to prove their commitment to religious freedom.

2. THE AMERICAN PEOPLE WANT TO SEE THE U.S. GOVERNMENT ADVANCE BASIC HUMAN RIGHTS AROUND THE WORLD.

Eighty-seven percent of respondents to a 2017 Gallup poll said promoting and defending human rights in other countries was a very important or somewhat important U.S. foreign policy goal.[11] And 70 percent of respondents to a 2021 Pew Research Center study said the United States should promote human rights in China, even if it harms economic relations with China.[12] It is significant such a large majority of Americans prioritize the promotion of human rights over economic ties with the second-largest economy in the world.

3. WORKING ON INTERNATIONAL RELIGIOUS FREEDOM IS AN OPPORTUNITY TO FOSTER BIPARTISAN COOPERATION.

Ever since the bipartisan passage of IRFA in 1998, the issue of international religious freedom has been a source of unity, with effective advocates residing on both sides of the aisle. Although today's American politics is suffering from hyperpartisanship and a divided culture, long-standing agreement concerning international religious freedom enables Democrats and Republicans to work together, even when they agree on little else.

Religious groups of all faiths face persecution around the world. This includes Christians in Nigeria, Uyghur Muslims in China, Yazidis in Iraq, and Hindus in Pakistan, just to name a few. Because the victims of religious persecution are diverse, the advocates for religious freedom are diverse as well. A broad coalition of non-profits associated with a number of different faiths regularly join forces in Washington, D.C. to advance the same international religious freedom policies.

Religious freedom is an essential part of America's heritage, and the United States should display leadership in promoting this fundamental human right. The "first freedom" enshrined in the Bill of Rights has been upheld by the U.S. Supreme Court and passed down to contemporary Americans intact. On the world stage, even Western countries that share our democratic values tend to wait for us to take the lead. Setting the example for parliamentarians across the globe is a role that Congress should embrace.

While our attention is often focused close to home, it is a mistake to brush aside international concerns. Just because they are not right in front of us at all times doesn't mean they are unimportant. And when they do arise, it is often overseas—involving questions of unstable regimes, weapons of mass destruction, and other weighty matters which keep us up at night.

WHAT CAN WE DO?

Considering the monumental scale of global persecution can be disheartening. Yet, hearing the stories of those who are suffering often drives us to ask ourselves, *what can I do about it?*

While much can be done to advance international religious freedom, we will offer three main action steps.

1. LEARN

In order to make a difference, we must first become informed. Read and listen to the stories of those who have been persecuted for their beliefs.

Learn about the countries with some of the worst religious freedom conditions. A helpful resource is Open Doors' annual World Watch List, which ranks the top 50 most dangerous places to be a Christian.[13]

You can also dig a little deeper and research how regimes abuse their people, how mob violence takes the lives of innocent people, and how oppressive laws dictate what people are allowed to believe. The State Department's annual International Religious Freedom Report[14] and the United States Commission on International Religious Freedom's annual report[15] are great places to learn about some of these types of persecution in specific countries.

Perhaps most importantly of all, listen to the stories of individuals who have stood for their faith against great odds. Many survivors of persecution have published impactful articles and books detailing their experiences. Learn from their stories and pay attention to how people helped them or how they wish people would have taken steps to help.

2. ADVOCATE

Some members of Congress promote international religious freedom because they are passionate about it. However, for members who are less familiar with the topic, calls or emails from constituents can help spur them to action. Your representatives will only know you care about promoting international religious freedom if you tell them. When elected officials become aware this issue is significant to you and others in your district, it will become important to them too.

Contact your members of Congress. They work for you, and they have a vested interest in hearing what you have to say. Their offices have staffers dedicated specifically to answering constituent communications. Your call or email will be noticed.

If you know of a specific bill you would like your representative to support, mention that. If you do not know of a bill on the topic you are interested in, articulate a specific issue, and express your desire to see it addressed. If your representative knows you are concerned about the plight, for example, of Coptic Christians in Egypt, Yazidis in Iraq, or Uyghur Muslims in China, they can look out for (or write) future bills that address these issues.

Those of us in free societies must use our voices to defend those who cannot defend themselves. In some countries, repressive governments have effectively silenced religious minorities. In these cases, especially, it is critical we speak up on their behalf.

3. PRAY

Our world often disparages prayer as an impractical means of help and doubts its impact. Such a view is a disservice to the power of prayer and ignores the pleas of persecuted believers around the world who ask others to pray for them.

When Pastor Andrew Brunson was held captive in a Turkish prison for his faith, he had a deep desire to know other people were praying for him and not forgetting him while he was detained. In his darkest moments, Brunson valued the prayers of those around the world. He said, "It was very moving to hear that Chinese and Iranian believers who have suffered so much were praying for me. I felt very unworthy."[16]

Those in seemingly hopeless situations may find hope in the knowledge believers around the world are lifting them up in prayer. For those who are imprisoned, threatened, intimidated, or forced to live in fear, the knowledge other believers around the world are praying for them can be a comfort.

But where do we start when there are so many needs across the globe? Here are a few tips to get you started in praying for the persecuted.

- *Pray for specific people, countries, and situations.*

When you know of a specific person abused or imprisoned for their faith, pray for them by name. Consider the cases of Huma Younus,[17] Wang Yi,[18] and Leah Sharibu.[19]

When you don't know of individuals in need of prayer, pray for situations. Pray for Christians facing blasphemy charges in Pakistan, for young girls held hostage by Boko Haram in Nigeria, for Christians detained in labor camps in North Korea, or churches in China facing harassment from the government. Voice of the Martyrs has a convenient Global Prayer Guide with a summary of the challenges in every country with laws targeting Christians and countries where Christians experience dangerous social hostility.[20]

There are hundreds of thousands of persecuted believers whose names the outside world may not know and may never discover. Yet, God knows their names and the trials they have suffered for Him. It's okay, and beneficial, to pray for the persecuted even when we are unaware of specific situations. These people need our prayers as well.

- *Consider what you might want prayer for if you lived in a persecuted context.*

Many Christians live in a country where it can be dangerous to follow Christ. Open Doors estimates that 340 million Christians live in such places. Not all methods of persecution are life and death. Many are relatable.[21] Christians may be facing discrimination in employment, as many do in Pakistan. Or, they may be attending a church service on a religious holiday with a gnawing fear of an attack, the likes of which are all too common in the Muslim world. Or, they may live in a restrictive country where they are afraid to share their faith.

Depending on the context, pray for persecuted believers the way you would want someone to pray for you if you were in the same situation. Pray that God would meet both their physical and spiritual needs.

- *Pray that religious freedom would become the universal standard across the globe.*

In addition to praying for persecuted individuals and situations, pray for greater religious freedom around that world.

Further, pray for the leaders of other countries that persecute believers—that they would have a change of heart and their plans to oppress religious groups would be thwarted. Also, pray for the leaders of free countries, including the

United States—that they would be given effective policy ideas and solutions to advance international religious freedom.

• *Remember why we pray for the persecuted.*

Scripture calls Christians to remember and to pray for the persecuted. In Ephesians 6:18–20, the apostle Paul instructs believers to "keep alert with all perseverance, making supplication for all the saints, and also for me, that words may be given to me in opening my mouth boldly to proclaim the mystery of the gospel, for which I am an ambassador in chains, that I may declare it boldly, as I ought to speak."

In this passage, Christians are asked both to pray for all other Christians as well as to pray for Paul, who was imprisoned for his ministry at the time he was writing. In prison, Paul was concerned for his Christian witness and requested prayer that he would have the right words to use. Similarly, we can pray that missionaries and believers in persecuted contexts would represent Christ well with their words and actions and be granted wisdom to operate in their contexts.

Grace Gao, whose father is a Christian human rights lawyer imprisoned in China, challenges individuals to do what they can, no matter how small, because our actions matter to those who are imprisoned and oppressed. She said:

> I wish everybody always has hope in their mind and to pray as much as you can and to pray for as many people as you can. Because for a lot of people who are in jail, I think the only thing that keeps them alive—it's [knowing] that someone outside is caring about them, is still praying for them. It's important. We can't forget those people, even though we don't know those people. They need our faith.[22]

For those who feel abandoned, the thought of someone out there praying can be more meaningful than we realize.

YOUR ACTIONS MATTER

Everyone everywhere ought to have the ability to choose their religion, change their religion, and live according to their faith. Whenever this basic human right is acknowledged and respected, whole societies benefit. Whenever this right is violated, whether by governments or by individuals, people suffer. This fact alone is a more than sufficient reason for the world to care about religious freedom.

Christians have an even greater reason to care about religious freedom than the world does. Scripture compels us to share the gospel and care for the persecuted church, the downtrodden, and those who cannot help themselves. Because God has allowed us to freely choose Him, it is good and right we follow His example by ensuring everyone everywhere has the freedom to believe, without government or social coercion.

The scope of religious persecution can be overwhelming. But to the persecuted, your actions matter, and you can do more than you know.

ABOUT THE
AUTHORS

Lela Gilbert is an award-winning writer who has authored or co-authored more than sixty books. She authored *Saturday People, Sunday People: Israel through the Eyes of a Christian Sojourner*, and co-authored *Persecuted: The Global Assault on Christians* with Nina Shea and Paul Marshall. Lela is Senior Fellow for International Religious Freedom at Family Research Council and Fellow at Hudson Institute's Center for Religious Freedom.

Arielle Del Turco. is the assistant director of the Center for Religious Liberty at Family Research Council, where she is responsible for international religious freedom policy and advocacy efforts. Through research and analysis, she crafts policy solutions and coordinates advocacy. Her work has appeared in *USA Today*, *RealClearPolitics*, *National Review*, and *Newsweek*.

LTG (RET.) Jerry Boykin was one of the original members of the U.S. Army's Delta Force. He was privileged to ultimately command these elite warriors in combat operations. Later, he commanded all the Army's Green Berets as well as the Special Warfare Center and School.

In all, General Boykin spent thirty-six years in the Army, serving his last four years as the Deputy Undersecretary of Defense for Intelligence. He is an ordained minister with a passion for spreading the Gospel of Jesus Christ and encouraging Christians to become warriors in God's Kingdom. He and his wife Ashley have five children and live in Virginia.

NOTES

INTRODUCTION

1. "Harassment of religious groups continues to be reported in more than 90% of countries," Pew Research Center, November 10, 2020, https://www.pewforum.org/2020/11/10/harassment-of-religious-groups-continues-to-be-reported-in-more-than-90-of-countries/.

2. "https://www.opendoorsusa.org/christian-persecution/world-watch-list/

3. Paul Marshall, *Their Blood Cries Out* (Dallas: Word Publishing, 1997).

4. https://www.opendoorsusa.org/christian-persecution/world-watch-list/

5. Article 18 of the Universal Declaration of Human Rights (UDHR), accessed December 2, 2021, https://www.un.org/en/about-us/universal-declaration-of-human-rights.

6. "International Religious Freedom Act of 1998," Wikipedia, accessed October 11, 2021, https://en.wikipedia.org/wiki/International_Religious_Freedom_Act_of_1998.

7. "From John Adams to Massachusetts Militia, 11 October 1798," National Archives – Founders Online, accessed October 11, 2021, https://founders.archives.gov/documents/Adams/99-02-02-3102.

CHAPTER 1: ASIA: PERSECUTION FROM ALL SIDES

1. "Police Violently Raid House Church in China," International Christian Concern, May 4, 2020, https://www.persecution .org/2020/05/04/police-violently-raid-house-church-china/.
2. Gao Feng, "State Security Police Raid House Church Meeting in Chinese Port City of Xiamen," Radio Free Asia, May 4, 2020, https://www.rfa.org/english/news/china/xiamen-church-05042020155239.html.
3. Leah Klett, "Police violently raid house church in China, drag out worshipers (video)," Christian Post, May 5, 2020, https://www .christianpost.com/news/police-violently-raid-house-church-in-china-drag-out-worshipers-video.html.
4. June Cheng, "House church on a hill," *World Magazine*, April 15, 2016, https://wng.org/articles/house-church-on-a-hill-1620602615.
5. "Early Rain Covenant Church," China Partnership, accessed June 7, 2021, https://www.chinapartnership.org/early-rain-covenant-church.
6. Early Rain Covenant Church, "95 Theses: The Reaffirmation of our Stance on the House Church," China Partnership, August 30, 2015, https://www.chinapartnership.org/blog/2015/08/95-theses-the-reaffirmation-of-our-stance-on-the-house-church.
7. Wang Yi, "My Declaration of Faithful Disobedience," China Partnership, December 12, 2018, https://www.chinapartnership. org/blog/2018/12/my-declaration-of-faithful-disobedience.
8. Paul Mozur and Ian Johnson, "China Sentences Wang Yi, Chinese Pastor, to 9 Years in Prison," *New York Times*, December 30, 2019, https://www.nytimes.com/2019/12/30/world/asia/ china-wang-yi-christian-sentence.html.

9. "Sichaun Church Members Detained During Easter Service," International Christian Concern, April 13, 2020, https://www. persecution.org/2020/04/13/sichuan-church-members-detained-easter-service/.

10. Mimi Lau, "South Korean missionaries fearful as crackdown on 'infiltration' in China gathers pace," *South China Morning Post*, June 10, 2018, https://www.scmp.com/news/china/policies-politics/article/2150057/south-korean-missionaries-fearful-crackdown.

11. "Constitution of the People's Republic of China – Adopted on December 4, 1982," accessed October 2, 2019, http://en.people .cn/constitution/constitution.html.

12. Ibid.

13. "World Watch List Report—China," Open Doors, accessed June 7, 2021, https://www.opendoorsusa.org/christian-persecution/world-watch-list/china/.

14. Nina Shea and Bob Fu, "China Cracks Down on Christians," Hudson Institute, December 12, 2018, https://www.hudson. org/research/14741-china-cracks-down-on-christians.

15. Charlotte Gao, "Chinese Communist Party Vows to 'Sinicize Religions' in China," *The Diplomat*, October 24, 2017, https:// thediplomat.com/2017/10/chinese-communist-party-vows-to-sinicize-religions-in-china/.

16. Lily Kuo, "In China, they're closing churches, jailing pastors – and even rewriting scripture," *The Guardian*, January 13, 2019, accessed September 17, 2021, https://www.theguardian.com/world/2019/jan/13/china-christians-religious-persecution-translation-bible.

17. Anugrah Kumar, "China shuts down Bible App, Christian WeChat as new crackdown policies go into effect," *Christian Post*, May 2, 2021, https://www.christianpost.com/news/china-shuts-down-bible-app-christian-wechat-accounts.html.

18. Kumar, "China shuts down Bible App."

19. Shen Hua, "China Conducts Two Trials in Crackdown on Audio Bibles," *Voice of America*, December 14, 2020, https://www.voanews.com/east-asia-pacific/china-conducts-two-trials-crackdown-audio-bibles.

20. "Brother Andrew's Story," Open Doors, accessed September 16, 2021, https://www.opendoorsusa.org/about-us/history/brother-andrews-story/.

21. Ian Johnson, "Decapitated Churches in China's Christian Heartland," *New York Times*, May 21, 2016, https://www.nytimes.com/2016/05/22/world/asia/china-christians-zhejiang.html.

22. "2018 Annual Report: Chinese Government Persecution of Churches and Christians in Mainland China," ChinaAid, 2018, https://drive.google.com/file/d/1deR6dkQpidTsJ0RheaZ2Y8Q-C4XVvEWZ/view.

23. Tang Feng, "Xi Jinping's Quotes Replace the Ten Commandments in Churches," *Bitter Winter*, September 14, 2019, https://bitterwinter.org/xi-jinpings-quotes-replace-the-ten-commandments/.

24. "Chinese Communist Party using CCTV to 'maintain social order' at churches," World Watch Monitor, March 23, 2017, https://www.worldwatchmonitor.org/coe/chinese-communist-party-using-cctv-to-maintain-social-order-at-churches/.

25. "China bulldozing churches and replacing holy imagery with Communist in religious crackdown," *South China Morning Post*, September 15, 2018, https://www.scmp.com/news/china/society/article/2164358/china-bulldozing-churches-and-replacing-holy-imagery-communist.

26. June Cheng, "The modern Chinese house church," *World Magazine*, May 31, 2018, https://wng.org/articles/the-modern-chinese-house-church-1618208677.

27. Cary Huang, "China must let the dark deeds of the Cultural Revolution come to light," *South China Morning Post*, May 13, 2016, https://www.scmp.com/comment/insight-opinion/

article/1943970/china-must-let-dark-deeds-cultural-revolution-come-light.

28. Brian Stiller, "The Evangelical Church in Vietnam: Beauty and resilience," August 28, 2018, accessed February 2, 2022, https://www.evangelicalfellowship.ca/Communications/Dispatches-from-Brian-Stiller/August-2018/The-Evangelical-Church-in-Vietnam-Beauty-and-resi.aspx.

29. "CNA: Government rewards citizens for reporting on house churches," ChinaAid, August 3, 2020, https://www.chinaaid.org/2020/08/cna-government-rewards-citizens-for.html.

30. "ChinaScope: Bitter Winter: CCP Actions to Ban Foreign Religions Will Continue throughout China," ChinaAid, June 13, 2019, https://www.chinaaid.org/2019/06/chinascope-bitter-winter-ccp-actions-to.html.

31. "ChinaScope: Bitter Winter."

32. Mimi Lau, "A rare glimpse into how an 'underground' Chinese Catholic church celebrates Christmas," *South China Morning Post*, December 26, 2016, https://www.scmp.com/news/china/policies-politics/article/2057253/rare-glimpse-how-underground-chinese-catholic-church.

33. Nina Shea, "The Vatican's Agreement with China Looks Even Worse Now," Hudson Institute, November 26, 2018, https://www.hudson.org/research/14711-the-vatican-s-agreement-with-china-looks-even-worse-now.

34. "Vatican-China Deal of 2018," *Bitter Winter*, accessed September 17, 2021, https://bitterwinter.org/Vocabulary/vatican-china-deal-of-2018/.

35. Shea, "The Vatican's Agreement with China Looks Even Worse Now"

36. Philip Pullella, "Vatican says China intimidating Catholics loyal to pope," Reuters, June 28, 2019, https://www.reuters.com/article/us-pope-china/vatican-says-china-intimidating-catholics-loyal-to-pope-idUSKCN1TT1MY.

37. Massimo Introvigne, "September 22: First Anniversary of the Vatican-China Deal," *Bitter Winter*, September 20, 2019, https://bitterwinter.org/september-22-first-anniversary-of-the-vatican-china-deal/.

38. Jason Horowitz, "Vatican Extends Deal with China Over Appointment of Bishops," *New York Times*, October 22, 2020, https://www.nytimes.com/2020/10/22/world/europe/vatican-china-bishops.html.

39. "China Tribunal," accessed September 16, 2021, https://chinatribunal.com/.

40. Joshua Lipes, "Survey: Three Million, Mostly Uyghurs, in Some Form of Political 'Re-Education' in Xinjiang," Radio Free Asia, August 3, 2018, https://www.rfa.org/english/news/uyghur/millions-08032018142025.html

41. Philip Wen and Olzha Auyezov, "Tracking China's Muslim Gulag," Reuters, November 29, 2018, https://www.reuters.com/investigates/special-report/muslims-camps-china/.

42. Michael Pompeo, "Genocide in Xinjiang," *Wall Street Journal*, January 19, 2021, https://www.wsj.com/articles/genocide-in-xinjiang-11611078180.

43. "China cuts Uighur births with IUDs, abortion, sterilization," Associated Press, June 29, 2020, https://apnews.com/article/269b3de1af34e17c1941a514f78d764c.

44. Bill Murphy, "China, officially atheist, could have more Christians than the U.S. by 2030," *Houston Chronicle*, February 24, 2018, https://www.houstonchronicle.com/news/houston-texas/houston/article/China-officially-atheist-could-have-more-12633079.php.

45. "Powerful Testimony from a Christian Survivor of North Korea," Family Research Council, June 7, 2019, https://frcblog.com/2019/06/powerful-testimony-christian-survivor-north-korea/.

46. "Report of the Commission of Inquiry on Human Rights in the Democratic People's Republic of Korea," United Nations, accessed September 17, 2021, https://www.ohchr.org/en/hrbodies/hrc/coidprk/pages/reportofthecommissionofinquirydprk.aspx.

47. "Report of the Commission of Inquiry on Human Rights in the Democratic People's Republic of Korea."

48. "A Prison Without Bars, U.S. Commission on International Religious Freedom, March 2018, accessed February 2, 2022, https://www.uscirf.gov/sites/default/files/APrisonWithoutBars-FINAL.pdf/.

49. "Prisons of North Korea," U.S. Department of State, August 25, 2017, https://www.state.gov/wp-content/uploads/2019/03/Prisons-of-North-Korea-English.pdf.

50. "Report of the Commission of Inquiry on Human Rights in the Democratic People's Republic of Korea."

51. "North Korea," U.S. Commission on International Religious Freedom, 2019, https://www.uscirf.gov/sites/default/files/Tier1_NORTHKOREA_2019.pdf.

52. "North Korea," Aid to the Church in Need, accessed June 7, 2021, https://acnuk.org/north-korea/.

53. Bio on Pastor A Dao, United States Commission on International Religious Freedom, accessed December 2, 2021, https://www.uscirf.gov/pastor-dao.

54. Leah Klett, "Vietnamese pastor released after 4 years imprisonment over religious freedom advocacy," *Christian Post*, September 21, 2020, https://www.christianpost.com/news/vietnamese-pastor-released-after-4-years-imprisonment-over-religious-freedom-advocacy.html.

55. James Carr and Glenn Grothman, "Hopes and fears for religious freedom in Vietnam," *The Hill*, August 20, 2020, https://thehill.com/blogs/congress-blog/religious-rights/512929-hopes-and-fears-for-religious-freedom-in-vietnam.

56. "United States Commission on International Religious Freedom Annual Report 2021," United States Commission on International Religious Freedom, 2021, https://www.uscirf.gov/sites/default/files/2021-04/2021%20Annual%20Report_0.pdf.

57. "The World Watch List," Open Doors, accessed June 7, 2021, https://www.opendoorsusa.org/christian-persecution/world-watch-list/.

58. "2020 Report on International Religious Freedom: Vietnam," U.S. Department of State, May 12, 2021, accessed February 2, 2022, https://www.state.gov/reports/2020-report-on-international-religious-freedom/vietnam/.

59. "United States Commission on International Religious Freedom Annual Report 2021," United States Commission on International Religious Freedom, 2021, https://www.uscirf.gov/sites/default/files/2021-04/2021%20Annual%20Report_0.pdf.

60. Samuel Smith, "Jailed pastor's son 'bludgeoned' with baton, detained by Vietnamese police amid US ambassador's visit," *Christian Post,* July 7, 2020, https://www.christianpost.com/news/jailed-pastors-son-bludgeoned-with-baton-detained-by-vietnamese-police-amid-us-ambassadors-visit.html.

61. Brian Stiller, "The Evangelical Church in Vietnam: Beauty and resilience," August 28, 2018, accessed February 2, 2022, https://www.evangelicalfellowship.ca/Communications/Dispatches-from-Brian-Stiller/August-2018/The-Evangelical-Church-in-Vietnam-Beauty-and-resi.aspx.

62. John Hayward, "Pakistani Court Rules 14-year-old Christian Girl Must Remain Married to Her Muslim Kidnapper," *Breitbart,* August 6, 2020, accessed March 22, 2021, https://www.breitbart.com/national-security/2020/08/06/pakistani-court-rules-14-year-old-christian-girl-must-remain-married-muslim-kidnapper/.

63. Arielle Del Turco, "Combatting Forced Marriage of Young Women in Pakistan," Family Research Council, March 2021, https://www.frc.org/forcedmarriage.

64. Engy Magdy, "A Christian Girl in Pakistan Pleas for Justice," *The Tablet,* September 16, 2020, https://thetablet.org/a-christian-girl-in-pakistan-pleas-for-justice/.

65. Inés San Martín, "Pakistani Catholic girl kidnapped and forced to marry seeks asylum in UK," *Crux,* February 5, 2021, https://cruxnow.com/church-in-asia/2021/02/pakistani-catholic-girl-kidnapped-and-forced-to-marry-seeks-asylum-in-uk/.

66. San Martín, "Pakistani Catholic girl kidnapped and forced to marry seeks asylum in UK."

67. "2019 Report on International Religious Freedom: Pakistan," U.S. Department of State, June 10, 2020, https://www.state. gov/reports/2019-report-on-international-religious-freedom/ pakistan/.

68. "2019 Report on International Religious Freedom: Pakistan."

69. "2019 Report on International Religious Freedom: Pakistan."

70. "Pakistan Penal Code (Act XLV of 1860)," Pakistani.org, 1860, accessed June 7, 2021, http://www.pakistani.org/pakistan/ legislation/1860/actXLVof1860.html.

71. "Pakistan Penal Code (Act XLV of 1860)."

72. "Blasphemy accusation in Pakistan sparks ransacking of Hindu temple, school," Reuters, September 16, 2019, https:// www.reuters.com/article/us-pakistan-blasphemy/blasphemy-accusation-in-pakistan-sparks-ransacking-of-hindu-temple-school-idUSKBN1W10MX.

73. Emily Sullivan, "Asia Bibi, Pakistani Woman Acquitted Of Blasphemy, Is Freed from Jail," National Public Radio, November 8, 2018, https://www.npr.org/2018/11/08/665531066/asia-bibi-pakistani-woman-acquitted-of-blapshemy-is-freed-from-jail.

74. Zia ur-Rehman and Maria Abi-Habib, "Sewer Cleaners Wanted in Pakistan, Only Christians Can Apply," *New York Times*, May 4, 2020, https://www.nytimes.com/2020/05/04/world/asia/ pakistan-christians-sweepers.html.

75. "Pakistan's Most Oppressed and the COVID-19 Pandemic," International Christian Concern, April 24, 2020, accessed June 8, 2021, https://www.persecution.org/2020/04/24/pakistans-oppressed-covid-19-pandemic/.

76. "Expectations of Justice Low for Grieving Family of Street Sweeper in Pakistan," *Morning Star News*, May 1, 2020, https:// morningstarnews.org/2020/05/expectations-of-justice-low-for-grieving-family-of-street-sweeper-in-pakistan/.

77. "Gunmen Shoot, Wound Daughter of Pastor Slain in 2015 in Eastern India," *Morning Star News*, April 21, 2020, https://morningstarnews .org/2020/04/gunmen-shoot-wound-daughter-of-pastor-slain-in-2015-in-eastern-india/.

78. Arielle Del Turco, "Religious Freedom Concerns in India Rise Amid Coronavirus Crisis," Family Research Council, April 21, 2020, https://www.frcblog.com/2020/04/religious-freedom-concerns-india-rise-amid-coronavirus-crisis/.

79. "Bishop of Truro's Independent Review for the Foreign Secretary of FCO Support for Persecuted Christians," Christian Persecution Review, 2019, https://christianpersecutionreview.org.uk/interim-report/.

80. "U.S. Pastor Allowed to Return Home from India after More than Seven Months," *Morning Star News*, May 21, 2020, https://morningstarnews.org/2020/05/u-s-pastor-allowed-to-return-home-from-india-after-more-than-seven-months/.

81. Shilu Manandhar, "Christians Say Police Target Them for Their Faith," *Global Press Journal*, January 24, 2021, https://globalpressjournal.com/asia/nepal/christians-say-police-target-faith/.

82. Rock Rozario, "Christians in Nepal persecuted by religious and political decree," *Union of Catholic Asian News*, May 7, 2021, https://www.ucanews.com/news/christians-in-nepal-persecuted-by-religious-and-political-decree/92379#.

83. Timothy Shah, "Nepal Religious Freedom Landscape Report," Religious Freedom Institute, October 14, 2020, https://www .religiousfreedominstitute.org/publication/nepal-religious-freedom-landscape-report.

84. "Four Christians in Nepal Arrested for 'Preaching Christianity,'" International Christian Concern, August 16, 2019, https://www. persecution.org/2019/08/16/four-christians-nepal-arrested-preaching-christianity/.

85. "Authorities Demolish Rupantaran Khristiya Church in Nepal," International Christian Concern, January 29, 2021, https://www

.persecution.org/2021/01/29/authorities-demolish-rupantaran-khristiya-church-nepal/.

86. Shah, "Nepal Religious Freedom Landscape Report,".

87. "Nepal," Open Doors, accessed September 17, 2021, https://www.opendoorsuk.org/persecution/world-watch-list/nepal/.

88. Danielle Preiss, "Why Nepal Has One of the World's Fastest-Growing Christian Populations," National Public Radio, February 3, 2016, https://www.npr.org/sections/goatsandsoda/2016/02/03/463965924/why-nepal-has-one-of-the-worlds-fastest-growing-christian-populations.

89. "Terror in Sri Lanka," CNN, April 2019, accessed June 8, 2021, https://www.cnn.com/interactive/2019/04/world/sri-lanka-attacks/.

90. Joanna Slater and Terrence McCoy, "Terror and trauma in Colombo: Sri Lanka's capital grieves," *Washington Post*, April 24, 2019, https://www.washingtonpost.com/world/asia_pacific/terror-and-trauma-in-colombo-sri-lankas-capital-grieves/2019/04/23/2b9b4382-6483-11e9-a698-2a8f808c9cfb_story.html.

91. Emma Green, "How Sri Lanka's Christians Became a Target," *The Atlantic*, April 24, 2019, https://www.theatlantic.com/international/archive/2019/04/sri-lankas-christians-faced-new-persecution/587842/.

92. "Sri Lanka," Open Doors, accessed June 8, 2021, https://www.opendoorsusa.org/christian-persecution/world-watch-list/sri-lanka-2/.

CHAPTER 2: AFRICA: "THERE'S A WAR GOING ON"

1. "Abducted Dapchi Girls in 'Boko Haram town' in Yobe, Claims Rep," *Sahara Reporters*, March 2, 2018, http://saharareporters.com/2018/03/02/abducted-dapchi-girls-boko-haram-town-yobe-claims-rep.

2. Ahmad Salkida, "EXCLUSIVE: Leah Sharibu speaks from captivity, asks Buhari to pity her (audio)," *The Cable*, August 27,

2018, https://www.thecable.ng/exclusive-leah-sharibu-speaks-from-captivity-asks-buhari-to-have-mercy-on-her.

3. "Leah Sharibu," The Voice of the Martyrs Canada, accessed September 14, 2021, https://www.vomcanada.com/ng-leah-sharibu.htm.

4. Lela Gilbert, "Leah Sharibu: Held Captive 3 Years for Her Christian Faith," Family Research Council, February 19, 2021, https://www.frcblog.com/2021/02/leah-shirabu-held-captive-3-years-her-christian-faith/.

5. Gilbert, "Leah Sharibu."

6. Femi Owolabi, "Report: Leah Sharibu gives birth in captivity for Boko Haram commander," *The Cable*, January 26, 2020, https://www.thecable.ng/report-leah-sharibu-gives-birth-in-captivity-for-boko-haram-commander.

7. Lela Gilbert, "The Crisis of Christian Persecution in Nigeria," Family Research Council, February 2021, https://www.frc.org/nigeria.

8. "Leah Sharibu," U.S. Commission on International Religious Freedom, accessed September 14, 2021, https://www.uscirf.gov/religious-prisoners-conscience/current-rpocs/leah-sharibu.

9. "2022 World Watch List," https://www.opendoorsusa.org/christian-persecution/world-watch-list/

10. Wole Oyebade, "Leah Sharibu: Remembering a forerunner of resistance," *The Gaurdian*, December 29, 2020, accessed September 14, 2021, https://guardian.ng/opinion/leah-sharibu-remembering-a-forerunner-of-resistance/.

11. Russell Heimlich, "Christianity and Islam in Sub-Saharan Africa," Pew Research Center, April 28, 2010, https://www.pewresearch.org/fact-tank/2010/04/28/christianity-and-islam-in-sub-saharan-africa/.

12. Harriet Sherwood, "Christian persecution rises as people refused aid in Covid crisis – report," *The Gaurdian*, January 12, 2021, https://www.theguardian.com/world/2021/jan/13/christian-persecution-rises-as-people-refused-aid-in-covid-crisis-report.

13. Lela Gilbert, "Multiple Beheadings in Mozambique: Is the World Indifferent?" *Providence*, November 16, 2020, https://providencemag .com/2020/11/multiple-beheadings-mozambique-world-indifferent/.

14. Lindsay Scorgie and Mallory Dunlop, "Congo officials claim that a rebel group is tied to the Islamic State. That could backfire," *Washington Post*, July 8, 2021, https://www.washingtonpost.com/ politics/2021/07/08/congo-officials-claim-that-rebel-group-is-tied-islamic-state-that-could-backfire/.

15. "Sudan," The World Factbook – Central Intelligence Agency, accessed September 14, 2021, https://www.cia.gov/the-world-factbook/countries/sudan/.

16. https://www.opendoorsusa.org/christian-persecution/world-watch-list/

17. "Religion of South Sudan," Britannica, accessed September 14, 2021, https://www.britannica.com/place/South-Sudan/Religion.

18. "Ethiopian Orthodox Church head says genocide is taking place in Tigray," Reuters, May 9, 2021, https://www.reuters.com/ world/ethiopian-orthodox-church-head-says-genocide-is-taking-place-tigray-2021-05-09/.

19. " https://www.opendoors.org/en-US/persecution/countries/

20. "African Christians at Risk as Persecution Intensifies," SOFREP, April 24, 2021, https://sofrep.com/news/african-christians-at-risk-as-persecution-intensifies/.

21. https://www.opendoors.org/en-US/persecution/countries/

22. Benoit Faucon, Nicholas Bariyo, and Joe Parkinson, "Islamic State Seeks Revival in Christian Countries," *Wall Street Journal*, April 15, 2021, https://www.wsj.com/articles/islamic-state-seeks-revival-in-christian-countries-11618498283.

23. Olivier Guitta, "A New Caliphate in Africa?" Akhbar al-Aan TV, April 13, 2021, https://www.linkedin.com/pulse/new-caliphate-africa-akhbar-al-aan-tv-13-apr-2021-olivier-guitta/.

24. "African Christians at Risk as Persecution Intensifies," SOFREP, April 24, 2021, https://sofrep.com/news/african-christians-at-risk-as-persecution-intensifies/.

25. Islamic Republic News Agency, https://www.irna.ir/.

26. Mona Alami, "Hezbollah allegedly training Nigeran Shiites to expand influence in West Africa," MEI, July 5, 2018, https://www.mei.edu/publications/hezbollah-allegedly-training-nigerian-shiites-expand-influence-west-africa.

27. Muhammad Fraser-Rahim and Mo Fatah, "In Somalia, Iran Is Replicating Russia's Afghan Strategy," *Foreign Policy*, July 17, 2020, https://foreignpolicy.com/2020/07/17/iran-aiding-al-shabab-somalia-united-states/.

28. Declan Walsh, Eric Schmitt, Simon Marks, and Ronen Bergman, "In a Dangerous Game of Cat and Mouse, Iran Eyes New Targets in Africa," *New York Times*, February 15, 2021, https://www.nytimes.com/2021/02/15/world/africa/iran-ethiopia-plot.html.

29. Ishaan Tharoor, "Iran's Ahmadinejad says the U.S. is out to get the Hidden Imam, who, uh, disappeared in the 10th century," *Washington Post*, June 24, 2015, https://www.washingtonpost.com/news/worldviews/wp/2015/06/24/irans-ahmadinejad-says-the-u-s-is-out-to-get-the-hidden-imam-who-um-disappeared-in-the-10th-century/.

30. Tonny Onyulo, "Churches, NGOs help Mozambicans displaced by Islamist insurgency," Catholic News Service, May 28, 2021, https://www.catholicnews.com/churches-ngos-help-mozambicans-displaced-by-islamist-insurgency/.

31. "ISIL-linked attackers behead 50 people in northern Mozambique," Al Jazeera, November 10, 2020, https://www.aljazeera.com/news/2020/11/10/isil-linked-attackers-behead-50-people-in-northern-mozambique.

32. Declan Walsh, "With Village Beheadings, Islamic State Intensifies Attacks in Mozambique," *New York Times*, November 11, 2020, https://www.nytimes.com/2020/11/11/world/middleeast/Mozambique-ISIS-beheading.html.

33. "2019 Report on International Religious Freedom: Mozambique," U.S. Department of State, accessed September 15, 2021, https://

www.state.gov/reports/2019-report-on-international-religious-freedom/mozambique/.

34. "Religion is shaping Cabo Delgado civil war," Mozambique News Reports & Clippings, April 30, 2020, https://www.open.ac.uk/technology/mozambique/sites/www.open.ac.uk.technology.mozambique/files/files/Mozambique_484-30Apr2020_Supplement-religion-vote.pdf.

35. Courtney Mares, "Catholic charity sends aid to Mozambique after reports of mass beheading," Catholic News Agency, November 11, 2020, https://www.catholicnewsagency.com/news/46557/catholic-charity-sends-aid-to-mozambique-after-reports-of-mass-beheading.

36. Andrea Morris, "'The World Has No Idea What Is Happening': Islamic Extremists Massacre, Behead in Mozambique Reign of Terror," CBN News, July 29, 2020, https://www1.cbn.com/cbnnews/world/2020/july/the-world-has-no-idea-what-is-happening-islamic-extremists-massacre-behead-in-mozambique-reign-of-terror.

37. https://www.opendoorsusa.org/christian-persecution/world-watch-list/

38. "Somalia 2019 International Religious Freedom Report," U.S. Department of State, https://www.state.gov/wp-content/uploads/2020/05/SOMALIA-2019-INTERNATIONAL-RELIGIOUS-FREEDOM-REPORT.pdf.

39. "https://www.opendoorsusa.org/christian-persecution/world-watch-list/

40. "https://www.opendoorsusa.org/christian-persecution/world-watch-list/

41. Rosie Scammell, "Eritrean gospel singer Helen Berhane was tortured for her beliefs. Now she's speaking up," Washington Post, December 29, 2015, https://www.washingtonpost.com/national/religion/eritrean-gospel-singer-helen-berhane-was-tortured-for-her-beliefs-now-shes-speaking-up/2015/12/29/9b5ffabe-ae5b-11e5-b281-43c0b56f61fa_story.html.

42. Kevin Zeller, "Eritrean soldiers destroy two refugee camps in Ethiopia," Mission Network News, July 12, 2021, https://www.mnnonline.org/news/eritrean-soldiers-destroy-two-tigray-refugee-camps/.

43. Danielle Paquette, "Islamist militants are targeting Christians in Burkina Faso: 'They are planting seeds of a religious conflict,'" *Washington Post*, August 21, 2019, https://www.washingtonpost.com/world/africa/islamist-militants-are-targeting-christians-in-burkina-faso-they-are-planting-seeds-of-a-religious-conflict/2019/08/20/3d689bf8-b91c-11e9-aeb2-a101a1fb27a7_story.html.

44. Lela Gilbert, "West Africa: Praying for a Miracle," *Juicy Ecumenism*, September 3, 2020, https://juicyecumenism.com/2020/09/03/lela-gilbert/.

45. Tola Mbakwe, "Churches in Burkina Faso abandoned as Christians flee violence from radical Jihadists," *Premier Christian News*, August 30, 2020, https://premierchristian.news/en/news/article/churches-in-burkina-faso-abandoned-as-christians-flee-violence-from-radical-jihadists.

46. "Mounting violence forces one million to flee homes in Burkina Faso," United Nations High Commissioner for Refugees, August 18, 2020, https://www.unhcr.org/news/briefing/2020/8/5f3b84914/mounting-violence-forces-million-flee-homes-burkina-faso.html.

47. "Pastor Tortured, Killed in Nigeria," International Christian Concern, July 28, 2021, https://www.persecution.org/2021/07/28/pastor-tortured-killed-nigeria/.

48. Baroness (Caroline) Cox and Revd David Thomas, "'YOUR LAND OR YOUR BLOOD'—The escalating persecution and displacement of Christians in northern and central Nigeria," Humanitarian Aid Relief Trust, November 2019, https://www.hart-uk.org/wp-content/uploads/2019/12/Nigeria-Visit-Final-Report_Nov-2019-1-1.pdf.

49. "Islamic Extremists Threaten to Kill Abducted Pastor in One Week if Ransom Isn't Paid," International Christian Concern, February 27, 2021, https://www.persecution.org/2021/02/27/islamic-extremists-threaten-kill-abducted-pastor-one-week-ransom-isnt-paid/.

50. Personal interview.

51. Emeka Umeagbalasi, "Nigeria Is a Killing Field of Defenseless Christians," Genocide Watch, April 13, 2020, https://www.genocidewatch.com/single-post/2020/04/13/Nigeria-Is-A-Killing-Field-Of-Defenseless-Christians.

52. Umeagbalasi, "Nigeria Is a Killing Field of Defenseless Christians."

53. "Fulani Herdsmen in Nigeria Kill More than 60 Christians in Five Weeks, Sources say," *Morning Star News*, April 5, 2020, https://morningstarnews.org/2020/04/fulani-herdsmen-in-nigeria-kill-more-than-60-christians-in-five-weeks-sources-say/.

54. Stephanie Busari, "Outcry after a Nigerian student dies from 'brutal attack' in church," CNN, June 1, 2020, https://www.cnn.com/2020/06/01/africa/attack-nigeria-student-church/index.html.

55. Lela Gilbert, "Nigeria's Christians and Their Endless Persecution," Family Research Council, May 11, 2020, https://www.frcblog.com/2020/05/nigerias-christians-and-their-endless-persecution/.

56. Lela Gilbert, "Is the World Ignoring a Christian Genocide in Nigeria?" Hudson Institute, April 21, 2020, https://www.hudson.org/research/15954-is-the-world-ignoring-a-christian-genocide-in-nigeria.

57. Joe Parkinson and Gbenga Akingbule, "Outside Nigeria's 'Green Zone,' Jihadists Rule the Road," *Wall Street Journal*, November 19, 2020, https://www.wsj.com/articles/outside-nigerias-green-zone-jihadists-rule-the-road-11605787200.

58. Lela Gilbert, "Christian Persecution: A Glaring Blind Spot in Nigeria and Beyond," Family Research Council, November 20,

2020, https://www.frcblog.com/2020/11/christian-persecution-glaring-blind-spot-nigeria-and-beyond/.

59. Paul Marshall, "Secular Myopia Warps the West's View of Nigeria," Hudson Institute, November 23, 2020, https://www.hudson.org/research/16526-secular-myopia-warps-the-wests-view-of-nigeria.

60. Lela Gilbert, "Nigeria Is Officially Declared a 'Country of Particular Concern'—and Not a Minute Too Soon," Hudson Institute, December 8, 2020, https://www.hudson.org/research/16550-nigeria-is-officially-declared-a-country-of-particular-concern-and-not-a-minute-too-soon.

61. U.S. Commission on International Religious Freedom, "USCIRF Welcomes the State Department's Designation of Nigeria among World's Worst Violators of Religious Freedom," press release, December 7, 2020, https://www.uscirf.gov/news-room/releases-statements/uscirf-welcomes-state-departments-designation-nigeria-among-worlds.

62. Lela Gilbert, "An Urgent Letter of Particular Concern," Family Research Council, December 8, 2021, https://www.frc.org/updatearticle/20211208/urgent-letter.

63. Tyler O'Neil, "Religious freedom advocates ask Biden to put Nigeria back on watchlist for anti-Christian violence," Fox News, December 7, 2021, https://www.foxnews.com/politics/biden-nigeria-religious-freedom-watchlist-anti-christian-violence-advocates.

64. "Frequently Asked Questions: IRF Report and Countries of Particular Concern," U.S. Department of State, https://www.state.gov/frequently-asked-questions-irf-report-and-countries-of-particular-concern/.

65. "Thousands flee attacks in Nigeria, clashes continue, says UN," ABC News, April 16, 2021, https://abcnews.go.com/US/wireStory/thousands-flee-attacks-nigeria-clashes-continue-77113591.

66. Col. (ret.) Dr. Jacques Neriah, "Africa Is a Jihadist Playground for the Resurgent Islamic State and al-Qaeda," Jerusalem Center for Public Affairs, March 1, 2021, https://jcpa.org/africa-is-a-jihadist-playground-for-the-resurgent-islamic-state-and-al-qaeda/.

67. Lela Gilbert, "Under Jihadi Siege, Christians in West Africa Are Praying for a Miracle," Hudson Institute, September 8, 2020, https://www.hudson.org/research/16362-under-jihadi-siege-christians-in-west-africa-are-praying-for-a-miracle.

68. Nick Turse, Sam Mednick, and Amanda Sperber, "Exclusive: Inside the Secret World of US Commandos in Africa," Pulitzer Center, August 11, 2020, https://pulitzercenter.org/stories/exclusive-inside-secret-world-us-commandos-africa.

69. Gilbert, "Under Jihadi Siege, Christians in West Africa Are Praying for a Miracle."

70. Mosa'ab Elshamy, "US General: 'Wildfire of Terrorism' on March in Africa," Military.com, June 19, 2021, https://www.military.com/daily-news/2021/06/19/us-general-wildfire-of-terrorism-march-africa.html.

71. Emily Estelle, "Why Experts Ignore Terrorism in Africa," *Foreign Policy*, April 19, 2021, https://foreignpolicy.com/2021/04/19/why-experts-ignore-terrorism-in-africa/.

CHAPTER 3: MIDDLE EAST: WARS AND RUMORS OF WARS

1. Lela Gilbert, "Persecuted Iranian Christian Mary Mohammadi Votes for Truth in Her Homeland," CBN News, June 14, 2021, https://www1.cbn.com/cbnnews/cwn/2021/june/persecuted-iranian-christian-mary-mohammadi-votes-for-truth-in-her-homeland.

2. "Fatemeh Mohammadi reported detained in Tehran prison as Trump highlights arrest," Article18, February 7, 2020, accessed September 21, 2021, https://articleeighteen.com/news/5547/.

3. https://www.opendoorsusa.org/christian-persecution/world-watch-list/

4. Patrick Wintour, "Persecution of Christians 'coming close to genocide' in Middle East – report," *The Guardian*, May 2, 2019, https://www.theguardian.com/world/2019/may/02/persecution-driving-christians-out-of-middle-east-report.

5. "Middle East-North Africa," Pew Research Center, April 2, 2015, https://www.pewforum.org/2015/04/02/middle-east-north-africa/.

6. Eli Kavon, "The triumph of the 'dhimmi,'" *Jerusalem Post*, October 10, 2016, https://www.jpost.com/opinion/the-triumph-of-the-dhimmi-469876.

7. "Jewish refugees expelled from Arab lands and from Iran," Ministry of Foreign Affairs – Israel, November 30, 2017, https://mfa.gov.il/MFA/ForeignPolicy/Issues/Pages/Jewish-refugees-expelled-from-Arab-lands-and-from-Iran-29-November-2016.aspx.

8. Lela Gilbert, *Saturday People, Sunday People: Israel through the Eyes of a Christian Sojourner* (New York: Encounter Books, 2012), vii, https://www.amazon.com/Saturday-People-Sunday-Christian-Sojourner/dp/159403639X.

9. https://www.opendoors.org/en-US/persecution/countries/

10. Lela Gilbert, "Iran's Furtive Occupation of Iraq's Christian Communities," Hudson Institute, March 17, 2019, https://www.hudson.org/research/14885-iran-s-furtive-occupation-of-iraq-s-christian-communities.

11. "Total death toll | Over 606,000 people killed across Syria since the beginning of the 'Syrian Revolution,' including 495,000 documented by SOHR," Syrian Observatory for Human Rights, June 1, 2021, https://www.syriahr.com/en/217360/?__cf_chl_jschl_tk__=pmd_xr7SzXK7o.mXFJ50a8oXkGPKPxRM6VedCs_GrG2HcHs-1632252439-0-gqNtZGzNAeWjcnBszQel.

12. Lela Gilbert, "Turkey's Christians Face Increasingly Dangerous Persecution," *Newsweek*, April 13, 2021, https://www.newsweek .com/turkeys-christians-face-increasingly-dangerous-persecution-opinion-1583041.

13. Saudi Arabia, Open Doors, accessed September 21, 2021, https://www.opendoorsuk.org/persecution/world-watch-list/ saudi-arabia/.

14. Mansour Borji, "A recipe for intolerance: Iran's blueprint for cracking down on Christians," Middle East Institute, December 9, 2020, https://www.mei.edu/publications/recipe-intolerance-irans-blueprint-cracking-down-christians.

15. "2019 Report on International Religious Freedom: Israel, West Bank and Gaza," U.S. Department of State, accessed September 21, 2021, https://www.state.gov/reports/2019-report-on-international-religious-freedom/israel-west-bank-and-gaza/.

16. Lela Gilbert, "An Outrageous Anti-Christian Attack in Egypt," Hudson Institute, June 2, 2016, https://www.hudson.org/ research/12539-an-outrageous-anti-christian-attack-in-egypt.

17. "Hundreds of Egyptian Muslims attack Christian woman and homes after rumours about her son," *The Telegraph*, May 26 2016, https://www.telegraph.co.uk/news/2016/05/26/hundreds-of-egyptian-muslims-attack-christian-woman-and-homes-af/.

18. Gilbert, "An Outrageous Anti-Christian Attack in Egypt."

19. https://egyptindependent.com/lady-of-karam-still-awaiting-verdict-for-those-who-stripped-her-naked/

20. Samuel Tadros, *Motherland Lost: The Egyptian and Coptic Quest for Modernity* (Stanford, CA: Hoover Institution Press, 2013), https://www.amazon.com/Motherland-Lost-Egyptian-Modernity-International/dp/081791644X.

21. Gilbert, "An Outrageous Anti-Christian Attack in Egypt."

22. Gilbert, "An Outrageous Anti-Christian Attack in Egypt."

23. Martin Mosebach, *The 21: A Journey into the Land of Coptic Martyrs* (Walden, NY: Plough Publishing House, 2019), 233–34,

https://www.amazon.com/21-Journey-into-Coptic-Martyrs/dp/0874868394.

24. Lela Gilbert, "Egypt's silent epidemic of kidnapped Christian girls," *Jerusalem Post*, December 5, 2018, https://www.jpost.com/opinion/egypts-silent-epidemic-of-kidnapped-christian-girls-573614.

25. Paul Marshall, "Are Egypt's Christians Persecuted? Why Some Copts Say No," *Religion Unplugged*, January 15, 2021, accessed September 21, 2021, https://religionunplugged.com/news/2021/1/15/are-egypts-christians-persecuted-why-copts-say-no.

26. Lela Gilbert, "Will Egypt's New President Sisi #BringBackOurCopticGirls?" Hudson Institute, June 19, 2014, https://www.hudson.org/research/10383-will-egypt-s-new-president-sisi-bring-back-our-coptic-girls-.

27. United Nations Human Rights, "Egypt must free Coptic Christian rights defender reportedly held on terror charges, say UN experts," press release, December 11, 2019, https://www.ohchr.org/EN/NewsEvents/Pages/DisplayNews.aspx?NewsID=25419.

28. Lela Gilbert, "Why American support for Kurdistan could soon become a matter of life and death," Fox News, May 7, 2015, https://www.foxnews.com/opinion/why-american-support-for-kurdistan-could-soon-become-a-matter-of-life-and-death.

29. Cathrin Schaer and Gasia Ohanes, "Can Pope Francis save Iraq's Christians from 'extinction'?" DW, May 3, 2021, https://www.dw.com/en/what-can-pope-francis-really-achieve-in-iraq/a-56769175.

30. Lela Gilbert, "Kurds, Christians and Barbarians at the Gate," Hudson Institute, October 23, 2014, https://www.hudson.org/research/10745-kurds-christians-and-barbarians-at-the-gate.

31. "President Trump: 'Abu Bakr al-Baghdadi is dead'," BBC News, October 27, 2019, https://www.bbc.com/news/av/world-50200383.

32. Jason Burke, "Isis-linked groups open up new fronts across sub-Saharan Africa," *The Guardian*, June 25, 2021, https://www.theguardian.com/world/2021/jun/25/isis-linked-groups-open-up-new-fronts-across-sub-saharan-africa.

33. This section is adapted from Lela Gilbert's "Iran's Furtive Occupation of Iraq's Christian Communities," Hudson Institute, March 17, 2019, https://www.hudson.org/research/14885-iran-s-furtive-occupation-of-iraq-s-christian-communities.

34. "After ISIS, Nineveh's Christians now face new threat from Shabak Shiite militias," *AsiaNews*, February 14, 2019, http://www.asianews.it/news-en/After-ISIS,-Nineveh%E2%80%99s-Christians-now-face-new-threat-from-Shabak-Shiite-militias--46250.html.

35. Zachary Laub, "Syria's Civil War: The Descent into Horror," Council on Foreign Relations, March 17, 2021, accessed September 21, 2021, https://www.cfr.org/article/syrias-civil-war.

36. Lela Gilbert and Arielle Del Turco, "Inside An Oasis Of Religious Freedom In Northeast Syria," *Religion Unplugged*, November 2, 2020, https://religionunplugged.com/news/2020/10/30/inside-an-oasis-of-religious-freedom-in-northeast-syria.

37. Lela Gilbert, "Ancient Christian Communities Caught In Syria's Crossfire Need Shelter This Winter," Hudson Institute, November 11, 2019, https://www.hudson.org/research/15471-ancient-christian-communities-caught-in-syria-s-crossfire-need-shelter-this-winter.

38. Lela Gilbert, "Trusting Trump and a lesson for the West: Proceed with caution," *Jerusalem Post*, October 22, 2019, https://www.jpost.com/opinion/trusting-trump-and-a-lesson-for-the-west-proceed-with-caution-605445.

39. Eric Schmitt, Maggie Haberman, and Edward Wong, "President Endorses Turkish Military Operation in Syria, Shifting U.S. Policy," *New York Times*, Updated October 15, 2019, https://www.nytimes.com/2019/10/07/us/politics/trump-turkey-syria.html.

40. Gilbert, "Trusting Trump."

41. Anurima Bhargava and Nadine Maenza, "U.S. Leaders Must Stand Against Turkey's Atrocities in Northern Syria," *Newsweek*, July 25, 2020, https://www.newsweek.com/us-leaders-must-stand-against-turkeys-atrocities-northern-syria-opinion-1520418.

42. Lela Gilbert, "Coronavirus, Turkish Attacks Threaten Kurds, Christians in Northeast Syria," Hudson Institute, April 14, 2020, https://www.hudson.org/research/15935-coronavirus-turkish-attacks-threaten-kurds-christians-in-northeast-syria.

43. "Syria: Aid Restrictions Hinder Covid-19 Response," Human Rights Watch, April 28, 2020, https://www.hrw.org/news/2020/04/28/syria-aid-restrictions-hinder-covid-19-response.

44. Gilbert, "Turkey's Christians Face Increasingly Dangerous Persecution."

45. Aykan Erdemir, "Scapegoats of Wrath, Subjects of Benevolence: Turkey's Minorities Under Erdoğan," Hudson Institute, April 19, 2019, https://www.hudson.org/research/14970-scapegoats-of-wrath-subjects-of-benevolence-turkey-s-minorities-under-erdo-an.

46. Daren Butler and Ece Toksabay, "Erdogan declares Hagia Sophia a mosque after Turkish court ruling," Reuters, July 10, 2020, https://www.reuters.com/article/us-turkey-museum-verdict/erdogan-declares-hagia-sophia-a-mosque-after-turkish-court-ruling-idUSKBN24B1UP.

47. Lela Gilbert and Human Rights Without Frontiers, "Turkey's Christians face increasingly dangerous persecution," International Institute for Religious Freedom, April 21, 2021, https://www.iirf.eu/news/other-news/turkeys-christians-face-increasingly-dangerous-persecution/.

48. "No justice for Chaldean priest in Turkey after his father goes missing and his mother turns up dead," *AsiaNews*, March 20, 2021, http://asianews.it/news-en/No-justice-for-Chaldean-priest-in-Turkey-after-his-father-goes-missing-and-his-mother-turns-up-dead-52658.html.

49. "German Pastor Hopeful in Fight to Remain in Turkey," *Morning Star News*, March 20, 2021, https://morningstarnews .org/2021/03/german-pastor-hopeful-in-fight-to-remain-in-turkey/.

50. Abdelrahman Ayyash, "The Turkish Future of Egypt's Muslim Brotherhood," The Century Foundation, August 17, 2020, https://tcf.org/content/report/turkish-future-egypts-muslim-brotherhood/?agreed=1.

51. Gilbert, "Turkey's Christians Face Increasingly Dangerous Persecution."

52. "Constantine's Church," Hagia Sophia, accessed September 21, 2021, https://www.hagiasophia.com/constantines-church/.

53. U.S. Commission on International Religious Freedom, "USCIRF Decries Decision to Change Status of the Hagia Sophia," press release, July 10, 2020, https://www.uscirf.gov/news-room/ releases-statements/uscirf-decries-decision-change-status-hagia-sophia.

54. "567th anniversary of conquest of Istanbul marked at Hagia Sophia," *Hurriyet Daily News*, May 30, 2020, https://www .hurriyetdailynews.com/istanbuls-conquest-celebrated-at-hagia-sophia-155180.

55. Gilbert, "Saturday people, Sunday people and the 'Mohammadian army.'"

56. Lela Gilbert, "It's Time to Reassess U.S. Policy Toward Turkey and Erdogan's Islamist Agenda," Family Research Council, June 22, 2020, https://www.frcblog.com/2020/06/its-time-reassess-us-policy-toward-turkey-and-erdogans-islamist-agenda/.

57. Nadav Shragai, "Turkey's Intrusion into Jerusalem," Jerusalem Center for Public Affairs, June 15, 2020, https://jcpa.org/article/ turkeys-intrusion-into-jerusalem/.

58. Seth J. Frantzman, "Could Egypt and Turkey be headed for war in Libya?" *Jerusalem Post*, June 21, 2020, https://www.jpost .com/middle-east/could-egypt-and-turkey-be-headed-for-war-in-libya-632167.

59. Lela Gilbert, "Erdogan's agenda: Neo-Ottoman ambition or pan-Islamist zeal?" *Jerusalem Post*, June 28, 2020, https://www .jpost.com/middle-east/erdogans-agenda-neo-ottoman-ambition-or-pan-islamist-zeal-633040.

60. Seth J. Frantzman, "Turkey's airstrikes in northern Iraq threaten Christian villages," *Jerusalem Post*, June 22, 2020, https://www .jpost.com/middle-east/turkeys-airstrikes-in-northern-iraq-threaten-christian-villages-632345.

61. Giulia Valeria Anderson, "Afrin: Turkey's Never-Ending War in Syria," Washington Kurdish Institute, June 8, 2020, https://dckurd .org/2020/06/08/afrin-turkeys-never-ending-war-in-syria/.

62. "Turkish-Greek relations tense amid fears of military showdown," *Arab News*, June 13, 2020, https://www.arabnews.com/ node/1689421/middle-east.

63. "Turkey," U.S. Commission on International Religious Freedom, 2021, https://www.uscirf.gov/sites/default/files/2021-05/ Turkey%20Chapter%20AR2021.pdf.

64. John Hudson and Kareem Fahim, "Biden calls mass killing of Armenians a 'genocide' in break with previous presidents," *Washington Post*, April 24, 2021, https://www .washingtonpost.com/national-security/armenia-genocide-biden-turkey/2021/04/24/b0f2394a-a46a-11eb-8a6d-f1b55f463112_ story.html.

65. Francis X. Rocca and Emre Peker, "Pope Francis Calls Armenian Deaths 'First Genocide of 20th Century,'" *Wall Street Journal*, April 12, 2015, https://www.wsj.com/articles/pope-francis-calls-armenian-slaughter-first-genocide-of-20th-century-1428824472.

66. Benny Morris and Dror Ze'evi, "When Turkey Destroyed Its Christians," *Wall Street Journal*, May 17, 2019, https://www.wsj .com/articles/when-turkey-destroyed-its-christians-11558109896.

67. "Chronology of the Armenian Genocide -- 1915 (April-June)," Armenian National Institute, accessed October 14, 2021, https:// www.armenian-genocide.org/1915-2.html.

68. Raffi Khatchadourian, "Remembering the Armenian Genocide," *New Yorker*, April 21, 2015, https://www.newyorker.com/news/daily-comment/remembering-the-armenian-genocide.

69. Jeff Jacoby, "Armenian genocide was also a jihad," *Boston Globe*, April 14, 2015, https://www.bostonglobe.com/opinion/2015/04/14/armenian-genocide-was-also-jihad/AqlzTutJ73IJWRnlG8V6lN/story.html.

70. "Turkey Declares Jihad," Today in World War I, November 14, 2014, https://today-in-wwi.tumblr.com/post/102656541418/turkey-declares-jihad.

71. "Armenia-Azerbaijan: Why did Nagorno-Karabakh spark a conflict?" BBC News, November 12, 2020, https://www.bbc.com/news/world-europe-54324772.

72. Anton Troianovski, "At Front Lines of a Brutal War: Death and Despair in Nagorno-Karabakh," *New York Times*, October 18, 2020, https://www.nytimes.com/2020/10/18/world/europe/Nagorno-Karabakh-war-Armenia-Azerbaijan.html.

73. "Armenia, Azerbaijan declare martial law amid heavy clashes in Nagorno-Karabakh," *DW*, September 28, 2020, https://www.dw.com/en/armenia-azerbaijan-declare-martial-law-amid-heavy-clashes-in-nagorno-karabakh/a-55068321.

74. "Erdoğan: Armenia biggest threat to peace in region," *Daily Sabah*, September 27, 2020, accessed October 14, 2021, https://www.dailysabah.com/politics/diplomacy/erdogan-armenia-biggest-threat-to-peace-in-region.

75. Lela Gilbert, "Erdogan's agenda: Neo-Ottoman ambition or pan-Islamist zeal?" *The Jerusalem Post*, June 28, 2020, accessed October 14, 2021, https://www.jpost.com/middle-east/erdogans-agenda-neo-ottoman-ambition-or-pan-islamist-zeal-633040.

76. Pierre Balanian, "Turkey sends 4,000 Syrian ISIS mercenaries to fight against the Armenians (VIDEO)," *Asia News*, September 28, 2020, http://www.asianews.it/news-en/Turkey-sends-4,000-Syrian-ISIS-mercenaries-to-fight-against-the-Armenians-(VIDEO)-51151.html.

77. Liz Cookman, "Syrians Make Up Turkey's Proxy Army in Nagorno-Karabakh," *Foreign Policy*, October 5, 2020, https:// foreignpolicy.com/2020/10/05/nagorno-karabakh-syrians-turkey-armenia-azerbaijan.

78. "Baroness Cox Statement on the conflict by Azerbaijan against Armenia and Nagorno Karabakh (Artsakh)," Humanitarian Aid Relief Trust, October 4, 2020, https://www.hart-uk.org/news/baroness-cox-statement-on-the-azerbaijan-war/.

79. "Grief and Courage in Nagorno Karabakh," Humanitarian Aid Relief Trust (HART), November 2020, https://www.hart-uk .org/wp-content/uploads/2012/11/Grief-and-Courage-in.pdf.

80. "Azerbaijan to Host Special Forces from Turkey, Pakistan in Drills," Radio Free Europe/Radio Liberty, September 11, 2021, https://www .rferl.org/a/31455296.html.

81. "Senior Iranian Ayatollah Mohammad Mehdi Mirbagheri: In Order for the Hidden Imam to Reappear We Must Engage in 'Widespread Fighting' with the West," MEMRI, July 31, 2019, https://www.memri.org/tv/iranian-assembly-experts-ayatollah-mirbagheri-jihad-fighting-allah-moral-hidden-imam-conflict-west-revolution.

82. Lela Gilbert, "Iran's aggression and the Shi'ite apocalypse," *Jerusalem Post*, August 17, 2019, https://www.jpost.com/opinion/irans-aggression-and-the-shiite-apocalypse-598904.

83. Saeed Ghasseminejad, "Iran's apocalyptic policy makers," *Times of Israel*, June 10, 2013, https://blogs.timesofisrael.com/a-military-strategy-for-apocalypse-soon/.

84. Lela Gilbert, "Iranian revolution, phase two: Hidden in plain sight," *Jerusalem Post*, April 8, 2019, https://www.jpost.com/opinion/iranian-revolution-phase-two-hidden-in-plain-sight-585966.

85. Gilbert, "Iranian revolution, phase two."

86. https://www.uscirf.gov/news-room/releases-statements/uscirf-condemns-irans-crackdown-bahai-community

87. https://www.opendoorsusa.org/christian-persecution/world-watch-list/

88. Daniel Pipes, "Iran's Christian Boom," *Newsweek*, June 24, 2021, https://www.newsweek.com/irans-christian-boom-opinion-1603388.

89. Gilbert, "Iran's aggression and the Shi'ite apocalypse."

90. Richard J. Goldstone, "Israel and the Apartheid Slander," *New York Times*, October 31, 2011, https://www.nytimes.com/2011/11/01/opinion/israel-and-the-apartheid-slander.html.

91. Eliezer Sherman, "Arab Israeli Diplomat: Even If Palestinians Have a State, They Will Not Be Free (VIDEO)," *The Algemeiner*, May 6, 2015, http://www.algemeiner.com/2015/05/06/arab-israeli-diplomat-even-if-palestinians-have-a-state-they-will-not-be-free-video/.

92. "VIDEO: An Arab Christian Explains Why He Serves in the IDF," *Israel Today*, January 19, 2020, https://www.israeltoday.co.il/read/arab-christians-serve-in-the-idf/.

93. "Hamas," Counter Extremism Project, accessed September 22, 2021, https://www.counterextremism.com/threat/hamas.

94. This section is adapted from Lela Gilbert's "Jerusalem Notebook: The Silent Struggle of Bethlehem's Christians," Hudson Institute, August 1, 2016, https://www.hudson.org/research/12696-jerusalem-notebook-the-silent-struggle-of-bethlehem-s-christians.

95. Jayson Casper, "Why Many Christians Want to Leave Palestine. And Why Most Won't," *Christianity Today*, August 4, 2020, https://www.christianitytoday.com/news/2020/august/palestinian-christians-survey-israel-emigration-one-state.html.

96. Robert Nicholson, "Why Are Palestinian Christians Fleeing?" *Providence*, March 1, 2016, https://providencemag.com/2016/03/why-are-palestinian-christians-fleeing/.

97. Gilbert, "Jerusalem Notebook."

98. Lela Gilbert, "Gazan Christians on Christmas: Escape from watchful eye of radical Muslims," *Jerusalem Post*, December 25,

2019, https://www.jpost.com/opinion/christmas-in-gaza-good-and-bad-news-612033.

99. Personal interview with Lela Gilbert.

100. "United Arab Emirates to open diplomatic ties with Israel, plans for annexation on hold," *World Israel News*, August 13, 2020, https://worldisraelnews.com/united-arab-emirates-to-open-diplomatic-ties-with-israel-plans-for-annexation-on-hold/.

101. Jen Kirby, "Pope Francis's mass in the United Arab Emirates was historic — and complicated," *Vox*, February 5, 2019, https://www.vox.com/2019/2/5/18211956/pope-francis-mass-united-arab-emirates-arab.

102. "Pope Francis wraps up UAE trip with stadium Mass," DW, May 2, 2019, https://www.dw.com/en/pope-francis-wraps-up-uae-trip-with-stadium-mass/a-47361175.

103. "Annual Report 2021," U.S. Commission on International Religious Freedom, https://www.uscirf.gov/sites/default/files/2021-04/2021%20Annual%20Report_0.pdf.

104. "Abrahamic Family House: Mosque, church, synagogue to share same space in UAE," *Khaleej Times*, September 22, 2019, https://www.khaleejtimes.com/news/general/mosque-church-synagogue-to-share-same-space-in-uae--.

105. Gordon Lubold and Felicia Schwartz, "U.S., Israel, U.A.E., Bahrain Sign Peace Accord," *Wall Street Journal*, September 15, 2020, https://www.wsj.com/articles/u-s-israel-u-a-e-bahrain-sign-peace-accord-11600191303.

106. "Sudan-Israel relations agreed, Donald Trump announces," BBC News, October 24, 2020, https://www.bbc.com/news/world-africa-54554286.

107. Steve Holland, "Morocco joins other Arab nations agreeing to normalize Israel ties," Reuters, December 10, 2020, https://www.reuters.com/article/israel-usa-morocco-int/morocco-joins-other-arab-nations-agreeing-to-normalize-israel-ties-idUSKBN28K2CW.

CHAPTER 4: AFGHANISTAN: A RELIGIOUS FREEDOM
DISASTER

1. "The fiasco in Afghanistan is a grave blow to America's standing," *The Economist*, August 21, 2021, https://www.economist.com/ leaders/2021/08/21/the-fiasco-in-afghanistan-is-a-grave-blow-to-americas-standing.

2. This section was adapted from Lela Gilbert's "Afghan Christians Are Facing a Taliban Reign of Terror," *Religion Unplugged*, August 20, 2021, https://religionunplugged.com/ news/2021/8/20/afghani-christians-are-facing-a-taliban-reign-of-terrornbsp.

3. Bethany Dawson, "COVID-19 rates are soaring in Afghanistan as healthcare facilities collapse, says health minister," *Business Insider*, September 11, 2021, https://www.businessinsider.com/ afghanistan-covid-19-rates-are-soaring-healthcare-facilities-collapse-2021-9.

4. Christine Rosen, "The Biden Administration's Vision of a Woke Taliban," *Commentary*, August 18, 2021, https://www .commentary.org/christine-rosen/the-biden-administrations-vision-of-a-woke-taliban/.

5. Gilbert, "Afghan Christians Are Facing a Taliban Reign of Terror."

6. "Afghanistan—The situation of Christian converts," Landinfo, April 7, 2021, https://landinfo.no/wp-content/uploads/2021/04/ Landinfo-Report-Afghanistan-Christian-Converts-070402021 .pdf.

7. https://www.opendoors.org/en-US/persecution/countries/

8. "Global Prayer Guide – Afghanistan," The Voice of the Martyrs, accessed October 14, 2021, https://www.persecution. com/globalprayerguide/afghanistan.

9. Christine Rousselle and Jose Torres Jr., "Terrified Christians in Afghanistan brace for attacks: 'We are coming for you'," Catholic News Agency, August 19, 2021, https://www.catholicnewsagency

.com/amp/news/248726/terrified-christians-in-afghanistan-brace-for-attacks-we-are-coming-for-you.

10. William Stark, "Fear and Uncertainty Dominate Thoughts of Afghanistan's Christians Living Under Taliban Rule," International Christian Concern, August 17, 2021, https://www.persecution.org/2021/08/17/fear-uncertainty-dominate-thoughts-afghanistans-christians-living-taliban-rule/.

11. Sanjeev Miglani, "Taliban executions still haunt Afghan soccer field," Reuters, September 12, 2008, https://www.reuters.com/article/us-afghan-stadium/taliban-executions-still-haunt-afghan-soccer-field-idUSSP12564220080913.

12. David D. Kirkpatrick and Rukmini Callimachi, "Islamic State Video Shows Beheadings of Egyptian Christians in Libya," *The New York Times*, February 15, 2015, accessed October 15, 2021, https://www.nytimes.com/2015/02/16/world/middleeast/islamic-state-video-beheadings-of-21-egyptian-christians.html.

13. Lela Gilbert, "Why Is the American Government Blocking Refugee Flights from Afghanistan?" *Religion Unplugged*, September 3, 2021, https://religionunplugged.com/news/2021/9/3/why-is-the-us-government-blocking-refugee-flights-from-afghanistan.

14. Susan Crabtree, "Fitful 48 Hours for Americans, Afghans Trying to Escape," *RealClearPolitics*, September 3, 2021, https://www.realclearpolitics.com/articles/2021/09/03/fitful_48_hours_for_americans_afghans_trying_to_escape__146354.html.

15. Crabtree, "Fitful 48 Hours for Americans, Afghans Trying to Escape."

16. Mindy Belz, "A closing door," *WORLD*, September 1, 2021, https://wng.org/articles/a-closing-door-1630514363.

17. Nancy A. Youssef and Gordon Lubold, "Last U.S. Troops Leave Afghanistan After Nearly 20 Years," *Wall Street Journal*, August 30, 2021, https://www.wsj.com/articles/last-u-s-troops-leave-afghanistan-after-nearly-20-years-11630355853.

18. Kyle Becker, "State Dept. Order 'Blocks' Private Flights for Americans Conducting Unauthorized Rescue Missions to Afghanistan: Report," *Becker News*, August 28, 2021, https://beckernews.com/state-dept-order-blocks-private-flights-for-americans-conducting-unauthorized-rescue-missions-to-afghanistan-report-41186/.

19. John Cardillo, Twitter, August 28, 2021, https://twitter.com/rln22/status/1431822006052397058.

20. Personal interview.

21. Matthieu Aikins and Jim Huylebroek, "Taliban Appoint Stalwarts to Top Government Posts," *New York Times*, September 7, 2021, https://www.nytimes.com/2021/09/07/world/asia/taliban-women-protest-kabul-afghanistan.html.

22. Ahmad Seir, Rahim Faiez, Kathy Gannon, and Joseph Krauss, "Taliban vow to respect women, despite history of oppression," Associated Press, August 17, 2021, https://apnews.com/article/afghanistan-taliban-kabul-1d4b052ccef113adc8dc94f965ff23c7.

23. Maggie Astor, Sharif Hassan, and Norimitsu Onishi, "A Taliban spokesman urges women to stay home because fighters haven't been trained to respect them," *New York Times*, August 24, 2021, https://www.nytimes.com/2021/08/24/world/asia/taliban-women-afghanistan.html.

24. Hannah Ellis-Petersen, "Female TV anchor who interviewed Taliban flees Afghanistan," *The Guardian*, September 1, 2021, https://www.theguardian.com/world/2021/sep/02/female-tv-anchor-who-interviewed-taliban-official-ends-up-having-to-flee-afghanistan.

25. Jaide Garcia and Jonny Hallam, "Taliban accused of murdering pregnant Afghan policewoman in front of her family," CNN, September 6, 2021, https://www.cnn.com/2021/09/06/asia/taliban-afghanistan-pregnant-policewoman-murder-intl/index.html.

26. Gayle Tzemach Lemmon, "Opinion: Listen to the voices of Afghan women," *Washington Post*, August 15, 2021, https://

www.washingtonpost.com/opinions/2021/08/15/listen-voices-afghan-women/.

27. Ayaz Gul and Ayesha Tanzeem, "Taliban Vow to Respect Women's Rights 'Within Islamic Law'," VOA News, August 17, 2021, https://www.voanews.com/a/south-central-asia_taliban-vow-respect-womens-rights-within-islamic-law/6209664.html.

28. Christiane Amanpour, Twitter, September 1, 2021, https://twitter.com/camanpour/status/1433128089802977282.

29. Peter Beaumont, "Afghan women to be banned from playing sport, Taliban say," *The Guardian*, September 8, 2021, https://www.theguardian.com/world/2021/sep/08/afghan-women-to-be-banned-from-playing-sport-taliban-say.

30. Susannah George, Haq Nawaz Khan, Rachel Pannett, Ezzatullah Mehrdad, Adam Taylor, and Karen DeYoung, "Taliban forms acting government in Afghanistan, saying permanent leadership to be named soon, as protests grow," *Washington Post*, September 7, 2021, https://www.washingtonpost.com/world/2021/09/07/afghanistan-kabul-taliban-updates/.

31. Haq Nawaz Khan, Ellen Francis, and Adam Taylor, "The Taliban is bringing back its feared ministry of 'vice' and 'virtue,'" *Washington Post*, September 8, 2021, https://www.washingtonpost.com/world/2021/09/08/afghan-vice-virtue-ministry/.

32. Beaumont, "Afghan women to be banned from playing sport, Taliban say."

33. Jack Bantock, Celine Alkhaldi, and Hilary Whiteman, "Afghan cyclist's fears realized as Taliban aims to forbid women from playing sport," CNN, September 8, 2021, https://www.cnn.com/2021/09/08/sport/afghanistan-cycling-cricket-taliban-spt-intl/index.html.

34. Celine Castronuovo, "State Department voices concerns over all-male Taliban government," *The Hill*, September 7, 2021, https://thehill.com/policy/international/571205-state-dept-voices-concerns-over-all-male-taliban-government.

35. "Afghanistan: Women protest against all-male Taliban government," BBC News, September 8, 2021, https://www.bbc.com/news/world-asia-58490819.

36. Kathy Gannon, "Taliban form all-male Afghan government of old guard members," Associated Press, September 7, 2021, https://apnews.com/article/middle-east-pakistan-afghanistan-arrests-islamabad-d50b1b490d27d32eb20cc11b77c12c87.

37. Arielle Del Turco, "After Biden Abandoned Afghan Women, His 'Women's Rights' Rhetoric Rings Hollow," Family Research Council, September 8, 2021, https://www.frcblog.com/2021/09/after-biden-abandoned-afghan-women-his-womens-rights-rhetoric-rings-hollow/.

38. "Full Committee Hearing – Examining the U.S. Withdrawal from Afghanistan," U.S. Senate Committee on Foreign Relations, September 14, 2021, https://www.foreign.senate.gov/hearings/examining-the-us-withdrawal-from-afghanistan-091421.

39. Eric Patterson, "What Is Really Going on in Afghanistan: The Plight of Christians and Religious Minorities," *Providence*, September 9, 2021, https://providencemag.com/2021/09/what-really-going-afghanistan-plight-christians-religious-minorities/.

40. Arielle Del Turco, "5 Ways to Pray for the People of Afghanistan," Family Research Council, August 17, 2021, https://www.frcblog.com/2021/08/5-ways-pray-people-afghanistan/.

41. Kelsey Zorzi, "Afghanistan's Christians are turning off phones and going into hiding," *The Hill*, August 23, 2021, https://thehill.com/opinion/international/568992-afghanistans-christians-are-turning-off-phones-and-going-into-hiding.

42. "What We Know about the 13 U.S. Service Members Killed in the Kabul Airport Attack," NPR, August 31, 2021, https://www.npr.org/2021/08/29/1032044382/what-we-know-about-the-13-u-s-service-members-killed-in-the-kabul-attack.

43. John Hinderaker, "Meanwhile, in Afghanistan," *Power Line*, September 12, 2021, https://www.powerlineblog.com/archives/2021/09/meanwhile-in-afghanistan.php.

44. This section was adapted from Lela Gilbert's "Why Religion and Radical Islam Are Essential to Understanding the Taliban," *Religion Unplugged*, September 12, 2021, https://religionunplugged.com/news/2021/9/10/why-religion-and-radical-islam-are-essential-to-understanding-the-taliban.

45. "The 9/11 Commission Report: Final Report of the National Commission on Terrorist Attacks Upon the United States," July 22, 2004, https://www.govinfo.gov/app/details/GPO-911REPORT.

46. "Terrorist Groups in Afghanistan," Congressional Research Service, August 17, 2021, https://crsreports.congress.gov/product/pdf/IF/IF10604.

47. Douglas Schorzman, "Who Are the Taliban's New Government Leaders? Here's What We Know," *New York Times*, September 8, 2021, https://www.nytimes.com/article/taliban-leaders-afghanistan.html.

48. Rod Nordland, "Death Toll in Kabul Bombing Has Hit 150, Aghan President Says," *New York Times*, June 6, 2017, https://www.nytimes.com/2017/06/06/world/asia/kabul-bombing-death-toll-increases.html.

49. Mark Mazzetti, Eric Schmitt, David E. Sanger, and Helene Cooper, "Behind P.O.W.'s Release: Urgency and Opportunity," *New York Times*, June 4, 2014, https://www.nytimes.com/2014/06/05/world/asia/concern-for-health-of-bowe-bergdahl-drove-prisoner-exchange.html.

50. "MEMORANDUM FOR Commander, United States Southern Command, 3511 NW 91st Avenue, Miami, FL 33172," Department of Defense, January 21, 2008, https://wikileaks.org/gitmo/pdf/af/us9af-000004dp.pdf.

51. Sohel Rana and Sumit Ganguly, "Taliban's Religious Ideology Has Roots in Colonial India," *Religion Unplugged*, August 25, 2021, https://religionunplugged.com/news/2021/8/25/talibans-religious-ideology-has-roots-in-colonial-india.

52. "Chaos, desperation at Kabul airport as Biden defends withdrawal from Afghanistan," Reuters, August 17, 2021, https://www .reuters.com/world/asia-pacific/talibans-rapid-advance-across-afghanistan-2021-08-10/.

53. "In the Taliban's Afghanistan, Signs of a Return to Hard-Line Islamic Rule," *Wall Street Journal*, October 6, 2021, https://www.wsj.com/video/series/news-explainers/in-the-talibans-afghanistan-signs-of-a-return-to-hard-line-islamic-rule/988A48E7-C3B7-4DB7-876C-F60BA91D773D.

54. "Full text: bin Laden's 'letter to America,'" *The Guardian*, November 24, 2002, https://www.theguardian.com/world/2002/nov/24/theobserver.

55. Cortney O'Brien, "'Watters World' panel explains consequences of Biden's 'dishonorable' departure from Afghanistan," Fox News, September 11, 2021, https://www.foxnews.com/media/watters-world-panel-blasts-dishonorable-departure-from-afghanistan.

CONCLUSION: HOW CAN WE MAKE A DIFFERENCE?

1. Tom Farr, "What in the World Is Religious Freedom?" Religious Freedom Institute, November 1, 2019, https://www .religiousfreedominstitute.org/blog/what-in-the-world-is-religious-freedom.

2. "The Bill of Rights: A Transcription," National Archives, accessed September 23, 2021, https://www.archives.gov/founding-docs/bill-of-rights-transcript.

3. "Universal Declaration of Human Rights," United Nations, accessed September 23, 2021, https://www.un.org/en/about-us/universal-declaration-of-human-rights.

4. "Trafficking of Women and Girls in China via Forced and Fraudulent Marriage," U.S. Department of State, December 8, 2020, https://www.youtube.com/watch?v=LDekpQ258Pc.

5. "'Give Us a Baby and We'll Let You Go,' Trafficking of Kachin 'Brides' from Myanmar to China," Human Rights Watch, March

21, 2019, https://www.hrw.org/report/2019/03/21/give-us-baby-and-well-let-you-go/trafficking-kachin-brides-myanmar-china.

6. Kathy Gannon, "AP Exclusive: 629 Pakistani girls sold as brides to China," Associated Press, December 7, 2019, accessed September 23, 2021, https://apnews.com/article/ap-top-news-pakistan-international-news-weekend-reads-lahore-c586d0f73fe249718ec06f6867b0244e.

7. "Trafficking of Women and Girls in China via Forced and Fraudulent Marriage," U.S. Department of State, December 8, 2020, https://www.youtube.com/watch?v=LDekpQ258Pc.

8. For more on this topic, see Arielle Del Turco and Travis Weber, "Why Religious Freedom Is a National Security Issue," Family Research Council, August 2021, https://www.frc.org/nationalsecurity.

9. Elena Schor and Hannah Fingerhut, "Religious freedom in America: popular and polarizing," ABC News, August 5, 2020, https://abcnews.go.com/Politics/wireStory/religious-freedom-america-popular-polarizing-72188535.

10. Arielle Del Turco, "Three Reasons Congress Should Embrace International Religious Freedom," International Christian Concern, https://www.persecution.org/2021/05/31/three-reasons-congress-embrace-international-religious-freedom/.

11. Justin McCarthy, "Top U.S. Foreign Policy Goals: Stem Terrorism, Nuclear Weapons," Gallup, February 16, 2017, https://news.gallup.com/poll/204005/top-foreign-policy-goals-stem-terrorism-nuclear-weapons.aspx.

12. Laura Silver, Kat Devlin, and Christine Huang, "Most Americans Support Tough Stance Toward China on Human Rights, Economic Issues," Pew Research Center, March 4, 2021, https://www.pewresearch.org/global/2021/03/04/most-americans-support-tough-stance-toward-china-on-human-rights-economic-issues/.

13. "World Watch List 2021," Open Doors, https://www.open doorsusa.org/christian-persecution/world-watch-list.

14. "2020 Report on International Religious Freedom," U.S. Department of State, accessed September 23, 2021, https://www.state.gov/reports/2020-report-on-international-religious-freedom/.

15. "Annual Report 2021," U.S. Commission on International Religious Freedom, https://www.uscirf.gov/sites/default/files/2021-04/2021%20Annual%20Report.pdf.

16. Jeremy Weber, "Unforgotten: Andrew and Norine Brunson," *Wheaton Magazine*, Spring 2019, https://magazine.wheaton.edu/stories/spring-2019-unforgotten-andrew-and-norine-brunson.

17. Steve Warren, "Report: Kidnapped Pakistani Christian Teen Forced to Convert to Islam Is Pregnant, Confined to Room," CBN News, July 22, 2020, https://www1.cbn.com/cbnnews/2020/july/report-kidnapped-pakistani-christian-teen-forced-to-convert-to-islam-is-pregnant-confined-to-room.

18. Paul Mozur and Ian Johnson, "China Sentences Wang Yi, Christian Pastor, to 9 Years in Prison," *New York Times*, January 2, 2020, https://www.nytimes.com/2019/12/30/world/asia/china-wang-yi-christian-sentence.html.

19. Samuel Smith, "Nigeria vows to 'redouble' efforts to free Leah Sharibu 2 years after Boko Haram abduction," *Christian Post*, February 19, 2020, https://www.christianpost.com/news/nigeria-vows-to-redouble-efforts-to-free-leah-sharibu-2-years-after-boko-haram-abduction.html.

20. "Global Prayer Guide," The Voice of the Martyrs, accessed September 23, 2021, https://www.persecution.com/globalprayerguide/.

21. "Christian persecution," Open Doors, accessed September 28, 2021, https://www.opendoorsusa.org/christian-persecution/.

22. Arielle Del Turco, "'They Need Our Faith,'" July 16, 2021, https://www.frc.org/updatearticle/20210716/need-faith.